Landscape Management

Landscape Management

Planting and Maintenance of Trees, Shrubs, and Turfgrasses

James R. Feucht
Professor, Landscape Plants
Colorado State University
Fort Collins, Colorado

Jack D. Butler
Professor, Turfgrass
Colorado State University
Fort Collins, Colorado

VNR VAN NOSTRAND REINHOLD COMPANY
New York

This book is dedicated to the memory of the late
F. L. S. (Steve) O'Rourke, world-renowned horticulturist
and close friend, who inspired and encouraged me to
prepare this text.

Van Nostrand Reinhold Company Inc.
115 Fifth Avenue
New York, New York 10003

Van Nostrand Reinhold Company Limited
Molly Millars Lane
Wokingham, Berkshire RG11 2PY, England

Van Nostrand Reinhold
480 La Trobe Street
Melbourne, Victoria 3000, Australia

Macmillan of Canada
Division of Canada Publishing Corporation
164 Commander Boulevard
Agincourt, Ontario M1S 3C7, Canada

16 15 14 13 12 11 10 9 8 7 6 5 4 3 2 1

Library of Congress Cataloging-in-Publication Data

Feucht, James R.
    Landscape management.

    Includes index.
    1. Arboriculture.   2. Turf management.
3. Landscape gardening.   4. Grounds maintenance.
I. Butler, Jack D.   II. Title.
SB435.F48   1987   635.9   87-12165
ISBN 0-442-22680-2 (pbk.)

Contents

Preface

Whether you are a student or you already work in landscape architecture, landscape contracting, nursery/landscape management, or arboriculture, you will find this book a useful reference. The book combines the essentials of several natural sciences, including plant anatomy, physiology, soils, and pest management to provide the working knowledge required to install and manage any landscaped area, be it a small residential property or large industrial complex.

A lack of communication, caused by inadequate understanding, between the architect/designer or contractor/manager and the client is the most common cause for the poor performance of plants in a landscape. Often, however, the cause for inferior performance or death of plants is blamed on the failure of the plants themselves. In all but a few instances, poor performance of plants in landscaped areas results from ignorance of how plants grow and how they respond to our manipulations of their environment.

The landscape manager usually suffers the consequences of poor plant selection, poor placement, or poor planting procedures. Most managers have little or no control over the situation, yet are often held responsible for the *entire* landscape. The manager is called upon to "save" the plants and keep them in top condition, sometimes against all odds.

The primary objective of this book is to create a common understanding about plants, their requirements, and their responses to the varied situations in which we place them. Whether you are the one who will choose the plants and planting procedures for a job, supply the plants required, or be responsible for their ultimate upkeep, the information in this book will help you to make informed decisions about landscape management, as well as to convey the necessary details of a particular task to all involved.

Acknowledgments

Appreciation is expressed to M. Thomasine (Tommie) Waidmann and Laurie Capelli, who spent many hours typing manuscripts and offered constructive suggestions for changes in wording and grammar of the text.

I appreciate the generous help of Dr. Alex L. Shigo (retired), Kenneth M. Dudzik (N.E. Forest Experiment Station, Durham, N.H.), and Eugene B. Eyerly (Eyerly and Associates, Denver, Colo.) in supplying many of the photographs used in the text. Dr. Shigo also gave freely of his time to review several chapters of the book, offering constructive criticism and improvements.

Appreciation is also expressed to Larry Keesen, Irrigation Consultant, Denver, for his review and constructive comments of chapter 3 on irrigation.

Thanks also to Dr. Kenneth M. Brink, Colorado State University, for moral support in making this book possible. His encouragement, through securing my sabbatical leave to allow me time to complete the book, is sincerely appreciated.

Appreciation is also expressed to the many students who have offered suggestions for improvement of the original, unpublished versions of this book used in courses at Colorado State University, University of Colorado at Denver, and Front Range Community College.

Landscape Management

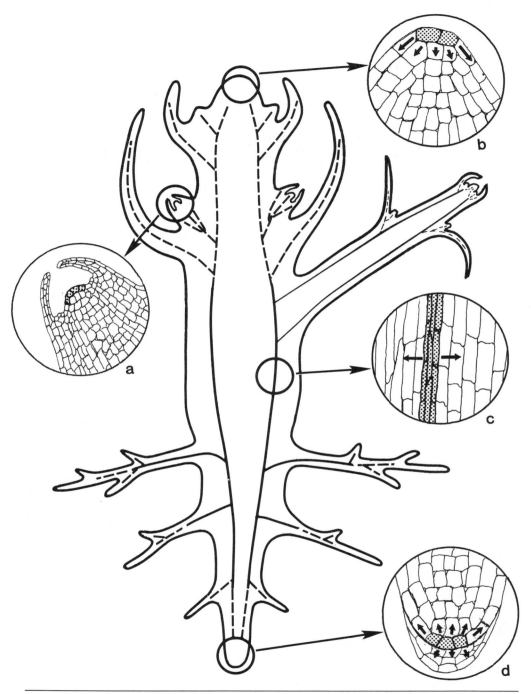

Figure 1-1. Composite representation of a plant to show meristems: (*a*) lateral bud; (*b*) terminal bud; (*c*) vascular cambium; (*d*) root tip.

1. 🌿

Plant Growth and Development

Plants, like all living things, are made up of cells. Groups of cells are arranged into specialized tissues. Tissues make up the organs (stem, leaf, root), and these make up the organism. Cells are generated from specialized dividing cell groups called *initials*. These initials form the growing points, or *meristems,* of shoots, flowers, fruits, and roots of all plants. Woody plants also have a meristematic area, the *cambium,* a more or less cone-shaped cylinder responsible for the diametric growth of stems and branches. Figure 1-1 illustrates meristems in plants.

Other specialized tissues in plants include the central stem core, the *pith;* vascular tissues for water and nutrient transport from the roots, the *xylem;* the food-conducting tissues, or *phloem;* and outer, protective layers, the *epidermis* or *periderm.*

Roots differ slightly in structure from stems in that most lack a central pith. In function, roots, of course, differ considerably in that they provide anchor in the soil and take up essential elements and water. Stems support leaves, flowers, and fruit. Leaves and some stems function as the food-manufacturing organs.

PLANT TYPES

Higher plants, excluding mosses, ferns, algae, and fungi, are usually separated into two basic types—*herbaceous* or *woody*—depending on the tissues they form.

Herbaceous plants generally form soft tissues throughout; woody plants form some soft tissues, but most become harder and lignified. Herbaceous annuals do not develop secondary tissues that allow for shoot enlargement in diameter. Herbaceous perennials develop secondary tissues only at the base of shoots; these result in budlike areas (*shoot primordia*) that generate new shoot growth each season. Because herbaceous annuals do not generate overwintering shoot primordia, they die when their life cycle is completed, usually shortly after flowering and seed production. Marigolds, zinnias, and sweet alyssum are examples of herbaceous annuals.

Some horticultural texts classify herbaceous plants according to their cold tolerance: annuals are intolerant, since they die in freezing weather, whereas perennials, having nonhardy tops but cold-hardy roots, lose only their shoot growth annually. This classification, though useful commercially in colder climates, has its limitations. Many so-called annuals sold in garden centers are actually herbaceous perennials. For example, petunia, geranium, and snapdragon, while treated as annuals in colder climates, are perennials in warmer climates. Some so-called annuals, even in northern climates, are really winter annuals, which germinate from seed in the fall, survive the winter as tiny plants, then go to seed and die in spring. Many of the weedy mustards and several grasses, such as cheatgrass (*Bromus tectorum*), are winter annuals.

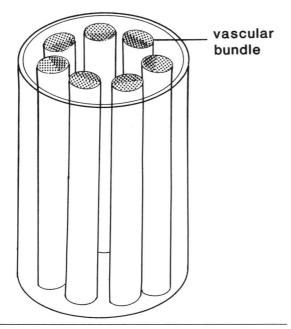

Figure 1-2. Vascular bundles of a monocot. Darkest areas represent the xylem.

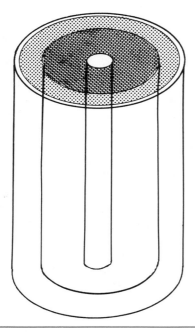

Figure 1-3. Vascular cylinder of a dicot. Darkest areas represent the xylem. Center cylinder is the pith.

Still other herbaceous plants behave as *biennials.* The first year from seed is nonflowering (vegetative). During the second season, the plant produces flowers and seed, then dies. The garden foxglove, canterbury bells, and moneywort are examples of biennials.

Woody Plants

Woody plants have a cambium, called the *vascular cambium,* in stems and roots that creates new conductive tissues (xylem and phloem) each season. In woody plants some tissues become lignified, or hardened, fairly quickly, especially the water- and mineral-conducting tissues (the xylem). The vascular cambium enables diametric growth of stems and roots not possible in annual herbaceous plants and only partly so in herbaceous biennials and perennials.

The arrangement of xylem and phloem (vascular tissues) in woody plants differs somewhat depending upon the type of plant. In woody plants such as the palm, the vascular system is in bundles, separated by large areas of fiber cells and thin-walled cells used for food storage called *parenchyma.* This arrangement is more or less typical in plants known as *monocots,* which include grasses, sedges, rushes, bamboo, and the numerous palms (fig. 1-2). Some monocots—grasses, sedges, and rushes, for example—are herbaceous; others, such as bamboo and palm, are woody.

Woody plants known as *dicots* usually have vascular tissues arranged in more or less a conical cylinder (fig. 1-3). Even this cylinder, however, is interrupted by rows of parenchyma cells known as *rays.* For purposes of this text, it is important to think of the rays as "walls" that divide a tree or shrub into distinct, but discontinuous, wedge-shaped compartments (fig. 1-4). Trees and shrubs are highly compartmented. In addition to the rays, the annual layers of xylem (sometimes called *growth rings*) form another compartment radially. Vertically, individual cells form yet another compartment. Evidence now is strong that even the pith, at least in young twigs in some woody plants, forms a distinct compartment too. Because trees and shrubs are compartmented, they have a unique advantage over animals and other plant types in walling off or "compartmentalizing" invading organisms (see chapters 5 and 7).

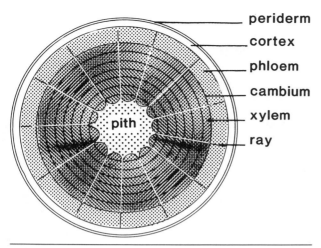

periderm
cortex
phloem
cambium
xylem
ray

pith

Figure 1-4. Traditional cross-sectional view of a woody plant.

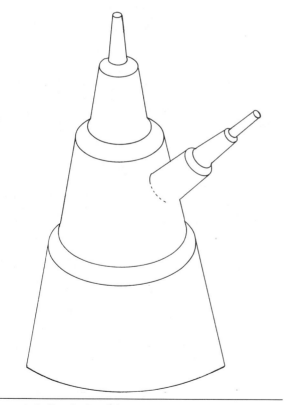

Figure 1-5. Depiction of tree structure as a series of cylindrical cones. Smallest cone is the oldest.

GROWTH STRUCTURE

In this chapter the discusssion of growth of woody plants will be limited to trees. The reader should keep in mind, however, that the discussion also applies to woody shrubs. Classification of woody plants as trees or shrubs is artificial, merely a convenience of man. Shrubs can be pruned to look and behave like small trees; trees can be pruned to look and behave like shrubs. Some texts define woody plants with a mul-tistemmed habit under 15 to 25 feet in height as shrubs and those over that height as multistemmed trees. From the standpoint of growth structure, however, there is no distinction between the two, although in genetic and biochemical makeup, there are distinct differences.

The oldest living things are woody plants. In the Sierra Nevada in California, some bristlecone pines (*Pinus aristata*) have been shown to be over 5,000 years old. More recent evidence indicates that some creosote bushes (*Sarcobatus vermiculatus*) are even older. Such longevity can occur in woody plants, but not in herbaceous plants and in animals, because of the structure and the manner in which woody plants develop defenses against outside forces.

Traditionally, a tree is usually shown as a cross section (fig. 1-4). Depiction of the *annual rings,* much used in science by dendrochronologists to date trees, while helpful, has led most to an incomplete conception of a tree. Trees grow in all dimensions. They are best viewed as cylindrical cones, one placed atop another (fig. 1-5). Thus, a tree is really a tree within a tree within a tree. Even this concept is difficult to comprehend unless a three-dimensional idea is kept in mind, for even the "cone" is interrupted by buds, leaf traces (vascular bundles leading to leaves), and branches.

Even the concept of branch attachment has been grossly misunderstood. Almost all texts on plant anatomy, horticulture, and general botany depict a tree and its branch as a continuous series of layers, as shown in figure 1-6. This concept is inaccurate and has resulted in serious mismanagement of trees through pruning, wound treatment, and even disease control. The correct view of stem and branch in longitudinal section is shown in figure 1-7. Notice that the xylem at the branch–stem union is not continuous except on the lower side.

Also notice that the pith is not continuous as has been traditionally shown. In young branches and stems, a pith protection zone is easily seen in some plants (fig. 1-8). There is also a difference in cell structure and arrangement of stem pith and branch pith. The significance of this is discussed in the chapters on pruning and disease control.

It has also been traditionally accepted that cambial activity proceeds more or less simultaneously on branches and stems (trunks). This concept has been proven false. In spring the growth of trees begins at the buds and progresses along branches toward the stems; this phenomenon is called *basipetal development.*

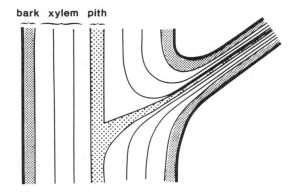

Figure 1-6. Traditional view of a trunk and branch attachment. The concept illustrated by this diagram is incorrect.

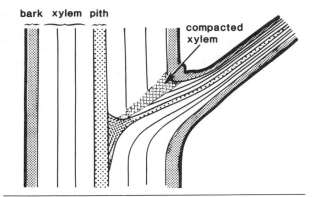

Figure 1-7. Correct view of a trunk and branch attachment indicates that the xylem of the branch and trunk is continuous only below the attachment and that the pith of the stem and branch is not continuous.

As cambial activity nears the stem, it does not develop over the union point of branch and stem in a cylinder, but rather sharply turns downward under the branch onto the stem in a narrow band. Weeks later, the stem cambium becomes active, producing xylem that envelops the base of the branch in a *collar,* as shown in figures 1-9 and 1-10 (Shigo 1984, 1985). This can be readily seen simply by peeling bark from a live stem and branch in late spring or early summer, when leaves are expanding or are fully expanded. Choose a stem and branch at least 1 inch in diameter for easier viewing. Since the xylem of both stem and branch develop first as uneven ridges, appearing somewhat stringy, the pattern of growth can be followed (fig. 1-11). Elm and oak are good species to choose for this bark-peeling exercise.

Figure 1-8. Pith projection zone in red maple (arrow), magnified 40×. (Courtesy Kenneth Dudzik, USDA N.E. Forest Experiment Station)

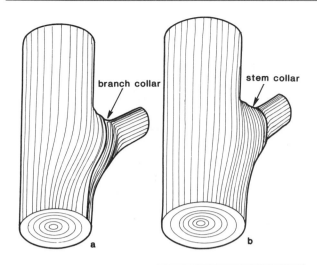

Figure 1-9. Diagram of xylem growth in peeled branches: (*a*) formation of branch collar in spring; (*b*) formation of stem collar in early summer.

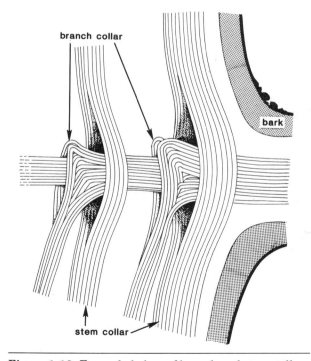

Figure 1-10. Expanded view of branch and stem collars as they would appear if growth rings were pulled apart at a branch.

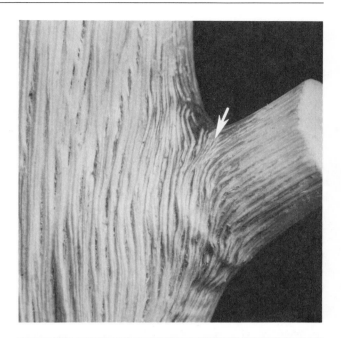

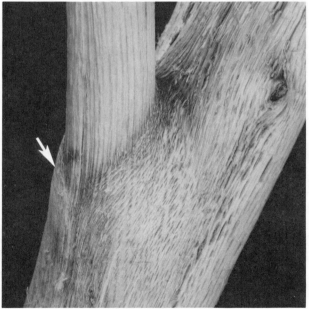

Figure 1-11. Stems and branches of white oak peeled of bark to show xylem development: (*left*) branch collar (arrow) in spring; (*right*) stem collar (arrow) in early summer. (Courtesy Kenneth R. Dudzik, USDA N.E. Forest Experiment Station)

GROWTH PROCESSES

Plants undergo three distinct processes during growth: *photosynthesis* (food manufacture), *respiration* (food utilization), and *transpiration* (water loss). All three processes are intimately linked, but each will be discussed separately.

Photosynthesis

In simple terms, photosynthesis uses energy captured from the sun to combine water and essential elements from the soil with carbon dioxide from the air to produce basic food for plant growth. The photoreceptor (energy receiver) is *chlorophyll,* which is present in certain cells of leaves and young stems. Photosynthesis is actually a very complex process involving numerous enzymes, catalysts, growth hormones, and at least sixteen elements. The complex biochemistry involved is of interest to biochemists, plant physiologists, and others wanting to delve into the intricacies of plant growth. For purposes of this book, however, readers only need to understand the simple, basic process and how environmental changes, soils, and man can influence it.

The basic requirements for photosynthesis include: light of the proper wavelengths and intensity, proper temperature, soil conditions that allow adequate water and nutrient supply, and an atmosphere with a supply of carbon dioxide. If any of these are suboptimal, photosynthesis is reduced or stopped altogether.

Adequate light is, of course, essential to the growth of any green plant. The intensity of light needed may vary, depending upon species. Oddly enough, very bright light destroys chlorophyll in plants. Sun-tolerant plants are those that are capable of maintaining an equilibrium between newly synthesized chlorophyll and that which has been destroyed by light. (Kramer and Kozlowski 1979). Sun-intolerant plants have more new chlorophyll in their leaves than tolerant species, but because they cannot maintain the equilibrium, leaves may bleach and perish under bright light. Many plants, however, can adapt to a change of sunlight exposure if it is not too sudden.

The quality of light is just as important as light intensity. Attempts to grow plants under blue or green light will fail. Red light, which lies at the other end of the spectrum, is required.

Light duration is also important, even acting to trigger certain processes in plants. Some plants will fail to flower if not given enough short days of light. Chrysanthemums and poinsettia are examples of such *short-day* plants. Others, *long-day* plants, fail to flower unless there are a certain number of days with light in excess of eight hours. Still others appear to be *day neutral* in that day length does not affect flowering. It is a common greenhouse practice to manipulate day length with artificial lights to force flowering of plants at any time of year.

Optimum temperatures for photosynthesis also vary from one kind of plant to another. Photosynthesis generally ceases in all plants when temperatures reach 110°F (60°C) or drop to as low as freezing.

Conditions of the soil also affect photosynthesis. If the soil is inadequate in minerals, even in just one of the thirteen elements needed, photosynthesis will be affected. Sometimes the elements needed are present in a soil in adequate amounts but are not available to the plant because of soil reaction (acidity or alkalinity) or water supply. Soils that are too wet or too dry or are very acid or alkaline are not conducive to mineral uptake (see chapter 2).

It should be pointed out here that elements, whether supplied by the soil or by applied fertilizers, *do not constitute plant food,* as is commonly suggested in commercial fertilizer advertising.

Respiration

During plant growth, some of the food made by photosynthesis is used to produce cells, enzymes, proteins, and other essential products in the process of respiration. The basic by-product released is oxygen. Most is released through openings in the leaves called *stomata* (fig. 1-12).

Respiratory activity increases when temperatures increase. Unlike photosynthesis, however, respiration continues to increase with increasing temperatures. The end result can be death of cells as the food supply is exhausted.

Not all carbohydrates made by plants during photosynthesis are used immediately; some are stored in the form of starches, fats, and lipids. This occurs when respiratory activity slows, as temperatures drop. As cooler temperatures as well as shorter days occur near the end of summer, plants in northern climates begin to accumulate stored food energy. In herbaceous perennials and biennial root crops, such as carrots and beets, the energy is stored in the root. In woody plants some is stored in the roots, but most will be found in the overwintering buds, twigs, and stems (or trunks). Thus, the energy needed to resume growth in spring is close at hand, not, as tradition has taught, at the base of the plant—"the sap rises in spring." The *bleeding* observed in some trees results not from sap moving up or down but from the conversion of stored food energy into sugars. This chemical process produces internal pressure in species such as grape, walnut, redbud, maple, and birch. When the pressure is sufficient and there are wounds, whether natural or man-caused, the sugary "sap" is secreted. Oozing of sap can also result when certain disease organisms cause internal fermentation of sugars. This is the case with a common bacterial disease known as slime flux, which is found in elm, poplar, willow, and many other trees (see chapter 8 for more information on this organism).

Respiratory activity in plants is increased by wounding, which stimulates a response by the plant to undergo chemical and physical changes. The changes serve to protect the plant from possible invasion of outside forces, such as disease organisms. Plants *do not* have the ability to heal wounds. They do, however, have varying degrees of chemical protection, built-in walls of defense and, if possessing vascular cambium, can cover or *compartmentalize* their adversary. This subject is discussed in greater detail in chapter 5.

Transpiration

Water loss in plants is a natural and essential function. Only when water is lost faster than it can be replaced does a plant suffer. Excess transpiration results in a water deficit within the plant. It may occur when soil is too dry or too wet, temperatures are excessive, humidity is low, wind velocities are rapid, or roots are disturbed.

Under certain conditions, plants can also be harmed if they fail to lose water at the proper rate. When plants are subjected to sudden changes from high water loss to virtually none, some leaf cells may become damaged due to excess inflation (turgidity) by the water. This commonly occurs to geraniums in greenhouses where the tops of the plants are cooled rapidly under conditions of high relative humidity. This injury, known as *edema* (also spelled oedema), is rare in nature. Some plants, particularly grasses, can release excess water directly through their leaf tips. This phenomenon, called *guttation,* occurs in Kentucky bluegrass and is often mistaken for dew.

Most water is lost through stomata in leaves and lenticels of bark. The remainder of the leaf surface is protected with a waxy layer, the *cuticle,* (see fig. 1-

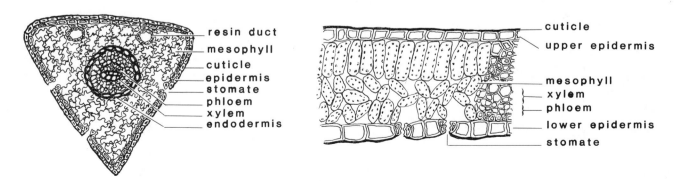

resin duct
mesophyll
cuticle
epidermis
stomate
phloem
xylem
endodermis

cuticle
upper epidermis

mesophyll
xylem
phloem
lower epidermis
stomate

Figure 1-12. Leaves in cross section: (*left*) pine needle; (*right*) deciduous plant.

12). This layer varies in thickness from one plant species to another; sometimes it varies even on the same plant. The cuticle can be penetrated by some microorganisms and insects and damaged by pollutants or injurious chemicals applied by man. Damage from pesticide applications and detergents or surfactants, which is relatively common, is often called *spray burn*.

In actuality, spray burn involves desiccation of a leaf or stem that results from excessive water loss caused by damage to the cuticle. For the same reason, droplets of water can cause leaf spots, or leaf burn. This type of damage is not caused by magnification of the sun's rays by the water droplet, as is popularly believed, but rather by salts and other contaminants in the water. When the water evaporates, the contaminants concentrate, causing damage to the cuticle. Water loss and subsequent death of cells in the affected areas then takes place.

TOLERANCE TO DROUGHT AND SALTS
Drought

The amount of water needed by a plant to sustain life in its cells is about the same whether the cell be from a cactus in a desert or a tree in the rain forest. The average water needed is about 800 pounds per pound of dry weight. However, species do differ in the mechanisms by which they cope with a dry period.

Some plants merely *escape* drought by virtue of their life cycle. Winter annuals, such as mustards and such spring-flowering bulbs as tulip, fit in this category. They grow in fall and spring when moisture is usually ample and temperatures are cool. In the hotter, drier season, they are dormant as seed or bulbs.

Other plants *endure* drought, mostly through structural modifications. Plants with reduced leaf size and thick cuticle, like cacti, are endurers. Others, like sage, have silvery foliage, which tends to reflect heat. Many succulents have infrequent or small stomata and a large water storage area. Examples include the stem of cacti and taproot of yucca. A *taproot,* incidentally, does not tap deep water sources, as often thought, but merely acts as an underground storage for both water and carbohydrates. Many desert plants have deep taproots but obtain water from their shallow lateral roots near the soil surface.

A special group of drought-endurers is sometimes classified as *evaders* (or *avoiders*). These plants have special mechanisms that cause the plant to defoliate during a drought, thus avoiding high water loss. Foliage regrows when moisture is more favorable. The single-leaf ash (*Fraxinus anomola*) of western deserts exhibits this behavior. Also included in this group are plants that have special cells within their leaves called *bulliform* cells. These cells, usually in the epidermal layer, are thinner-walled than most. When drought occurs, the cells become flaccid, causing the leaf to curl under and thus serving to reduce the exposed leaf surfaces. Curl-leaf mountain mahogany (*Cercocarpus ledifolius*) and many grasses are examples. Some plants, such as rhododendrons, also react this way in cold weather.

Most plant scientists now agree that there is no truly drought-resistant plant, at least not without one or more of the mechanisms just mentioned. Perhaps the closest to it are the lichens, which are actually fungi and algae in a mutual association called *symbiosis*. They can survive together on rocks fully exposed to heat for extended periods.

High Tolerance to Salts

There are two basic types of salt-tolerant plants: those that can tolerate salt sprays to their foliage and those that can thrive in soils high in salts.

Coastal plants, such as seagrape and bayberry, can withstand almost constant sprays from ocean water. Most such plants have cuticles on their leaf surfaces that repel salty water.

Plants that thrive in saline soils are, in a sense, drought endurers. High salts in soil cause extreme problems to most plants because water cannot move into the roots—in fact, it will move out of the roots, a process called *plasmolysis*. Much is yet to be learned about how plants cope with soil salinity. It is believed that most salt-enduring species simply slow down growth processes to reduce water needs. It is also known that some plants such as saltbrush (*Atriplex*) secrete excess salts.

It is not surprising that many desert plants have evolved salt-enduring as well as drought-enduring mechanisms, as most soils in arid areas have a tendency to be high in salts.

WATER MOVEMENT IN PLANTS

Perhaps the most important single factor in plant growth and development is the movement of water within the plant.

Plants absorb large quantities of water through roots and even small amounts through leaves. Only about 5 percent of the water is actually used in metabolic activities for growth. The rest is lost by transpiration through lenticels in the bark of woody plants, stomata in the leaves, and to some extent directly through the cuticle.

Plants, especially trees, are large users of water because the vast surface area of their leaves results in high rates of transpiration. It was found, for instance, that a 47-foot-tall silver maple (*Acer saccharinum*) had over 175,000 leaves with a combined leaf area of 7,260 square feet (Kozlowski 1971). Willows and cottonwoods along a ditch or stream may take up as much as 40 inches of water in a growing season (Spurr 1964).

Path of Water Movement

Water, along with mineral elements from the soil, enters a plant through small roots and root hairs. Root hairs, in plants that have them, are extensions of single epidermal cells. Conifers and other plants without root hairs have, in their place, symbiotic fungi called mycorrhiza, which are thought to assist in water and mineral uptake by plants.

Water and minerals then move through several layers of root tissue to the xylem vessels and tracheids, through which they move to branches, leaves, flowers, and fruit. For some time it was thought that water moved only in the most recently formed ring of xylem (usually called sapwood). It is now known, however, that xylem tissue can remain active for water transport for several years in some trees.

The ascent of water and minerals may not be in a straight path. Rudinsky and Vite (1959) reported that the pathway may be spiral (as in spruce), interlocked (more or less zigzag), or straight. The variations are the result of the structural formation of the xylem cells. This phenomenon is worth remembering because it is useful in diagnosing plant problems, as discussed in chapter 13.

Water and Nutrient Ascent

Exactly how water reaches the tops of tall trees has been a subject of much controversy for centuries. Early investigators thought that water was "pumped" by contraction of the medullary rays. Others ascribed to the theory that movement and subsequent bending of cell walls created a suction, causing water uptake. Still others, as late as 1900, theorized that water is taken up only in live tissues; this was called the vital theory. In the early 1900s, the root pressure theory was proposed to explain water movement in plants.

The vital theory was soon abandoned when it was shown that dead cells could take up water just as readily as live ones. The root pressure theory, which was based upon observation of sap flow from wounds in late winter (as in sugar maples, birch, redbud, grapes, and walnut), was also discounted by most scientists when it was found that few species developed root pressure and those that did failed to produce pressure when growth resumed (Kozlowski 1961). What was being observed, of course, was the conversion of stored carbohydrates (starches, mostly) into sugars, which resulted in pressure within the plant, as discussed earlier in this chapter. It should be kept in mind that at the time the root pressure theory was popular, it was also thought that sap went down in the fall and rose in spring. This has subsequently resulted in many fallacious practices in horticulture and arboriculture.

More modern concepts, based on extensive studies and the use of radioactive isotopes, have replaced these early theories. It has been found that the ascent of sap involves several mechanisms, including transpiration loss of water, capillarity, and the cohesive force of water. As water is lost, capillarity in the small tubes (vessels and tracheids) causes water to move to replace that which was lost. The strong cohesive force of water in capillary tubes is responsible for water columns as high as a tree to maintain an unbroken continuum.

Some scientists questioned this "cohesive force of water" theory, indicating that air bubbles in the vessels and tracheids would break the cohesiveness of water. Research has shown, however, that even where there are air bubbles in xylem vessels and tracheids, trees have more than enough cells to overcome this problem (Kozlowski 1961).

The cohesive force of water can be demonstrated by the following simple exercise. Place some water on a small pane of glass, put another pane of glass on top, and then try to pull the two panes apart. Considerable force is necessary to separate the two unless they are slid sideways. This is because water forms a molecular bond in the small space and large surface area between the glass panes. The same concept, which also applies to "super glues," accounts for the strong affinity of water in cells of plants.

COLD HARDINESS

Resistance of plants to cold temperatures is of great concern to horticulturists, foresters, and arborists. In most landscape plantings and "urban forests," the plants used to come from varying habitats. It is not uncommon to find plantings containing fewer than 10 percent indigenous species and over 90 percent introduced or exotic ones. With such mixed plantings, it is important to choose species that come from areas comparable in climatic conditions to the area being planted. Usually, however, such mixed groups contain a wide variation in cold hardiness as well as adaptability to soils and exposure. As a result, periodic severe freezes in some areas of the country will kill some plants in a landscape but not others.

Selecting plants for cold hardiness is not as simple as choosing plants from areas of similar climate, because even microclimatic conditions can make a difference. Plants produced from seed will also vary genetically in cold hardiness. Seed of a species collected from a native habitat in a southern, warmer climate will generally produce less hardy plants than seed of the same species from a more northern climate. Thus, it is important to know the origin of plants before attempting to use them in a landscape site.

Even the tissues of plants vary in hardiness. Flower buds of forsythia and peach, for example, are generally less hardy than vegetative buds on the same plants. Roots are less hardy than top growth. A plant that may sustain air temperatures of $-40°F$ ($-40°C$) may have roots capable of withstanding only $0°F$ to $-5°F$ ($-18°C$ to $-21°C$). This, of course, poses special problems to nurserymen trying to overwinter container-grown stock or using plants in raised planters in northern climates.

Mechanisms of Cold Injury

Much research is being done on the mechanisms of cold injury in plants. No simple concept explains why cold injures one plant and not another or just how injury takes place within a plant. Simulations of cold injury in laboratory experiments cannot necessarily be correlated with what actually happens under natural conditions. Studies of what happens in living cells is difficult because the very preparation needed to view cells microscopically alters the natural conditions. Nevertheless, most researchers today agree that cold injury to cells involves intracellular freezing (within the cell) or extracellular freezing (between cells or in the spaces between cells).

It has been thought that intracellular freezing under rapid cooling can cause ice crystals to form within the cell, leading to physical rupturing of the cell membranes. Whether or not this commonly occurs in nature is still questioned.

Research has shown that most freeze injury is actually a desiccation of the cell caused by extracellular freezing (Li and Sakai 1978; Weiser 1970; Kramer and Kozlowski 1979). Even plants that undergo extracellular freezing can survive if it occurs slowly.

The speed at which freezing occurs, temperatures achieved, duration of cold, condition of plant tissues, and genetic variability are intertwining factors that determine cold hardiness and resistance to frost.

Acclimation of Plants to Cold

Studies by Weiser (1970) have shown that woody plants typically undergo three stages of cold acclimation. The first stage takes place before frost occurs and may be triggered by either shortening days or cool temperatures or both. This is a gradual change of metabolic activity, which correspondingly alters the chemical composition in plant cells. The second phase occurs when there is a killing frost. Following a frost, changes occur in sugars, proteins, amino acids, and other metabolic products that increase the cold resistance of the cells. Sugars are converted to stored energy in the form of starches; fats and lipids increase. In the third phase, occurring during very cold temperatures, "binding" of water in cells occurs. This enables hardy plants to withstand very low temperatures. In a sense, water is supercooled to the extent that it does not freeze in the usual sense. The degree of hardiness achieved appears to be largely dependent upon the rate of cooling. Plants subjected to rapid cooling may not develop as much hardiness as others of the same species that are subjected to gradual cooling.

Although this description of acclimation is an oversimplification of a very complex process, it does suggest several important points to remember from the standpoint of landscape management:

1. Choose plants that are known to be from hardy sources. For example, green ash trees from Tennessee may be less hardy than those from Wisconsin.
2. When purchasing plants from nursery suppliers, make sure that the stock, even though considered hardy for the originating area, has been properly acclimated to local conditions. For example, nursery stock shipped from Oregon in spring may not be properly acclimated to midwestern conditions and may be in a more active state of growth than local conditions dictate.
3. Newly received plants from distant suppliers should be acclimated for several days to weeks, depending upon conditions, before planting at a site. Acclimation in a lath house or unheated greenhouse is usually sufficient.

Sunscald, Frost Cracks, and Ring Shakes

A common problem in newly planted trees is the development of a condition known as sunscald. The term *sunscald* is somewhat unfortunate because it implies that the rays of the sun burn the bark of a tree. This is not the case. Sunscald, sometimes called *southwest disease,* is actually a dehydration of bark tissues resulting from sudden temperature changes. It occurs mostly in late December through late February. At that time of year, many trees have satisfied cold dormancy requirements and cells can become active if temperatures are suitable.

If the weather is sunny, cells in the bark on the southwest exposure of a tree may become metabolically active in response to warmth. This results in a loss of cold hardiness. If nighttime temperatures are freezing, as is often the case in northern areas, the sudden temperature drop causes extracellular freeze injury (movement of water out of cells) and subsequent dehydration. Insulative tree wrap is therefore used as a standard nursery practice on young, thin-barked trees. The tree wrap is designed to keep temperatures of the bark from changing rapidly.

Frost cracks occur in trees because of sudden changes in temperature or even from drought stress (fig. 1-13). Contrary to popular belief, however, they start on the *inside* of a tree as a result of defects from earlier injury (Shigo 1983, 1984). In other words, in the unlikely event it was possible to find a tree with no defects, the tree would not develop frost cracks, regardless of temperature extremes or water stresses.

Figure 1-13. Old frost crack in a red oak. Crack started from a defect inside the tree. (Courtesy Alex L. Shigo [ret.], USDA N.E. Forest Experiment Station)

Ring shakes are separations along thin-walled cells in the region between annual growth rings (fig. 1-14). When an injury occurs as a result of cold temperatures, the barrier zone between growth rings develops boundaries. The boundary is relatively weak, and thus separation of rings may occur.

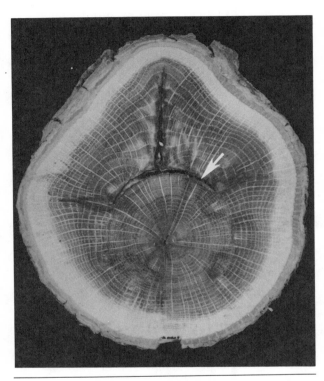

Figure 1-14. Ring shake in oak (arrow). Note that a frost crack radiates from the ring shake. Frost cracks and ring shakes begin from defects inside the tree, not from the outside. (Courtesy Alex L. Shigo [ret.], USDA N.E. Forest Experiment Station)

REFERENCES

Eames, A. J., and MacDaniels, L. H. 1947. An Introduction to Plant Anatomy. New York: McGraw-Hill Book Co.

Esau, K. 1953. Plant Anatomy. New York: J. W. Ley & Sons, Inc.

Kozlowski, T. T. 1961. The movement of water in trees. For. Sci. 7:177–92.

————. 1971. Growth and Development of Trees. Vol. 1— Seed Germination, Ontogeny and Shoot Growth. New York: Academic Press.

Kramer, P. J., and Kozlowski, T. T. 1979. Physiology of Woody Plants. New York: Academic Press.

Li, P. H., and Sakai, A., ed. 1978. Plant Cold Hardiness and Freezing Stress: Mechanisms and Crop Implications. New York: Academic Press.

Romberger, J. A. 1963. Meristems, growth and development in woody plants. USDA Tech. Bull. 1293.

Rudinsky, J. A., and Vite, J. P. 1959. Certain ecological and phylogenic aspects of the pattern of water conduction in conifers. For. Sci. 5:259–66.

Shigo, A. L. 1983. Tree defects: A photo guide. USDA N.E. Forest Exp. Sta. Report NE-82.

————. 1984. Tree decay and pruning. J. Arboriculture 8:1–12.

————. 1985. How tree branches are attached to trunks. Can. J. Bot. 63 (8):1391–1401.

Spurr, S. H. 1964. Forest Ecology. New York: Ronald Press.

Weiser, C. J. 1970. Cold resistance and injury in woody plants. Science 169:1269–78.

Zimmerman, M. H., and Brown, C. L. 1971. Trees: Structure and Function. New York: Springer-Verlag.

2.

Soils and Plant Fertility

Variations in soils lead to some of the most perplexing problems encountered by landscape managers. Soil takes many years to develop under natural conditions; it is easily destroyed by disturbance but not easily reclaimed. It has been estimated that one inch of topsoil in the semi-arid prairies of the west takes about 100 years to form. In more humid, higher rainfall areas, soil may form more quickly because of the more dense vegetation.

While it is possible to grow plants without soil, such "soilless culture" is limited to greenhouses.

What we call soil is the upper few inches or feet of the earth's crust. This portion is in constant contact with the atmosphere and is subject to weathering. The action of water as a solvent, freezes and thaws, oxygen, carbon dioxide, acids, and the decomposition of plants and animals contribute to weathering. The type of parent material—rock—and the way in which it is weathered determines the soil type formed.

SOIL LAYERS AND TOPSOIL

A natural soil profile will usually have three distinct layers, or horizons. The *A* horizon is the most weathered and constitutes what is normally called *topsoil*. The *B* horizon, a transition area, is usually referred to as *subsoil*. The *C* horizon has little or no soil development and is the area of accumulated salts, lime, and other materials.

The term topsoil is often used in very vague ways. Nurserymen, landscape contractors, and landscape architects often call for topsoil in specifications without further definition. This has led to many planting jobs with relatively poor soil because almost any available soil can pass as topsoil. Because topsoils vary so much, specifications should not be vague. Good specifications spell out the major requirements, including the texture, organic content, parameters of available nutrients, and drainage characteristics of the soil.

Most sites to be landscaped have been severely disturbed by building activities, utility trenching, and grade changes. It is not uncommon to find the site totally stripped of the upper soil layers, leaving only subsoil. Removal and stockpiling of the upper soil layers during construction is practiced by many landscape architects. While commendable, this activity is often performed incorrectly and can lead to bigger problems later. Soil is sometimes stockpiled around or near existing trees. This practice will lead to the death of the trees because the added soil layers reduce oxygen exchange to tree roots. Stockpiled soil that is later applied over the site in varying thicknesses can also lead to problems. When stockpiled soil is applied over a subsoil, particularly one that has been compacted by construction and grading equipment, the movement of water is interrupted by the layering. This creates a perched water table effect and can lead to accumulated salts, as discussed later in this chapter.

To avoid this layering effect, stockpiled soils and soils brought to a site as topsoil should be partially incorporated into the subsoil. One method is to apply about one-third of the soil, rototill, plow, or disc into the subsoil, then apply the remainder. This allows for a more natural soil transition.

ESTIMATING SOIL TEXTURE

The ideal soil has about 50 percent air space and 50 percent solids. The solids consist of organic matter (OM) and minerals. Many soil texts indicate that an ideal soil should be about 45 percent minerals and 5 percent OM, but in addition to ratios of minerals to OM, it is also important to consider the composition of the mineral component and arrangement of the particles and their aggregate sizes.

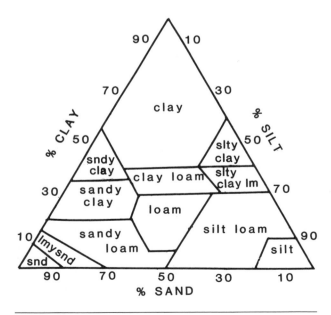

Figure 2-1. Soil texture triangle. The percentages of sand, silt, and clay determine texture.

Texture can be estimated by a simple "feel" test. Roll some slightly moistened soil between thumb and forefinger. If it forms a firm ball, feels smooth, and becomes very sticky when moistened, it is high in clay. If it feels grainy and does not hold a ball, it is more sandy. A more precise test, of course, can be conducted by a soils laboratory, where the soil particle sizes are accurately separated by screening into clay, sand, and silt.

If budget or time does not permit a laboratory test, but a texture determination more accurate than the feel test is desirable, the following fairly simple procedure can be used:

1. Take a representative sample of the soil in question (about 1 pint is sufficient).
2. Dry the soil and pulverize with a roller (rolling pin or wooden mallet) to break down the largest clods.
3. Add 1 cup of the sample to a quart jar.
4. Add water to cover the soil completely by at least 2 inches.
5. Add 1 teaspoon of nonsudsing detergent.
6. Place lid on jar and shake the mixture thoroughly.
7. Allow to settle for at least three days. (The clay may take weeks to settle fully, but three days yields most of it.)
8. Measure the thickness of sand (bottom layer), silt (middle layer), and clay (top layer). For each layer, multiply the thickness by 100 and divide by the total thickness of all three layers. This will give the approximate percentage of each layer. These values will not be quite accurate because some of the clay is still suspended.
9. Use a triangular texture chart (fig. 2-1) to determine soil texture.

The best soil texture for landscaped areas is a sandy clay loam.

AMENDING A SOIL

Building a good soil, starting with the typical excavator, or subsoil, found in most landscape developments cannot be done properly in a year, or even two. Soil improvement is a continual process. It often takes ten years or more to make a productive soil. Unfortunately, few invest the time and effort to do this. Amendments, however, still help.

If soil is too sandy or too high in clay, the solution to both extremes is essentially the same—add organic matter. In a sandy soil, organic matter acts much like a sponge to hold moisture and minerals. In clay, organic matter helps to aggregate the finer particles, allowing for larger pore spaces and thus improving aeration and drainage.

It is possible, especially in clay soils, to create a soluble salt problem by adding too much organic matter at once. This is especially true if some sources of manure are used. The general rule of thumb is to incorporate no more than 3 cubic yards of organic matter per 1,000 square feet of soil each year. This is equivalent to 1¼ inches of amendment on the soil surface before it is tilled in.

Coarse sand also can be used to break up a clay soil. Avoid using fine-textured masonry sand. The danger in using sand alone is in not adding enough. Too small a quantity added to clay can aggravate the situation by forming a bricklike substance. Normally, sand must be added to reach or exceed one-third the soil volume before it will help to break up the clay.

All amendments should be thoroughly tilled into the soil, making a uniform mixture.

Organic Amendments

The best organic amendments include relatively coarse peats, partially decomposed compost, and aged barnyard manure. The type of manure is not important, but it should be at least one year old if planting in the amended soil is anticipated soon after incorporation of the manure. Fresh manure usually is too high in ammonia, which injures plant roots. If manure has a strong acrid odor, avoid using it or let the amended ground lie fallow for several months before planting. Because of high salts, repeated use of most feedlot manures should be avoided unless the salts can be leached first. Dairy cattle manure generally is lower in salt content.

Coarse sphagnum peat is a good amendment but is quite expensive compared with manure or compost. Avoid using "native" sedge peats unless they are mixed with coarser material.

Most peat on the market is processed. It is air-dried, pulverized if needed, and sometimes screened. It is sold in bags or compressed in bales. It may be sold by weight or by cubic foot or yard. Peat sold by weight is usually bagged and *seems* less expensive until one actually compares cost to volume. Peat sold in compressed bales by volume (cubic foot) goes much farther than most bagged peat.

Peat in compressed bales is usually sphagnum peat from Canada, northeastern United States, Florida, or occasionally Europe. All are relatively expensive, with European peats being almost prohibitively expensive.

Rocky Mountain peats are sedge peats. They are blacker than sphagnum peats and usually lower in organic matter. They also tend to be to too finely pulverized. Such finely pulverized peats tend to act like a glue between soil particles and can actually hinder aeration and drainage.

Peats vary considerably in organic content and in pH. An analysis of peats from different sources is shown in table 2-1. When using peat to amend a soil, keep in mind that the organic content is the most important factor. Calculate value accordingly.

Inorganic Amendments

In addition to coarse sand, inorganic amendments include calcine clay products (such as Turface), pulverized volcanic rock (scoria), perlite (heat-treated limestone), and diatomaceous earth. These materials are compar-

Table 2-1. Organic Content and pH of Peats from Different Sources

Peat Source	Organic Matter (%)	pH
Canadian (sphagnum)	96.4	3.3
Michigan (sphagnum)	94.4	3.9
Colorado (sedge peats)		
Cripple Creek	64.6	5.9
Grand Mesa	60.6	6.0
Palisade	58.2	4.2
Leadville	56.8	5.2
Gunnison	52.5	6.8
Colorado Springs	46.8	5.0

Source: Unpublished data, Charles M. Drage, Department of Horticulture, Colorado State University.

atively expensive and probably practical only for amending small plots or small amounts of potting soils.

Lime, gypsum, and sulfur are sold as inorganic soil amendments. Whether or not they are useful depends upon the existing soil conditions. In soils of low pH (acidic), the use of lime will increase pH where desired. This practice is most commonly used for turfgrasses in the midwestern and eastern states.

Gypsum can be useful in soils high in adsorbed sodium and is discussed in further detail later in this chapter. Gypsum also helps certain tight, clay soils to aggregate, thus improving drainage. Unfortunately, gypsum is mistakenly thought to aid drainage in all clay soils. Gypsum will *only* aggregate a clay soil that is low in calcium (such as some of the kaolinite clays of the eastern states). It will not work on the bentonites of the semi-arid and arid climates because they already have a high calcium content; no reaction can occur to cause aggregation. Instead, more calcium in the form of a salt, calcium sulfate, is added.

Sulfur can be added to acidify a soil, but it is not usually practical on a large scale. It also depends upon how high the pH is initially. This is discussed further in the section on soil reaction.

WATER MOVEMENT IN SOIL

The rate at which water moves through a soil depends not only on the pore space sizes but also on the particle sizes of the soil and the degree of aggregation. Soils high in clay have many very small particles and tend to also have small pore spaces. At the same time, such soils also have tremendous surface area and strong surface tension. Very sandy soils are just the opposite. To understand water movement in soils, it is best to examine a soil from the standpoint of surface tension rather than porosity.

Water itself exerts a cohesive force or tension. The thinner the film of water, the greater the tension. When water is distributed as a film on soil particles, a tremendous affinity between water and particle results.

Water moves through gravel or sandy soil quickly, not only because of the large spaces between particles, but also because of the low tension between water and particle. Overlay a sandy or gravelly soil with a soil high in clay content, however, and water will tend to stay in the soil above the gravel because of the greater tension (fig. 2-2).

Conversely, overlaying a loam on a band of compacted

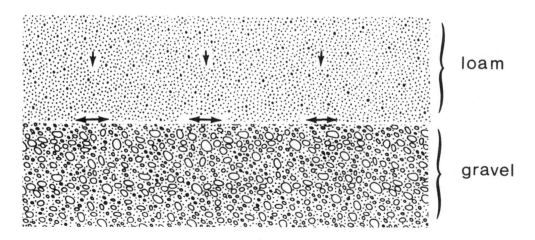

Figure 2-2. Movement of water (arrows) when loam is layered over gravel. Higher tension in the loam prevents water from moving into gravel.

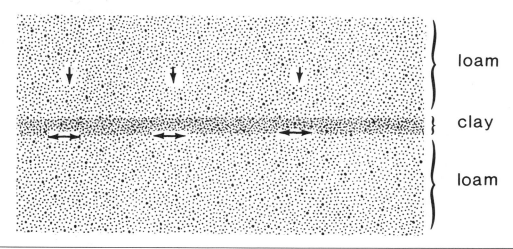

Figure 2-3. Movement of water (arrows) when a clay layer interrupts a loam soil. Higher tension in clay will prevent downward water movement.

clay will result in movement of water into the clay until all of the pore space in the clay is filled. The water will not readily move out of the clay, however, because the clay soil band has the greater tension of the two soils (fig. 2-3).

Soil–water tension has considerable practical implications in landscape horticulture and is discussed more thoroughly in chapter 4.

SOIL REACTION

Soil reaction is expressed in terms of pH, which is a measure of acidity or alkalinity. The major factors influencing soil reaction include rainfall, drainage, nature of the parent material, quality of irrigation, type and frequency of fertilizer applications, and length of time a soil has been cultivated or managed.

In simple terms, the pH scale runs from 0 to 14. The value of 7 is neutral; below 7, acid; and above 7, alkaline, or basic. Actually, the pH scale is logarithmic. A pH of 0 means that the solution contains 1 gram of H^+ (hydrogen) ions per liter (the presence of H^+ ions makes the solution acid). A solution of pH 1 has $\frac{1}{10}$ gram of H^+ ions per liter; pH 2, $\frac{1}{100}$ gram; pH 3, $\frac{1}{1,000}$ gram, and so on. At pH 7 the solution contains

$\frac{1}{10^7}$ H^+ ions per liter, while at pH 14 it contains $\frac{1}{10^{14}}$ gram. The *pH scale is not linear*. A drop of one pH unit (say from 4 to 3) means that the H^+ concentration has changed from $\frac{1}{10,000}$ gram per liter to $\frac{1}{1,000}$. This is a ten-fold increase. Remember, then, that a change of one pH unit means a *ten-fold* change in acidity.

The reason that 7 is the neutral point on this scale is that when a solution contains $\frac{1}{10^7}$ gram H^+ ions per liter, it is balanced by an equal number of OH^- ions. (The presence of these OH^- ions tends to make the solution basic.) Above pH 7 there are more OH^- than H^+ ions, so the solution is basic.

What is the effect of soil reaction on plant growth? Naturally a neutral environment (pH 7) is ideal for a large number of plants. Many soils, however, are acid or basic and can still support good plant growth. Plant growth can occur anywhere in the pH range of 3.5 to 10.0. For most plants, soil reactions in the pH range of about 6.0 to 8.3 require no special practices if the right plants are chosen for the soil. The optimum pH for most plants is 6.5 to 7.5. Acid-loving species, such as rhododendron, azalea, and many conifers need soils with a pH of 5.0 to 6.0 (fig. 2-4). Some plants, including Kentucky bluegrass, actually do best in slightly alkaline conditions. A list of selected plants and their optimum pH range is shown in table 2-2.

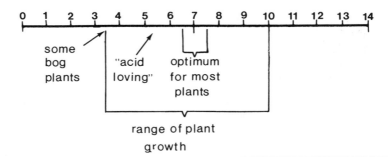

Figure 2-4. Soil pH range for plants.

Table 2-2. Optimum pH Range of Selected Landscape Plants

Plant	pH
Ageratum	6.0–7.0
Anemone	5.0–6.0
Apple	5.0–6.5
Ash, American	6.0–7.5
Aspen	3.8–5.5
Aster, alpine	5.5–7.0
Aster, New England	6.0–8.0
Azalea	4.5–6.0
Baby's breath	6.0–7.5
Bachelor's button	6.0–7.5
Balloon flower	5.0–6.0
Barberry, Japanese	6.0–7.5
Basswood (linden)	6.0–7.5
Bearberry (kinnickinnick)	4.5–6.0
Beautybush	6.0–7.5
Birch, European	4.5–6.0
Bleedingheart	6.0–7.5
Blueberry, highbush	4.0–5.5
Boxwood	6.0–7.5 (6.5 max)
Buffaloberry	6.0–8.0
Calendula	5.5–7.0 (8.5 max)
Candytuft, perennial	5.5–7.0 (8.0 max)
Canterberry bells	6.5–7.0
Cherry, sour	6.0–7.0
Chokeberry (*Aronia*)	5.0–6.0
Chrysanthemum	6.0–7.5 (8.2 max)
Cinquefoil (*Potentilla*)	6.0–7.0
Cockscomb (celosia)	6.0–7.5
Coleus	6.0–7.0
Columbine, Colorado	6.0–7.0
Coral bells	6.0–7.0
Cosmos	5.0–8.0
Cottonwood, fremont	6.0–8.0
Crocus	6.0–8.0
Currant, red	5.5–7.0

Table 2.2, *continued.*

Plant	pH
Daisy, ox-eye	6.0–7.5
Daisy, shasta	6.0–8.0
Delphinium	6.0–7.5
Dogwood, flowering	5.0–7.0
Dogwood, yellow twig	6.0–7.0
Euonymus, winged	5.5–7.0
Fern, maidenhair	6.0–8.0
Firethorn	6.0–8.0
Foxglove	6.0–7.5
Gaillardia	6.0–7.5
Geranium, domestic	6.0–8.0
Hackberry	6.0–8.0
Hawthorn, Paul's scarlet	6.0–7.0
Hemlock	5.0–6.0
Hen and chickens	6.0–8.0
Holly, American	5.0–6.0
Honeylocust	6.0–8.0
Honeysuckle, tatarian	6.5–8.0
Iris, German	6.5–7.5
Iris, Japanese	5.5–6.5
Juniper, common	5.0–6.5
Juniper, creeping	5.0–6.0
Kentucky coffeetree	6.0–8.0
Lilac, common	6.0–7.5
Lilac, Persian	6.0–8.0
Lily, regal	6.0–7.0
Lobelia	6.0–7.5
Lupine, garden	6.5–7.5
Magnolia, saucer	5.0–6.0
Maple, silver	5.5–6.0
Maple, sugar	6.0–7.5
Mint	7.0–8.0
Myrtle, crape	5.0–6.0
Ninebark	6.0–7.5
Oak, bur	5.0–6.0

Table 2.2, *continued.*

Plant	pH
Oak, English	6.0–8.0
Oak, pin	5.0–6.5
Oak, red	4.5–6.0 (7.5 max)
Pansy, tricolor	5.5–6.5
Peony	6.0–7.5
Periwinkle, perennial	6.0–7.5
Phlox (divaricata)	6.0–8.0
Pine, mugo	5.0–6.5
Pine, white	4.5–6.0 (7.5 max)
Poppy, oriental	6.0–7.5
Primrose (polyantha)	5.5–7.0
Pyrethrum	6.0–7.5
Rhododendron, Carolina	4.5–6.0
Rose, hybrid tea	5.5–7.0 (7.5 max)
Rosemary, bog	3.0–5.0
Snapdragon	6.0–8.0
Spirea, VanHoutte	6.0–7.0
Spruce, Colorado	6.0–7.0
Spruce, Norway	5.0–6.0
Stonecrop, showy	5.5–7.0
Sumac, staghorn	5.0–6.0
Sweet William	6.0–7.5
Tamarix	6.5–8.0
Tree-of-heaven	6.0–7.0
Verbena	6.0–8.0
Violet, sweet	6.0–7.5
Walnut, black	6.0–8.0
Willow, pussy	6.5–8.0
Yarrow	6.5–8.0
Yellowwood	6.0–8.0
Yew, Japanese	6.0–7.0
Zinnia	5.5–7.5

Source: Adapted from Michigan State College (1941).

Base Exchange

To understand the fundamental problem of soil reaction, one must understand the concept of *base exchange.* First, it must be recognized that the clay particles in soils have a large total surface area because of their small size. With most common rocks it would require a cube of about 2.2 inches on each side to weigh a pound. This cube would have a total surface area of about 29.4 square inches. If we cut this cube up into particles, 0.1 micrometer on a side (that would be $\frac{1}{2,540,000}$ of an inch), the total surface area would be 113,000 square feet or about 2.6 acres. A loam soil

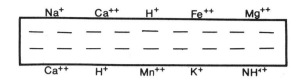

Figure 2-5. Soil colloid (micelle) with minerals adsorbed to colloid surface.

may actually contain several acres of surface *per pound* of soil. This surface is charged and chemically active. It is the heart of positively charged plant minerals in the soil. Thus, it is a storehouse of soil fertility.

A diagrammatic representation of a soil particle charged with various chemical elements is shown in figure 2-5. Some of the important ions that may be held in this manner are calcium (Ca^{2+}), magnesium (Mg^{2+}), iron (Fe^{2+}), manganese (Mn^{2+}), potassium (K^+), copper (Cu^+), sodium (Na^+), ammonia (NH_4^+), and hydrogen (H^+).

Soils vary in reaction depending on the ions present. If one or another ion predominates, or is present in excess, the pH and/or structure of the soil may be detrimental to plant growth. However, by the addition of certain soil amendments, the excess ion may be exchanged for (replaced by) another, leading to improved soil. Three commonly encountered soil conditions are acid soils, calcium clay soils, and sodic soils.

Acid Soils

In the case of acid soils, the major ion attached to soil particle surfaces is H^+ (fig. 2-6). These H^+ ions are in equilibrium with those in the surrounding soil solution, causing the solution to be acid. In order to reduce acidity, we must reduce the concentration of H^+ in solution *and* on the surface of the soil clay. In order to do this, we add lime ($CaCO_3$), which furnishes a

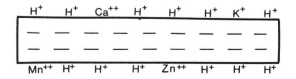

Figure 2-6. Acidic colloid with excess of hydrogen ions (H^+).

source of Ca^{2+} (dissolved calcium). The H^+ reacts with the CO_3^{2-} (carbonate) portion of the lime to form carbon dioxide and water, as follows:

$$2H^+ + CaCO_3 \longrightarrow Ca^{2+} + H_2O + CO_2$$

or

$$\text{Acid} + \text{Lime} \longrightarrow \underset{\text{calcium}}{\text{Soluble}} + \text{Water} + \underset{\text{dioxide}}{\text{Carbon}}$$

Calcium Clay Soils

When Ca^{2+} is predominant, pH will be neutral or slightly alkaline, and the soil particles will tend to cling together. This tendency to cling is very important because it is the basis for aggregation, structure, or good soil tilth. This fact, however, has also led to the common belief in some arid areas that adding gypsum (calcium sulfate) to clay will result in aggregation of clay. Unfortunately, as mentioned earlier, gypsum does not work in clays typical in arid areas because they are already high in calcium. Thus, Ca clay soil plus gypsum ($CaSO_4$) results in Ca clay soil with more calcium. The addition of gypsum to such soils may, in fact, increase salinity. Gypsum is useful only in sodic soils, as discussed in the next section.

To improve a clay soil high in calcium, incorporate organic matter. Although this may or may not alter pH, it will improve aggregation and thus drainage.

Sodic Soils

A third common soil condition is a predominance of sodium (Na^+) attached to the soil particles (fig. 2-7). When this condition occurs, the pH is usually high, above 8.5. Unfortunately, pH is not an exact indicator of sodium problems and high sodium may exist without high pH. When sodium is attached (adsorbed) to over 15 percent of the charges on the soil surface, the soil is referred to as *sodium affected* or *sodic*. A soils laboratory will report this as the SAR (sodium adsorption ratio). The term *alkali* is also used here but may be misleading since the word is also used, though incorrectly, to refer to soluble salts.

The effect of sodium is twofold. First, excessive sodium is directly toxic to plant growth. This effect varies with different kinds of plants. Second, sodium-affected soil particles do not cling together in aggregates. Normal soil contains crumbs, or aggregates, which act as very large soil particles. The pore spaces between these aggregates are large, allowing free movement of air and water. The effect of excessive sodium attached to the soil particles is to prevent clinging, therefore breaking down the aggregates. This results in a loss of the large pores between aggregates and restricts movement of water and air. Such soils form hard clods, are very sticky when wet, and take water very poorly. A comparison of aggregated and sodic soils is depicted in figure 2-8.

The purpose of sodic soil amendments is to provide a source of soluble calcium to replace the sodium on the exchange complex. This chemically is expressed as follows:

$$\text{Na clay} + Ca^{2+}\text{ salt} \longrightarrow \text{Ca clay} + Na^+\text{ salt}$$

The dissolved sodium salt must then be removed by water moving through the soil profile, that is, leached out. Heavy irrigation is often sufficient for this purpose. If heavy irrigation is not possible because the land will not drain and will simply remain flooded, drainage must be improved. Refer to the section on reducing salts later in this chapter for more details.

When gypsum is used to supply water-soluble calcium,

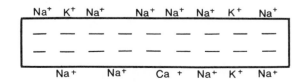

Figure 2-7. Sodic condition with excess of sodium ions (Na^+) adsorbed to colloid surface.

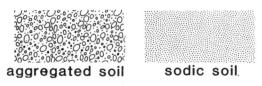

aggregated soil   sodic soil

Figure 2-8. Comparison between an aggregated and sodic soil. Sodic soils become very compacted and poorly drained.

the chemical reaction that takes place is illustrated as follows:

$$CaSO_4 + Na\ clay \longrightarrow Na_2SO_4 + Ca\ clay$$

The sodium sulfate must be removed so that a calcium clay will form. Formation of the calcium clay will result in a more desirable soil structure. Calcium chloride ($CaCl_2$) also is very effective as a sodic soil amendment but is too expensive for most situations.

Sulfuric acid (H_2SO_4) is sometimes used as an amendment for sodic soils, but it is very costly and somewhat hazardous to the user. Lime ($CaCO_3$) must be present in the soil for H_2SO_4 to be effective. The reaction of the acid with lime forms gypsum, thus changing an insoluble form of calcium (lime) to a soluble form (gypsum), as follows:

$$\underset{\text{(insoluble)}}{H_2SO_4 + CaCO_3} \longrightarrow \underset{\text{(soluble)}}{CaSO_4 + H_2CO_3}$$

The gypsum that is formed reacts as in the previous equation to form a calcium clay, and the replaced sodium must be removed by leaching.

Elemental sulfur has been used to form soluble calcium salts in limey soils. It must be oxidized by the soil bacteria to sulfuric acid as shown by the following reaction:

$$2S + 3O_2 + 2H_2O \longrightarrow 2H_2SO_4$$

This process may take several months. The sulfuric acid, in turn, reacts with lime in the soil to form gypsum. Lime sulfur is usually considered as reacting essentially the same as elemental sulfur.

Iron sulfates, both ferric and ferrous, are sometimes used as soil amendments to limey sodic soils. Their reaction can be represented in the following manner:

$$FeSO_4 + 2H_2O \longrightarrow Fe(OH)_2 + \underset{\text{(sulfuric acid)}}{H_2SO_4}$$

Under alkaline conditions, $Fe(OH)_2$ is very insoluble and the equilibrium of the reaction is shifted to the right. The H_2SO_4 then reacts with lime in the soil to form gypsum. Alum [$Al_2(SO_4)_3$] reacts in a similar manner. Limestone, of course, contains calcium, but the water solubility of $CaCO_3$ in alkaline soils is so low that it is usually of little value as an amendment for the replacement of sodium.

Remember: Sulfur, lime sulfur, iron sulfate, and aluminum sulfate *all require the presence of lime* in the soil to be effective as amendments on sodic soils. The major objective is to supply a source of soluble calcium, which can then exchange with excess Na^+ on soil particles. Table 2-3 lists the amounts of various amendments required to supply 1,000 pounds of soluble calcium. Price comparisons can then be based on these data.

SOLUBLE SALTS

Weathering of primary minerals is the indirect source of nearly all the soluble salts in virgin soils. In landscaped situations, inorganic fertilizers, manures high in salts, and well water may also add considerably to salt content.

The major soluble salts in saline (high-salt) soils are sodium, calcium, magnesium, sulfates, chlorides, and

Table 2-3. Amounts of Various Soil Amendments Required to Supply 1000 Pounds of Soluble Calcium

Amendment	Purity[a] (%)	Amount (lb)
Gypsum ($CaSO_4 \cdot 2H_2O$)	100	4300
Calcium chloride ($CaCl_2 \cdot 2H_2O$)	100	3700
Sulfur (S)	100	800
Sulfuric acid (H_2SO_4)	95	2600
Iron sulfate ($FeSO_4 \cdot 7H_2O$)	100	6950
Aluminum sulfate ($Al_2SO_4 \cdot 13H_2O$)	100	5550
Lime–sulfur solution	24[b]	3350

Source: Bower (1959).

a. If the amendment has a purity different from that indicated on the table, determine the amount needed to supply 1000 pounds of soluble calcium by dividing the percentage of purity given in the table by the percentage of purity of the material to be applied, and multiply this value by the number of pounds shown in the table. For example, if gypsum, having a purity of 80 percent is used, then (100/80) × 4300 = 1.25 × 4300 = 5400 lb would be needed.

b. Expressed as sulfur. Because lime–sulfur solutions have indefinite chemical compositions, their purity is expressed in terms of sulfur content.

bicarbonates. Effects of excess salts on plants are both osmotic and ionic.

Effects of Saline Soils

Plants grown in saline soils often are relatively small in size and dark bluish-green in color (salt effect); they also may have brown leaf margins. The salt effect is essentially a water deficiency induced in the plants by the osmotic properties of the salts, causing a reversal of water movement so that water moves out of the roots. This is called *plasmolysis*.

High salts can result in a deficiency of calcium induced by partial exclusion of calcium from the plant in the presence of excess magnesium. Other changes in nutrient availability can also occur depending upon the concentration of various ions as well as the pH. High salts, however, can occur at low as well as high pH.

Reducing Salts in Soils

In saline soils, soluble salts can be removed only by leaching with water. In most cases of high salts, subsurface drainage (internal drainage), as well as surface drainage, is poor. Before salts can be leached, both surface and internal drainage must be improved. Subsurface drainage can be improved by "opening" a compacted soil with organic amendments and removing excess surface water with drainage tile systems or French drains. French drains are merely silt trenches filled to the surface with gravel. The trenches move the water away from a low spot or area where accumulation of water occurs.

Subsurface drainage tile systems are more elaborate and more costly. They are used to reduce saturated areas of subsoil water. The often-used term *tiling* came from the old practice of placing perforated clay tiles (dry-laid) in trenches, which were then filled in with some gravel. More modern methods use less bulky and less expensive perforated plastic corrugated pipe. This pipe comes in continuous rolls of 2-, 4-, or 6-inch diameter and is very lightweight. It can be quickly installed by one person.

Perforated pipe (or tile) is laid in gravel-lined trenches into or below a water table. Pipe systems placed above a water table will do no good. This, in fact, is a common error in the use of perforated pipe. Many landscape managers have been disappointed in the results of elaborate perforated pipe installations because the purpose of the system was misunderstood. In order for a perforated pipe system to work, it must be installed in the area of saturation. It must also have a low point for outlet, and the entire system must have a minimum slope of 0.1 foot per 100 feet. This type of system will not remove excess surface water.

Perforated pipe systems are usually installed in a specific pattern depending on topography. Three basic patterns are common: natural (contour), herringbone, and grid. A combination of these is possible on a single site.

Natural and herringbone patterns are used in gullies and sloped areas; the grid pattern is employed in more flat terrain. In some cases, especially where no drain outlet is possible, a sump (dry well) is used to collect water from drain systems. This is simply a gravel-filled pit. It should be located in an out-of-the-way area and not close to buildings or plantings that cannot take occasional inundation with water. Sumps also tend to accumulate soluble salts that could be damaging to adjacent plantings.

Where installation of subsoil drainage systems is impractical, economically not feasible, or impossible, high-salt conditions can be circumvented with berm plantings. With this technique, all major trees, shrubs, flowers, and other plantings are put on mounds of soil above the salty soil. It is a usual practice to bring in new soil that has been tested to make sure salt levels are below 2.0 milimhos per centimeter (this unit of measure is for electrical conductivity and is used by soils laboratories to measure soil salinity). To prevent the upward movement of salts into the new soil through capillarity, a barrier is placed on the old saline soil before new soil is added. Anything that will break capillarity, has porosity, and does not decompose will do the job. Placing commercially available fiber mats on a few inches of coarse gravel is the preferred practice (fig. 2-9).

PLANT NUTRITIONAL REQUIREMENTS

Adequate nutrition is required for proper growth of plants. Even though plants of different species require somewhat different amounts of nutrients, all plants require the same types. If even one nutrient is lacking or in insufficient supply, the normal functions of a plant are impaired. In addition to water, oxygen, carbon dioxide, and nitrogen, at least twelve minerals are essential in varying amounts for plant growth. These minerals, often incorrectly called plant foods, are the raw materials supplied to the soil as fertilizer.

Plants need more nitrogen (N) than any other mineral: about 20,000 parts per million are found in the "average" dried leaf tissue. Potassium (K) and calcium (Ca) are next, each present at about 15,000 parts per million. Leaf contents of magnesium (Mg), phosphorus (P), and sulfur (S) are about 2,000 to 3,000 parts per million each; iron (Fe), boron (B), manganese (Mn), zinc (Zn), and copper (Cu) are all present at 100 parts per million or less. Molybdenum (Mo) is usually found in tissues at 1 part per million or less. Plants also take up chlorine (Cl) and sodium (Na), but their roles are not fully understood.

Elements needed in quantities in excess of 1,000 parts per million are considered *macronutrients;* those needed at less than 1,000 parts per million as *micronutrients.* Table 2-4 lists major known functions of essential elements in plants and their occurrence in plant tissues.

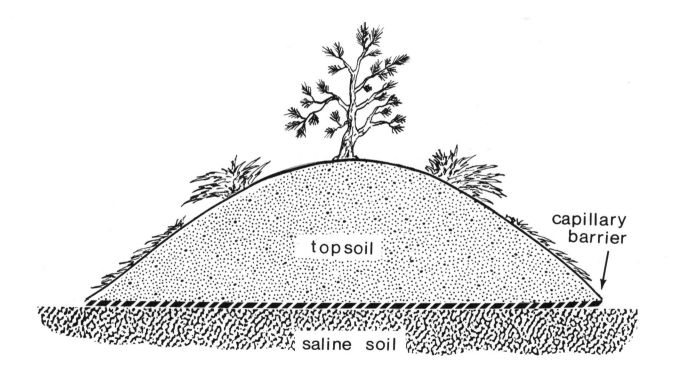

Figure 2-9. Berm planting above a saline soil. Capillary barrier may be a gravel layer, landscape fabric, or both.

Table 2-4. Functions of Essential Plant Elements[a]

Element	Occurrence in Plant	Functions
Boron (B)	Cytoplasmic cell membranes	Cell wall permeability; cell divisions and differentiation; translocation of sucrose (sugars)
Calcium (Ca)	Cytoplasm; calcium pectate salts of organic acids and phosphates	Activator of enzyme systems; calcium pectate part of middle lamella; calcium precipitates organic acids
Carbon (C)	All organic compounds; bicarbonate ion	Carbon is the key element in all organic molecular structures
Copper (Cu)	Tyrosinase cofactor	Tyrosinase is involved in reduction of molecular O_2; activator and inhibitor of several enzyme systems
Hydrogen (H)	All organic compounds; bicarbonate ion	Involved and part of same functions as carbon
Iron (Fe)	Peroxidase Fe^{2+} in cytoplasm and nucleus; catalase components in cytochromes	Peroxidase breaks down peroxides and C_2O_2 to oxidizable substances; activator of enzymes; essential in the synthesis of chlorophyll
Magnesium (Mg)	Chlorophyll; cocarboxylase enolase cofactor; cytoplasm, nucleus, and mitochondria	The center of chlorophyll molecule; cocarboxylase is a coenzyme of carboxylases; activator of several enzymes
Manganese (Mn)	Cytoplasm and nucleus; arginase activator	Activates enzymes; arginase converts arginine to urea; ascorbic acid synthesis
Molybdenum (Mo)	Nitrate reductase cofactor	Reduction of nitrate to ammonia
Nitrogen (N)	Proteins, chlorophyll, and many organic compounds	Structural component; important in assimilation of sugars
Oxygen (O)	Most organic compounds; bicarbonate ion	Final receptor of hydrogen in aerobic respiration; anion absorption and exchange
Phosphorus (P)	Phospholipids; nucleoprotein phosphates; sugar phosphates	Constituent of cytoplasmic membranes; adenosine phosphates necessary for synthesis of sugars, adenosine and biphosphide starches, and proteins; photosynthesis
Potassium (K)	Most if not all plant tissues	Carbohydrate synthesis and translocation; interferes in K metabolism
Sulfur (S)	Cystine and cysteine; glutathione; glycosides	Present in all proteins; glutathione acts as hydrogen carrier in respiration; glycosides tie up food reserves that might otherwise be toxic to the plant
Zinc (Zn)	Enzymes; cytoplasm as Zn^{2+}	Enzymes necessary for the synthesis of tryptophan, the precursor of IAA (indole acetic acid); breakdown of HCO_3^-; activator of proteolytic enzymes

a. Chlorine (Cl) and sodium (Na) are believed to have essential functions in plants. While their role in influencing the intake of other elements is undisputed, their precise functions within plants are still not clearly understood.

MINERAL UPTAKE BY PLANTS

The mechanisms by which plants obtain nutrients from the soil is still not fully understood. The use of radioactive isotopes to trace movement of substances in plants has, however, added significantly to our understanding of nutrient uptake, a very complex subject. It is known that nutrients are taken into a plant in the simple form of ionic salts. Absorption by plants involves at least four simple steps:

1. Movement of ions (in solution) from soil to root surfaces
2. Ion accumulation in roots
3. Radial transport of ions to root xylem
4. Translocation to shoots via the xylem

According to two common theories, the movement of ions from the soil to root surfaces apparently occurs by two processes, both based on ionic exchange (also called base exchange), that is, actual exchange of one ion by another. These theories apply only to roots in soils having colloidal clay or organic matter, since sand and silt have little or no capacity to exchange ions. One theory, the soil solution theory, proposes that the CO_2 given off by roots combines with water to form carbonic acid (H_2CO_3). This weak acid gives up hydrogen ions (H^+), which displace adsorbed ions on soil particles. The ions released by this exchange then become available to the plant root and are absorbed through the usual osmotic (diffusion) process. The *contact theory* bypasses soil solution and proposes a direct exchange of ions between root surface and soil surface. In this case, the ions are attracted to the root much like iron particles are attracted to a magnetic surface.

Nutrient availability is affected not only by the amount and kinds of ions in soil solution or adsorbed on the soil particles, but also by the pH and its effect on the overall chemistry of the soil—in other words, the soil reaction. The relative relationship between pH and mineral availability is shown in figure 2-10.

In soils of high pH, iron chlorosis is one of the more common ailments, especially in turf and certain trees

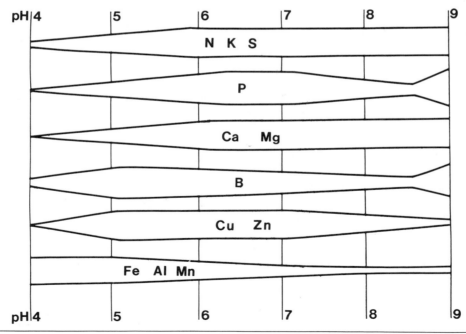

Figure 2-10. Relative availability of minerals at various pH levels. The wider the bar, the more available the mineral.

and shrubs such as maple, oak, and hawthorn. This situation is not readily corrected because of the buffering action of the soil. For trees, at least, it is better to select plants that tolerate the soil conditions than to try to change the soil. Most deciduous trees and shrubs will thrive in soils of moderate fertility. Soils that, by standard test, show nitrogen at 12 to 15 parts per million, phosphorus at 7 to 10 parts per million, and potassium at over 150 parts per million are usually adequate.

Poor performance in woody landscape plants is more often caused by physical soil factors than by low soil fertility. Such physical factors affect water and mineral availability.

SOIL MOISTURE AND MINERAL AVAILABILITY

Just as water movement in the soil is affected by surface tension, as discussed earlier, the availability of water and of minerals in the water to plants is affected by surface tension. The energy required by a plant to "pull" water away from soil particles varies to some degree with plant type. One method of measuring this energy is in atmospheres or negative pressure. One atmosphere is a force of approximately 14.2 pounds per square inch. Most plants reach a wilting point if the tension of the water is 15 atmospheres, or about 213 pounds per square inch, of negative pressure. A soil at field capacity exerts about ⅓ atmosphere; one that has reached hygroscopic dryness, about 31 atmospheres. Plants that tolerate drought can apparently "retrieve" water from a soil in excess of 15 atmospheres.

Soil texture makes a big difference in surface area and thus also changes the availability of water and minerals to plants at a given amount of total water in the soil. As shown in figure 2-11, clay soils hold more water at higher tension than loams or sandy soils. Thus, it is possible for a plant to wilt in one soil sooner than in another even though the amount of total moisture is the same. It is important in management of landscape plants and nursery stock to keep this principle of soil–water physics in mind; it is the primary factor in water management.

Water deficits in plants result not only in a wilting but also in overall interruption of basic plant processes

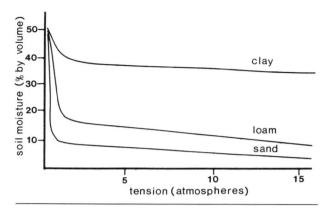

Figure 2-11. **Relationship between soil moisture and soil tension for soils of different texture. Clay soils hold more water at higher tension than do loams and sandy soils.**

including photosynthesis and respiration. One cannot assume, however, that a plant in a dry soil is undergoing a water deficit, because high internal water deficits may not occur if atmospheric conditions (that is, high humidity, no wind, and cool temperatures) cause a reduction in evapotranspiration. Some plants also have built-in mechanisms to cope with dry periods as discussed in chapter 1. Such plants avoid a water deficit and thus also avoid associated nutritional problems.

FERTILIZING LANDSCAPE PLANTS

Most trees and shrubs require only moderately fertile soil. Turf and flowers are more demanding, however, and usually require greater amounts of added nutrients to perform well. Some nutritional disorders (chlorosis, marginal scorch) can be used as a guide to soil fertility, but a soil test is generally advised to check fertility levels periodically.

Unfortunately, there are no strict rules to follow in a fertility management program. Some guidelines, however, can be offered. It must be remembered that these are merely guidelines, not strict levels that must be obtained to grow satisfactory plants.

Total Soluble Salts and pH

For trees, shrubs, and most herbaceous garden plants, an acceptable soil test would indicate a pH between 6.5 and 8.0 (above 7.5 is not usually satisfactory for trees prone to iron chlorosis). Salts should be below 2.0 milimhos per centimeter, although some plants, such as Russian olive and most junipers, can thrive in soils with higher salt levels.

If your soil test shows a soluble-salt reading above 2.0 milimhos per centimeter, you will find that sensitive plants, such as roses, most maples, pines, froebel spirea, most viburnums, and others, will develop poor foliage color and often a marginal browning that indicates salt injury. When the salt reading is between 4.0 and 8.0 milimhos per centimeter, injury will show in nearly all landscape plants. Bluegrass turf will grow poorly at 4.0 milimhos per centimeter or higher, although some cultivars are more salt-tolerant than others.

Table 2-5 lists plants considered the most tolerant to salts. These should be selected where salt levels cannot be reduced by leaching and draining. Where reduction of soluble salts is possible through improved drainage and leaching with water, the amount of water needed can be estimated from the guidelines in Table 2-6.

If the soil test also includes a test for sodium, it will include a sodium adsorption ratio (SAR). If the SAR

Table 2-6. Suggested Amounts of Water to Apply to Reduce Soluble Salts

Initial Salt Reading (mmho/cm)	Water to Apply (in.)
2.0– 4.0	3
4.1– 6.0	6
6.1– 8.0	8
8.1–10.0	10
10.1–15.0	12
over 15.0	usually not practical

Table 2-5. Salt-Tolerant Plants

Trees with moderate salt tolerance
(4–6 mmho/cm)
Boxelder (*Acer negundo*)
Gray birch (*Betula populifolia*)
Hackberry (*Celtis occidentalis*)
European ash (*Fraxinus excelsior*), also called blue ash
Blue ash (*F. quadrangulata*)
Juniper (*Juniperus scopulorum*); *J. virginiana* (eastern red cedar) considered more tolerant than *J. scopulorum*
Goldenrain (*Koelreuteria paniculata*)
Osage-orange (*Maclura pomifera*)
Black locust (*Robinia pseudoacacia*)
Japanese pagodatree (*Sophora japonica*), also called Chinese scholartree
Siberian elm (*Ulmus pumila*)

Trees with high salt tolerance
(6–8 mmho/cm)
Tree-of-heaven (*Ailanthus altissima*)
Shadblow (*Amelanchier canadensis*), also called serviceberry
Cockspur hawthorn (*Crataegus crus-galli*)
Russian olive (*Elaeagnus angustifolia*)
Arbor-vitae (*Thuja occidentalis*)
Japanese black pine (*Pinus thunbergi*)
Wafer-ash (*Ptelea trifoliata*)

Shrubs with moderate to high salt tolerance
(*above 8 mmho/cm)
*Four-wing saltbush (*Atriplex canescens*)

*Groundsel (*Baccharis halimifolia*)
Peashrub (*Caragana arborescens*)
*Scotch broom (*Cytisus scoparius*)
Silverberry (*Elaeagnus commutata*)
Cherry Elaeagnus (*E. multiflora*)
*Salt-tree (*Halimodendron halodendron*)
*Sea buckthorn (*Hippophae rhamoides*)
Juniper (*Juniperus chinensis* 'Pfitzer')
Tatarian honeysuckle (*Lonicera tatarica*)
*Bayberry (*Myrica pennsylvanica*)
*Common buckthorn (*Rhamnus cathartica*)
Glossy buckthorn (*R. frangula*)
*Rugosa rose (*Rosa rugosa*)
*Buffaloberry (*Shepherdia canadensis*)
VanHoutte spirea (*Spiraea vanhouttei*)
*Tamarisk (*Tamarix gallica; T. parviflora*)
*Seagrape
Japanese shore juniper (*Juniperus conferta*)

Grasses
(ranked from lowest to highest, 8–18 mmho/cm)
Creeping bentgrass (*Agrostis palustris*)
Western wheatgrass (*Agropyron smithi*)
Tall wheatgrass (*A. elongstrum*)
Canada wildrye (*Elymus canadensis*)
Bermudagrass (*Cynodon dactylon*)
Alkaligrass (*Puccinellia airoides*)
Saltgrass (*Distichlis stricta*)
Alkali sacaton (*Sporobolus airoides*)

is 15 or more, the soil is sodic. Correction of this problem has already been discussed.

Most soil tests show levels of important elements in parts per million. The principal ones include nitrogen, phosphorus, potassium, zinc, iron, manganese, and copper. Calcium, in the form of calcium carbonate (lime) may be expressed only in terms of high, medium, or low.

Nitrogen

As a general rule, the organic matter (OM) content is taken into consideration when determining how much nitrogen needs to be added. Organic matter, expressed as a percentage of total soil, contains 95 percent of all soil nitrogen. For each percentage point of OM, about 30 pounds of nitrate (NO_3^-) nitrogen per acre will be released. Each part per million of nitrate nitrogen is equivalent to about 3.6 pounds per acre-foot. To determine the amount of total nitrogen, multiply the percentage of OM by 30 and the parts per million of nitrate by 3.6, and add the resulting values. For example, a soil with a 2 percent OM and 7 parts per million of NO_3^- would have 85.20 pounds total nitrogen per acre-foot (2 times 30 plus 7 times 3.6).

This level is considered nearly adequate for most trees and shrubs, which do well on about 2 pounds of nitrogen per 1,000 square feet, or approximately 88 pounds nitrogen per acre. Turfgrasses require about twice as much nitrogen.

If soils are low in organic matter, they are also commonly low in nitrate nitrogen unless commercial fertilizers have already been added. Soils having low nitrate nitrogen and of heavy clay texture are best improved with organic matter rather than commercial inorganic fertilizers where possible. The OM will increase the nitrogen level and improve soil texture at the same time. Inorganic sources of nitrogen should also be avoided if salts are high because the fertilizer will tend to elevate salt levels even more.

Some organic sources of nitrogen should also be avoided, principally fresh manures and feedlot manures. The latter are usually high in soluble salts. The best organic source is aged dairy manure.

Organic matter is normally applied at a rate of up to 3 cubic yards per 1,000 square feet.

Phosphorus

Available phosphorus (P_2O_5) is greatly dependent on pH. In alkaline soils, phosphorus is usually present but in unavailable forms such as calcium phosphate and oxides of phosphorus. It may also be deficient in very acid soils where it has been leached. Phosphorus deficiency is common in decomposed granite soils in the Rocky Mountains and sandy soils of coastal areas. It is often low in the decomposed granite soils of the mountains as well as some of the heavier-textured clays.

Most trees and shrubs will thrive on about 0.5 pound P_2O_5 per 1,000 square feet or 22 pounds per acre. Turf and herbaceous plants require about twice as much. A soil test indicating 7 parts per million or above is generally adequate for woody plants. For herbaceous plants and turf, the phosphorus test level should be about 14 parts per million.

To increase phosphorus levels, use sources such as treble superphosphate (60 percent P_2O_5) or diammonium phosphate (21 percent N, 53 percent P_2O_5). About 2 pounds of material per 1,000 square feet will increase the level of phosphorus by 3.5 to 4 parts per million.

Potassium

Potassium is usually plentiful in alkaline soils and even in those that are somewhat acid. It is usually low or deficient in very sandy, well-drained soils and in very acid soils in high rainfall areas. When test levels go below 100 parts per million, corrective measures may be needed, especially in turfgrasses. The most common source of potassium is potassium chloride KCl (60 percent K_2O). For every 50-part-per-million increase in K_2O desired, add about 1 pound of KCl.

Micronutrients

Zinc, iron, copper, and manganese are needed in small amounts. The availability to plants of all four are affected by excessive lime (high pH). The most frequent problem is iron unavailability.

Little is known about the actual needs of trees and shrubs for these trace elements. Studies on fruit trees have led to some fairly reliable methods of arriving at fertilizer recommendations for these elements, but the recommendations cannot be readily translated to plants in a landscape situation.

It is generally accepted that soil test levels of iron below 10 parts per million will cause yellowing (chlorosis) in some cultivars of bluegrass turf. Trees that become chlorotic at this level are acid-loving species such as pin oak, silver maple, and some hawthorns.

Adequate availability of iron and other trace elements depends not only on soil pH and species requirements, but also on the mobility of the elements in plants. This can result in considerable discrepancy between plant response and soil test results. For example, trees under drought stress may show "typical" iron chlorosis (yellow with green veins), yet a soil test may indicate good iron availability. Therefore, when interpreting soil tests, especially those for Zn, Fe, Mn, and Cu, all factors should be considered before attempting to correct a potential deficiency.

FERTILIZING MATURE SHADE TREES

Shade tree fertilization did not receive much scientific attention until the 1950s. Prior to that time, most studies were confined to fruit trees and trees under forest conditions. Since 1950 numerous studies have attempted to develop satisfactory methods to apply mineral elements to large trees in landscaped situations.

Comparative studies have been conducted of various application methods: surface application; placing dry fertilizer in holes made with an auger, punch bar, or other device; liquid injection into the soil with a hydraulic "soil needle"; foliar feeding; and direct implantation into the xylem of the tree. In spite of all the research done, no single method has proven best for all situations. For the most part, however, those doing detailed comparative studies agree that surface broadcast applications are best for trees in lawn areas. Except for the disadvantage that some fertilizers also contain weed killers that can be injurious to trees, the broadcast method has the advantages of being rapid, of providing even distribution of fertilizer, and of being easier to carry out than other methods.

Soil application, either by placing dry fertilizer in holes or by liquid soil injection, has the obvious disadvantages of requiring special equipment, being time-consuming, and resulting in poor or uneven distribution. Dry fertilizers in holes, including the popular "tree spikes," tend to cause placement of concentrated salt in a small area. Distribution of the minerals requires a soil with good capillarity and copious amounts of water. In lawn areas, this method also causes "burn" spots or excessive greening, making an unsightly pattern. Hydraulic soil injection has some advantages over dry fertilizer placement, especially in heavy clay soils. The hydraulic technique will tend to deep water and aerate the root zone.

Injection of minerals directly into a tree also has disadvantages. It causes an open wound that is subject to pathogen or insect invasion, results in poor distribution within the tree, and is very time-consuming. In addition, special equipment and a certain amount of training is required with this application method.

Liquid injection, as in the Mauget method, and dry implant "capsules" such as Medicaps must be placed into roots near the flare of a tree rather than in the trunk to obtain the best distribution of the minerals. Injection and implant methods are generally reserved for special treatments such as iron and manganese deficiencies and for injecting systemic pesticides.

Foliar "feeding" is receiving considerable attention because it is fast, relatively inexpensive, and does not require equipment any more special than a spray rig, which most arborists already have. That minerals do absorb through the foliage has been amply demonstrated. Results, however, vary with the species, climatic conditions, solution used, and the overall condition of the tree.

Foliar applications are the "quick fix" for trees suffering a nutritional problem or overall low vigor. It is a short-term and thus very cosmetic approach. The method is useful in providing instant nutrients in recently planted trees whose roots are damaged.

It must be remembered, however, that applying liquid fertilizers to the foliage of a plant is actually applying a soluble salt, or combination of salts. A burn resulting from the plasmolytic effect of the solution drying and concentrating on the leaves can happen. Burning is usually only a problem where the solution was too strong to start with or was applied on a hot day.

REFERENCES

Bower, C. A. 1959. Chemical amendments for improving soils. USDA Agric. Bull. 195.

Hausenbuiller, R. L. 1978. Soil Science: Principles and Practices, 2nd Ed. Dubuque, IA: Wm. C. Brown Co.

Lyon, T. L., Buckman, H. O., and Brado, N. C. 1952. Nature and Properties of Soil. New York: Macmillan.

Michigan State College. 1941. Soil reaction preferences of plants. Agric. Exp. Stn. Spec. Bull. 306.

U.S. Department of Agriculture. 1957. Soil: The 1957 Yearbook of Agriculture.

3.

Irrigation Practices

Supplemental irrigation is required in most landscaped areas. Even in more humid, high rainfall areas, occasional periods of drought may occur, making it essential to supply water to sustain plant life. In semi-arid and arid areas, irrigation is a constant need and a major responsibility of the landscape manager.

It is not the intent of this book to discuss the details of the design and engineering of irrigation systems. This is best accomplished through consultation with professional irrigation design engineers at the planning stage. Landscape managers should, however, understand some basic principles and know how to troubleshoot irrigation problems.

FACTORS AFFECTING IRRIGATION

Several variables affect watering frequency, distribution of water, and efficiency of water use when irrigating. Climatic and soil conditions, as well as equipment design variables, must be taken into consideration when installing an irrigation system.

Soil Conditions

Soil type, drainage, and *salinity* determine the rate at which water can be applied. (Review the sections "Water Movement in Soils" and "Reducing Salts in Soils" in chapter 2.) If the soil to be irrigated is a clay, irrigation must be applied slowly to prevent waste from runoff. It may be necessary to repeat short watering cycles in the same area. In very sandy soils, water can be applied more rapidly, but care should be taken that the

water is not added for too long a period and lost below the root zone.

A simple procedure for determining the ability of the soil to accept water and the best application rate can be conducted as follows:

1. Choose space considered typical of the soil in the area.
2. Set a sprinkler in the center of the space. An impulse-type sprinkler is best, although the type of head is not too important for this test.
3. Water the area thoroughly until water begins to run off or appears to puddle, not soaking in readily.
4. Shut water off and wait approximately 24 hours. Then place shallow containers (about 2 inches deep and 6 inches in diameter) in five widely spaced locations in the irrigated area.
5. Apply water until runoff or puddling appears, making note of the time it took.
6. Measure the water in the containers, add the results, and divide by five. The average amount of water applied and the time it took can be used as a general guide for future irrigations to avoid excess applications of water.

Depth of water penetration can also be estimated using the same test. Simply check soil moisture to at least 6-inch depth prior to the first irrigation. Check moisture again after the first and second irrigations. In heavy clay soils, depth penetration may not be much greater after the second irrigation than after the first because of slow percolation.

For more precise measurements, water-measuring devices can be used. They are of three types: bimetal electrical conductivity probes, electrical conductivity wires embedded in gypsum blocks, and tensiometers. The first two types, using electrical conductivity, are relatively inexpensive, provide instant readings on a meter, and can be placed at almost any soil depth. They are not as accurate as tensiometers, however, because the salts in a soil will influence the conductivity readings. Soils high in salts will have higher than normal readings.

Tensiometers are quite accurate if installed according to the manufacturer's recommendations. These devices have a clay cup of known permeability at the tip of a plastic cylinder, which is filled with water and capped with a tight seal. As moisture decreases in the soil, water moves out of the clay cup. The resulting tension creates a partial vacuum on the water column in the cylinder. This is measured with a vacuum gauge attached to the top of the cylinder. Readings are usually in centibars (cbar); 100 centibars equals 1 atmosphere. A reading of zero on the gauge means saturation. Even though the wilting point of most plants is around 1,500 centibars, plants usually have water stress problems when the soil–water tension exceeds 25 to 30 centibars. The ideal for most plants is between 10 and 25 cbar. Below 10 cbar, water may exchange too much soil air, resulting in oxygen starvation to plant roots.

Tensiometers are, however, more difficult to install than electrical conductivity devices. They usually require frequent maintenance of the clay cups because of clogging, and they are somewhat limited to shallow soil depths. They are also vulnerable to theft and cannot normally be used in freezing weather. A newer type, called a Hydrovisor, which is now available, does not have a problem with freezing (Keesen 1985).

Infrared devices are now being developed that may help take the guesswork out of watering trees and shrubs. While still in the development and testing stages, these devices hold promise for quick and accurate determinations of soil moisture levels. Until better methods are available, relatively accurate watering guidelines for trees and shrubs are best obtained through the use of tensiometer or conductivity devices. Another way is simply to dig down occasionally to determine moisture levels in the deeper root zones of trees and shrubs.

The latter is still the most practical method for landscape managers.

Air Temperature and Wind

As would be expected, the warmer the temperature and the greater the wind velocity, the more water is lost. Both evaporation from the soil and transpiration from plants increase under these conditions. This loss must be taken into consideration when irrigating. Measurement of *evapotranspiration* rates is easily done with a *lysimeter*. This is a soil-filled plastic bucket that is sunk into the ground so that the rim is level with the soil surface. It is usually placed in a turf area with turf also growing in the bucket. Periodic removal and weighing of the bucket with soil and turf contents is done to calculate the evapotranspiration (ET) rate. This provides a very accurate record of water loss (or gain) and can be used to regulate watering frequency and rate of application.

In some areas, particularly near large urban populations, an ET rating is calculated on a regular basis and publicized through local news media. These ratings, however, are usually accurate only within a short distance from the lysimeter location.

Although ET ratings are practical for determining water needs of turf, they are not very useful for trees and shrubs. In fact, trees and shrubs growing in turf areas often suffer from either overwatering or underwatering while the turf thrives when watering is based on ET ratings. This is because ET ratings only measure water loss from a relatively shallow soil.

Sprinkler Head Spacing

In the installation of either an underground sprinkler system or moving hoses, the spacing between sprinkler heads and amount of overlap must be carefully considered in order to achieve the most uniform water distribution possible. No permanent underground sprinkler system is perfect because of the effects of soil type and wind. Wind influences water distribution greatly. In addition, the type of head, droplet size, angle of spray, and age or condition of the head significantly influence water distribution.

Before installing a system, study prevailing winds

during the normal irrigation season. It is usually possible to establish an average wind direction and velocity, which can be used in determining the overlap needed for more even water distribution. Many systems allow for a 50 percent overlap.

Sprinkler heads can be checked for water distribution by using the same shallow containers described earlier. Place one container close to the head, others at about 5-foot intervals. Water as usual and measure the water depth in each container. Heads that show uneven water distribution should be replaced or, if possible, adjusted. Failure to do so will result in water profile patterns such as those in figures 3-1 and 3-2. Inadequate overlap and the effect of wind is illustrated in figures 3-3 and 3-4.

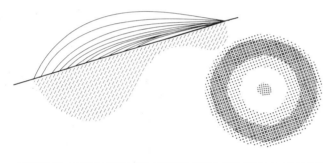

Figure 3-1. Soil profile and overhead view of a sprinkler with poor water distribution near its head. The darkest area in the overhead view will be the greenest in a turf.

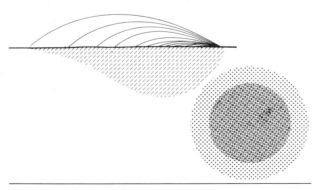

Figure 3-2. Soil profile and overhead view of a sprinkler with poor water distribution distant from its head. The darkest area in the overhead view will be the greenest in a turf.

TROUBLESHOOTING IRRIGATION PROBLEMS

A major concern of landscape managers is determining the cause of uneven color in turfgrasses. The problem often lies in poor irrigation but is mistaken for diseases, nutrient deficiencies, or even turf insects. Indeed, these problems are often brought about by uneven irrigation.

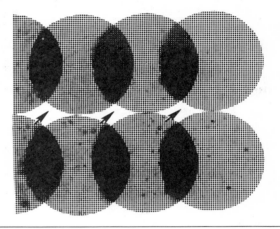

Figure 3-3. Overhead view of water distribution with heads too far apart. Arrows indicate typical dry diamond-shaped areas in turf; the darkest areas would be the greenest.

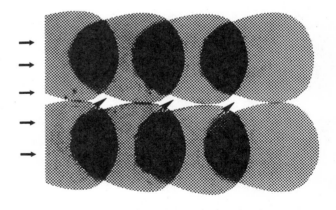

Figure 3-4. Overhead view of water distribution influenced by wind. Wind direction is shown by arrows at left. Center arrows point to typical elongated diamond-shaped dry spots in turf; the darkest areas would be the greenest.

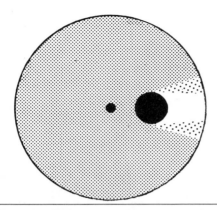

Figure 3-5. Overhead view of water distribution interrupted by an obstacle such as a tree (large circle).

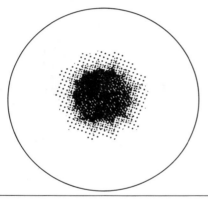

Figure 3-6. Overhead view of water distribution when the head is too deep in the ground. The darkest area would be the greenest in a turf.

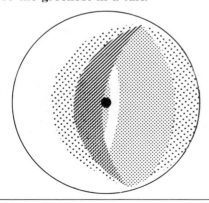

Figure 3-7. Overhead view of water distribution when the head is tilted. The darkest area would be the greenest in a turf.

In addition to uneven distribution patterns resulting from faulty heads and wind, some common patterns in turf will result from tilted heads, interference from trees and other obstructions, pop-up heads too deep into the ground, or partially clogged heads. Figures 3-5, 3-6, and 3-7 show typical patterns in turf from these causes.

To help sort out possible causes for uneven irrigation, it is best to make a sketch of the growth (color) patterns observed in the turf, locating the irrigation heads, trees, shrubs, and other structures on the sketch. Such a diagram can help to isolate which heads may need cleaning, replacement, or adjustment and whether or not spacing or obstructions are a factor. If irregular patterns in the turf do not seem to correlate with sprinkler head problems, other causes such as poor nutrition, buried debris in soil, and pests should be examined.

DRIP IRRIGATION

Drip irrigation has become popular in landscape sites, particularly in areas where water is scarce or expensive. The primary objective of drip systems is to apply water only to the plants intended and not the areas between. Most systems use very low pressure (20 pounds per square inch or less) and employ a series of small plastic tubes and specially designed outlets called *emitters*. Emitters can be selected to apply water at rates as low as 0.5 gallon per hour.

To function properly, water used in drip systems must be free of sediment. To ensure water purity, always connect the main line with a 150-mesh filter. Otherwise clogged emitters become a constant maintenance headache.

Drip systems are usually controlled with automatic timers and low-flow solenoid valves. A pressure-reducing valve is also necessary. It is also wise to install blowout valves. Almost any combination of emitter types, sizes, and gallonage can be put together in a system to meet water needs of individual plants in a landscape. The number and type of emitters permitted per system depend on the pressure used, the size of tubing, and the distance and elevation change. Friction loss, as in any irrigation system, must be known and calculated into the system. Otherwise emitters at the ends of a series may fail to deliver the proper amount of water. Irrigation equipment manufacturers can supply information to help in calculating friction losses.

Advantages and Disadvantages

In addition to saving water, drip systems that are properly installed can supply a more constant moisture level to plant roots than overhead systems. They are also much less expensive. An additional advantage is the flexibility allowed. Systems can be easily redesigned and installed by adding new emitters where needed or removing them where they are no longer needed.

Because drip systems apply water directly to the soil, uneven patterns resulting from wind are not a factor, as is the case with overhead irrigation. Uneven patterns are common, however, because of differences in soil capillarity and clogged emitters.

To some extent, drip systems can be concealed. This has advantages from the standpoints of aesthetics, vandalism, and liability, particularly in public areas. There are limits, however, on the amount of concealment that should be attained in a drip system; those that are too concealed are also more difficult to maintain. If emitters are concealed under a mulch, for instance, the time used just in locating and checking the condition of the emitters can offset the value of a concealed system. Some managers have elected to sacrifice some aesthetics and risk vandalism by making the system more visible, and so more easily serviceable.

In addition to the need for constant maintenance and the problems with vandalism, drip systems have other disadvantages when compared with overhead systems. Perhaps the biggest disadvantage is the limited life of some drip systems. This disadvantage, however, is overcome by good planning and sound engineering before installation. Except where used in confined areas such as raised planters, drip systems should be considered temporary unless provisions are made to expand the entire installation as plants grow. This is particularly true of tree and shrub plantings in open areas where roots are not confined. While the drip system itself will tend to restrict the lateral spread of tree and shrub roots, eventually the roots will outgrow the emitters. When this happens, it is best to abandon the drip system, or if practical, add more tubing and emitters.

Using Drip Systems in Nurseries and Greenhouses and for New Plantings

Drip systems of many types and combinations are widely used by nurserymen, florists, irrigation consultants, and landscape contractors. Among the most popular and least expensive is the so-called *spaghetti system.* From a main water line of polyvinyl chloride (PVC) pipe or black plastic (polyethylene), lateral lines of plastic pipe (0.5- to 1.0-inch diameter) are run close to the plants needing water. Connected with the laterals may be several multiple tubing adaptors to which small (1/8- to 1/4-inch diameter) tubing is attached. These are commonly called *spaghetti tubes.* The small tubes of varying lengths are then placed over the root zones of the plants to be irrigated. This convenient system makes it possible to water several plants from one multiple adaptor or apply water in a relatively uniform pattern over the root zone of a single large plant. Emitters are not usually used at the ends of the tubing, but special soft, vinyl caps (bug caps) with a slit tip may be added to reduce clogging.

The major problem with using drip systems in nurseries and new landscape plantings involves the failure to install a sufficient number of emitters per plant. Another problem occurs when emitters are located too close to the trunks of trees, where they will not be effective in applying water to the root zone.

For small herbaceous and woody ground covers, an overhead system is usually more practical. For 1-gallon container stock, one emitter per plant is usually sufficient; for 5-gallon container stock and trees and shrubs with rootballs over 8 inches in diameter, two or more emitters are usually needed to provide uniform water distribution. Balled-and-burlapped trees may require up to six emitters per plant, spaced evenly near the outside edge of the root ball.

The number of emitters required, of course, depends on the lateral spread of water provided. This varies with soil type. Fine-textured soils (high in clay) will have a wider distribution of water than sandy soils. A simple check of water distribution two or three days after the system has been installed and turned on will determine where more emitters need to be added.

Drip Systems in Saline Soils

Problems may be encountered with drip systems in soils high in natural salts. Since drip systems apply low volumes of water at slow rates, a *salt front* may develop at the edges of the wetted area. This is because water evaporates at nearly the same rate as it is applied. In profile, a salt front has the general shape of an ellipse. Salts can accumulate in this front to the point that plant roots are injured or killed by plasmolysis. It is a particularly serious problem in arid and semi-arid areas where high evapotranspiration rates are common.

To determine whether a salt buildup is occurring, dig a shallow trench radially from near an emitter to a point that slightly exceeds the wetting front. Salts are often visible as a white or light-colored band in the soil. In order to reduce the effects of salts, periodic heavy irrigation with overhead sprinklers or flooding of the surface soil is recommended.

GENERAL IRRIGATION RECOMMENDATIONS

Whether using overhead or drip systems, the following recommendations should be kept in mind:

1. Know the water-holding capacity of the soil. Water applied beyond the saturation point not only wastes water but risks serious oxygen starvation of plant roots. Water applied too lightly also is wasted through evaporation, and little will be used by the plant.
2. Install a system that fits the needs of the plants and the exposure that the plants must sustain. This may mean entirely different irrigation equipment in one area of a landscape from another. It also means separate controls. Plants with northern and eastern exposures, for instance, will usually need less frequent water applications than those with southern or western exposures; those in windy areas more than those in protected sites; and so forth.
3. Schedule regular inspections of irrigation heads and emitters. Look for patterns of irregular water distribution and correct the problem immediately.
4. Inspect and clean in-line filters regularly. This is particularly important with overhead spray systems using ditch water and with all drip-type installations. Even potable city water can eventually clog the filters.
5. Systems operated by time clocks should be changed according to climatic conditions. If controlled by tensiometers and similar moisture sensors, check regularly to make sure that the instruments are in proper working order.
6. With drip systems, flush main lines and laterals at least twice per season.
7. Heads of overhead systems should be checked weekly, preferably right after mowing of turf.
8. Check soils for potential salt buildup at least once per season. If soils have a tendency to increase in soluble salts, it may be an indication of inadequate water application. (Keep in mind, however, that frequent fertilizer applications can also increase salt levels, even when irrigation water is applied at the correct rates.)
9. Unless the system has been installed as frost-free or freezing is not likely, all lines, whether for overhead sprinklers or drip, must be drained during freezing weather. It is best also to blow the lines free of any residual water with compressed air. It is not necessary, however, to drain small spaghetti tubes used in drip systems.

REFERENCES

Keesen, L. 1985. Water management–are we doing our best? Colo. Green 1(3):16–23.

Morey, M. 1981. Spring irrigation precautions insure performance. Weeds, Trees and Turf 20(4, April):31–34.

Sarsfield, A. C. 1981. Irrigation devices for water conservation. Grounds Maintenance 16(5, May):14–22.

Smith, R. C. 1986. Sprinkler and drip irrigation systems: A detailed overview. Am. Nurseryman 163(March):68–70.

Tobey, S. 1984. Drip irrigation: What, why and how. Landscape and Irrigation 8(10):85–102.

4.

Planting and Transplanting

Anyone who transplants trees and shrubs, whether bare root, balled and burlapped, or by mechanical tree-moving devices, should not only know the proper procedures for digging the plant and operating the equipment, but should also have a good understanding of the biological processes carried on in a plant. These processes have a great bearing on the success or failure of any transplanting operation.

When a tree is transplanted, some injury always occurs to the root system. Some of this is the result of severing the roots by the spade, but a great deal of injury is also the result of damage to smaller roots and root hairs by vibrations and movement of the soil ball.

PHYSIOLOGICAL EFFECTS OF TRANSPLANTING

If we could crawl into a plant when it is being moved from one place to another, we would observe obvious and drastic changes. Outwardly, we see no visible change, unless the plant later wilts and dies, because when a plant is disturbed, the first changes are subtle chemical changes, termed *physiological changes,* that immediately affect the overall metabolism in the plant. The changes can be likened to those that occur within our own bodies when we get chilled; at first our resistance is lowered, an invisible change, and then hours or perhaps days later visible symptoms of a head cold appear.

Internal Water Deficit

One of the most obvious changes that takes place when a plant is disturbed is the interruption of normal water and mineral uptake by roots. Such roots cannot function because they have been separated from their water and mineral source, the soil. At the same time, the top of the plant continues, at least for a while, to use water and mineral elements faster than the root system can replace them. This results in an immediate internal water deficit in the plant. In addition, photosynthesis tends to shut down if the plant is in leaf. Dormant plants, not in leaf, undergo less drastic changes.

If the conditions for regrowth of damaged roots and conditions of the atmosphere surrounding the plant top are not favorable, the plant goes into what is known as *transplant shock.* The degree of shock depends upon soil and atmospheric conditions as well as the state of growth of the plant. For instance, a plant moved bare root (no soil attached) while in full leaf on a hot, dry day will experience greater shock and will have less chance of survival than one moved with soil attached to the roots in a dormant state on a cool, moist day. Consequently, bare-root material is handled only during the short dormant season in early spring. Container-grown (canned) nursery stock has become the major way of marketing because it allows moving and planting over a longer period of time and enables the nursery business to maintain sales almost year-round.

Evapotranspiration

As discussed in chapter 1, the loss of water is a normal process in plants. This continuous process changes in rate according to atmospheric conditions, water uptake rate from the soil, and the type and condition of the plant. Water loss from a plant, evapotranspiration, is determined by three major factors: the temperature of the air surrounding the leaf and stem surfaces; the relative humidity; and the velocity of air movement, or wind.

Plants lose water most rapidly when air temperatures are high, humidity is low, and wind velocity is strong because humidity is so much greater at the plant's surface than in the surrounding air. If the plant is in full leaf, it will lose water faster than when not in leaf, but significant water loss will occur even in plants that are dormant. This is why watering is frequently advised during dry winter periods. In many parts of the northern United States, the driest periods are often the winter months. Water may have been applied with supplemental irrigation during the growing season, but in freezing conditions, the irrigation system is shut down and drained. This sudden withdrawal of water plus desiccating cold winds can lead to severe winter injury. Such injury is particularly pronounced in evergreen species in the more arid and cold northern states.

ROOT ZONE ENVIRONMENT

In addition to the function of support, roots play a major role in supplying both water and mineral elements to the tree. Roots are continuously dying and being replaced. Except when they are in frozen soils, roots continuously grow into new areas of the soil. New root growth and elongation takes place near the tips, forming root hairs, which are delicate extensions of cell walls. Many plants, such as conifers, do not have root hairs but rely on mycorrhiza (symbiotic fungi) to aid in water and mineral uptake. The proper environment for mycorrhiza is just as important as for root hairs.

For normal root growth to take place, the root tip must have a favorable soil environment. Different species of plants require different environments, and these requirements determine to a great extent the ability of a plant to withstand transplanting. For the most part,

the level of oxygen (or air) in the soil required by a given species determines its ability to produce new roots in different environments. For example, swamp species such as swamp white oak, bald cypress, and many of the willows can develop new roots under soil conditions of relatively low oxygen content. It is undoubtedly for this reason that many swamp species also do well in heavy clay soils even though the moisture level is considerably less than that in a swamp. Swamp species do not necessarily like more water; rather, their roots tolerate *lower oxygen levels*. On the other hand, plants with mycorrhizal relationships, like pines, do very poorly in soils of low oxygen, probably because of the high oxygen requirements of symbiotic fungi.

The relationship between oxygen level in a soil and the regrowth of roots is the most important consideration in transplanting. A tree that has been transplanted must have the ability to develop new roots in a short period of time. These roots will grow in favorable soil zones only. The natural tendency of roots, however, is to grow down and not upward, although roots do grow upward under certain conditions. If a tree has been adjusted to a given soil and then the roots are covered with a heavy clay, regrowth of roots is hindered by a lack of oxygen. Such roots will not reestablish themselves, and the tree will die. In some trees, this can take as long as three years; in others, it occurs within a growing season. A further discussion of the effects of transplanting to differing soils is presented later.

Let us suppose that we move a plant under the most favorable of conditions: while it is dormant, with a ball of soil, when air temperatures are cool and humidity is high. Losses can still be expected unless we pay attention to the soil atmosphere. In many ways, the soil conditions necessary for successful transplanting are more complex and less understood than the requirements of the air surrounding the tops of the plant. This is understandable, since we do not see what goes on with the roots underground. It is also understandable in the light of all the myths perpetuated down through the ages about roots, their needs, and the planting advice extended by some "experts."

For example, you may have read or heard that when you plant a tree you *must* remove all the air pockets. This is generally done by stomping on the soil used in the hole as backfill. Such a practice not only damages more roots than the transplanting process but also drives out air needed by the roots to regenerate themselves. It is particularly serious when heavy clay soil is packed around the roots.

You may also have read in some old nursery planting guides that you should plant 2 inches deeper than the soil ball purchased from the nursery. This practice also does much to reduce chances for survival of nursery stock. This recommendation seems to have come from some old whims; nobody to date has provided a satisfactory explanation for it. Planting deeper, especially in heavy clay soils, *reduces* the ability of the plant to regenerate roots. In effect, the plant suffocates.

Internal Soil Drainage

Even if a tree has been successfully dug, maintaining a reasonable root system, transplant failure can still occur if attention is not paid to the type of soil and other conditions of exposure in which the tree is to be placed. Ideally, a tree growing in a sandy, well-drained soil should be transplanted only to a sandy, well-drained soil. This, of course, is not always practical and may not allow the planting of a wide variety of species in some landscapes. Trees, however, can adapt slowly to a new soil environment if some alteration of the soil aeration and drainage is performed.

Pines, for example, require a well-drained, well-aerated soil. If moved to a heavy clay soil without making provisions for drainage or gradual adaptation, they will die from oxygen starvation within one to three years. The small amount of backfill, or slurry, used in transplanting procedures with a spade digger is not sufficient to provide a well-drained transitional rooting medium if the tree is placed at the same level as it was before transplanting. Therefore, trees transplanted from well-drained sites to poorly drained sites should be placed as much as 2 to 4 inches above existing grade. This practice helps compensate for the poorer drainage of the new environment, thus giving the tree more time for root regrowth and adaptation. On very poorly drained sites, however, avoid the use of pines and other species that cannot tolerate such conditions, or provide subsoil drainage with tiles and/or gravel (French) drains (fig. 4-1). Subsoil drainage is discussed in chapter 2.

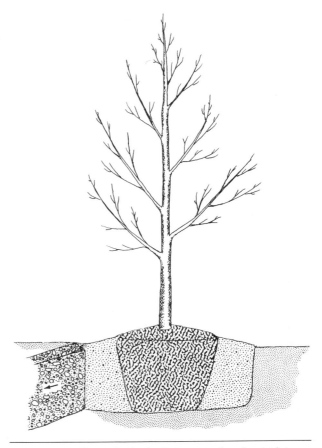

Figure 4-1. French drain for a newly planted tree. Note that the root ball is elevated several inches above the surrounding grade.

A common, but not valid, practice is to put gravel at the bottom of the hole and then backfill with the surrounding soil. This is a poor practice, especially in a heavy soil, because you are doing nothing more than putting gravel at the bottom of a hole that has no outlet. Furthermore, gravel alone has a poor capacity for capillary movement of water and thus provides a water barrier in the same way that a hard pan or a rock stratum would. In order for water to move through such a layer, the amount of water above the gravel must be sufficient to break the surface tension in the overlying soil and cause it to move through the gravel. In a heavy soil, this amount of water usually reduces the oxygen level to a point where the roots drown.

Amending Backfill

When planting a tree, shrub, or flower garden in heavy clay or a too sandy soil, adding organic matter can improve the physical as well as the nutritional conditions. As with almost everything else we do to alter natural conditions, we can go to extremes and create problems. Adding too much organic matter all at once to a soil can create undesirable effects. Since organic matter can act much like a sponge, too much may result in excess water-holding capacity. Some forms of organic matter may also contain high amounts of harmful salts. Such is the case with most feedlot manure. Other sources of organic matter, like peat, may repel water at first (when dry), then absorb too much all at once and withhold it from plant roots.

Soil Interface Effects

When two different soils are brought into contact, interface phenomena affect both the *direction* and *rate* of water movement. To understand what happens, one must first have a clear idea of how water moves in soils of different porosities and why. Water moves through an open sandy soil much more readily than through a tight clay soil, not just because the pore spaces in clay soils are smaller than those in sandy soils, but also because the tension created between the film of water and soil particles in clay restricts flow. Thus, a clay soil holds water more tightly and tends to draw water *away* from soils of greater porosity. Let us apply this concept to some of the common planting situations.

Balled Nursery Stock

Suppose you plan to plant a balled and burlapped tree obtained from a nursery, where it was growing in a loamy, well-drained soil. Since the tree was balled and burlapped, you would also be bringing some nursery soil to the new location. The new location has a heavier, clay-type soil. Several weeks or perhaps even months after planting, you find that the tree appears to be drying up in spite of weekly watering. Probing near the root ball, you discover that the soil is indeed dry but the surrounding clay soil is wet. This is because the clay soil tends to draw water *away* from the soil ball of the tree.

The opposite effect is also common when you plant a tree whose root ball soil is much heavier than the site soil. Such plants quickly drown because water tends to move *into* the soil ball. Both of these soil interface effects are illustrated in figure 4-2.

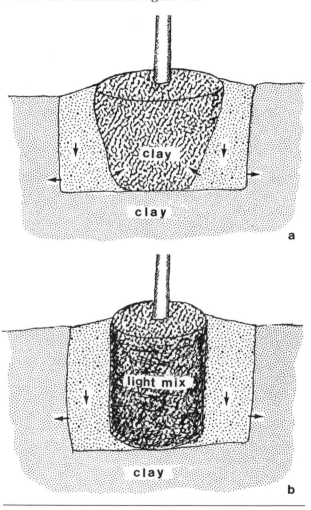

Figure 4-2. Soil–root ball interface effects when the site soil is a heavy clay-type soil: (*a*) when the root ball also is from a clay soil, water will tend to move into the clay (arrows) and saturate the root ball; (*b*) when the root ball is from a light mix, such as peat, water will tend to move away from the ball (arrows).

Container Stock in Soilless Mixes

Container-grown nursery stock, now a common means of culturing, has led to an even bigger soil–water relationship problem. In order to reduce the weight of containers, thus reducing loading and transplant costs, most container-grown stock is in lightweight mixes of bark, peat, or similar materials. Many are completely free of soil. As a result, the water-holding capacity is often very low, and such stock requires frequent, even daily, waterings in the nursery. When a plant under these conditions is removed from its container and planted at the site, water applied following planting moves rapidly through the root ball. If the surrounding soil is slow to drain, water collects in the base of the planting pit and can result in oxygen starvation of the roots. At the same time, roots near the surface of the soil ball may dry up (fig. 4-3).

In still other container-grown plants, particularly those high in peat, water may fail to wet the soil ball after planting because the peat itself will tend to shed water if it has been allowed to become dry on the surface.

Roots are often the most healthy and abundant in the bottom of containers. The best roots are usually found near the drainage holes when good aeration is present. Therefore, when stock in 5-gallon or larger containers is planted, the best mass of roots is usually too deep, limiting the oxygen supply. It is not uncommon even in relatively well-drained soils to find that the deep roots, those at the bottom of the container, have rotted away a few weeks or months after planting. This deep-root suffocation and the problems associated with poor water-holding capacity of container-grown stock can be alleviated by the relatively new technique of *root-ball splitting* (also called *butterfly method*), which is described in the next section.

Split-ball Technique

Use of the split-ball technique (Gouin 1983) helps to avoid the soil interface effects described in the previous section and to prevent root girdling, which often occurs to container-grown stock years after planting. The basic steps of this technique are as follows:

1. Slip the plant from container and lay it on its side on a firm soil. Using a sharp, square-edged spade, cut the ball all the way through from the bottom to approximately one-half the distance to the top of the ball (fig. 4-4a).
2. Make the planting hole twice as wide as the height of the ball, but only half as deep.
3. Place a mound of backfill soil in the center of the hole.
4. "Butterfly" the halves of the ball over the soil mound (fig. 4-4b).
5. Firm the plant by pushing downward on top of both sides of the split ball with your hands. *Do not use your feet.*
6. Finish adding backfill and water thoroughly.

For at least the first 30 days after planting, it may be necessary to water frequently and lightly. To reduce water frequency, adding a 4-inch-deep wood-chip mulch is advised. *Do not* use polyethylene plastics over the root zone. If weeds are a problem, use one of the landscape fabrics.

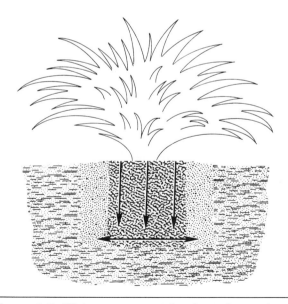

Figure 4-3. Water movement in planted container-grown stock with artificial soil mixes. Water will tend to move through artificial soil mixes and accumulate at the bottom of the planting pit (arrows). The upper part of the ball dries out, and the lower part becomes too wet.

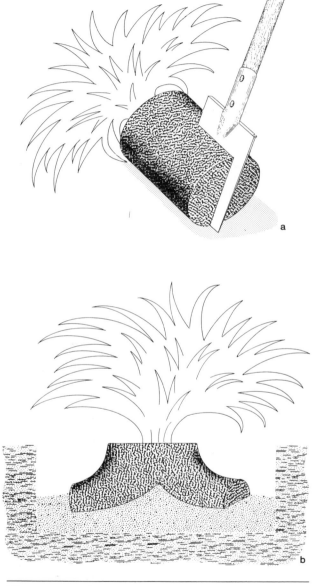

Figure 4-4. The split-ball (butterfly) technique. (a) Remove the container and lay the root ball on its side on a firm surface. Split with a sharp square-edged spade halfway up from bottom. (b) Prepare a shallow trench, place some backfill in the bottom, and "butterfly" the ball. Finish adding backfill.

SOME PLANTING GUIDELINES

If you remember that plant roots *must* have air to thrive, along with a balance of soil and water, that clay soils tend to hold water tightly at the expense of proper air, and that heavier soils can pull water away from porous soils, then you can alter the planting situation to adjust for potential problems.

Regardless of soil conditions, remove containers, even wire baskets and fiber pots, from all container-grown plants. With balled and burlapped stock, cut the twine around the base of the tree.

Heavy Clay Soil

1. Always dig the planting hole at least 12 inches wider than the root ball, but 2 to 4 inches *more* shallow. This practice forces you to plant higher than the surrounding area, so that *excess* surface water will move away from the plant. By placing the ball on firm ground, not backfill, it cannot settle and result in a too-deep planting. Planting high also places the roots in a more favorable environment for proper aeration.
2. Check the type of soil in the root ball. If it is a heavy clay like the site soil, amend the backfill only a little with coarse organic matter. Too much amendment can cause the soil ball to remain too wet. It has also been found that overamended soils can be worse than no amendment at all because they tend to cause root containment (Whitcomb et al. 1976; Schulte and Whitcomb 1975).
3. Avoid heavy tamping when placing the backfill. Use the blunt handle end of your shovel to remove only large air pockets. Avoid puddling of soil with water. Water after all backfill has been put into hole.
4. Do not use fertilizers in backfill.
5. Have your client (or employee) check water needs weekly by digging down around root ball. Caution them to avoid frequent light sprinklings.

Well-drained and Sandy Soil

1. Dig the hole wider than the soil ball but no deeper.
2. If the root ball is claylike and the site soil is very sandy, add some organic matter and some heavier

soil, not exceeding one-third volume of each, to the backfill.
3. If the root-ball soil is a lightweight peat, as with many container-grown plants, add up to one-third volume of coarse organic matter to the backfill. The split-ball method may also be used in this situation.
4. Check water needs as described above for clay soils. Sandier soils may need water more frequently.

MECHANICAL TREE DIGGERS

The development of machines capable of digging and moving large trees all in one operation has made "instant shade" a reality. It is also one of the most abused practices in landscape contracting, largely because it does not require horticultural skills to operate the hydraulic levers and other mechanical devices of a tree-digging machine. As long as the machine can slice through the soil and roots and lift the weight of the tree and soil ball, the tree can be moved.

To move a tree *successfully,* however, requires horticultural skills. The person in charge of the tree-digging operation must be aware of soil conditions, extent of root spread of the trees to be dug, environmental factors already discussed that affect transplanted plants, and the laws of the state that govern nursery standards.

Several types of machines are in use today, including hydraulically driven *spades* and chain-driven *clam shells.* The spade type is the most common and operates with four or more triangular-shaped blades on steel tracks. The size of ball dug is fixed by the maximum opening size of the blades. Machines vary in size from under 30 inches in diameter up to 84 inches. Thus, a 44 tree spade will dig a ball of soil with the widest portion at the top measuring 44 inches, and a 66 tree spade will dig a 66-inch ball. The actual root-ball size, however, is smaller and depends upon the feeder root depth of the plant to be dug. For practical purposes, the root ball dug by the machine should be measured 6 inches below the top of the soil line, because of the slope of the spade. A 44 tree spade thus digs only a 33-inch root ball, and a 66 tree spade digs a 58-inch root ball. Some machines introduced in the late 1970s dig a soil ball with nearly parallel sides in the top portion. Such machines would therefore dig a root ball of corresponding size.

It is important that root-ball size be determined when tree-digging machines are used because the ball must conform with minimum standards of the American Association of Nurserymen as well as local standards. The minimum standard for *collected stock* (stock dug from the wild) is 8 inches of root ball per inch of trunk caliper for needled evergreens and 9 inches per caliper inch for deciduous stock. A pine dug from the wild with a 44 tree spade, for instance, would be limited to trees of 4.12-inch caliper (33 divided by 8 equals 4.12). Caliper measurement is made 6 inches above ground.

Following minimum standards, of course, does not guarantee that the tree has adequate roots. In many cases of collected stock, it is impossible or at least not economically feasible to dig a ball large enough to ensure adequate roots.

Trees and shrubs dug from native stands (collected stock) or trees grown for several years undisturbed will normally have most of their feeder roots extending well beyond the capability of machines or even hand-digging. Watson and Himelick (1982, 1983) reported that as little as 2 percent of the original root system is recovered in machine-dug Norway maple, green ash, and ginkgo. It was further shown by Watson (1985) that a 4-inch-caliper tree will take about five years to replace a root ball of the same size as the one prior to transplanting. A 10-inch-caliper tree will take up to thirteen years to replace the original root system.

Special planting procedures are required for machine-dug trees. A common but *unacceptable* method is to dig the hole for the tree with the same or similar machine. The dug tree is then "glove fit" into the hole using a slurry of soil and peat to fill the cracks. This practice, of course, does not allow for soil preparation, and the slurry creates a coating not unlike a peat pot on the outside of the ball. This, in turn, causes an interruption of root development and forms a water barrier (interface) as described earlier.

The correct way to prepare a hole for a machine-dug tree is either to hand-dig a standard planting pit with vertical sides or remove the sloped sides of a machine-dug hole. The tree is lowered into the hole and backfilled one-third. This backfill is firmed *before* the machine spades are removed.

The same procedure applies to trees dug with a

machine, burlapped, and placed in a wire basket for storage or transport to the site. Preferably, wire baskets should be removed completely; at the very least the top two rows of mesh should be removed.

CONTAINERS AND WIRE BASKETS
Container-grown Plants

The trend in the nursery business is increasingly toward use of plants grown and sold in containers or transported in supporting wire baskets. In addition to soil interface problems in containerized stock, as discussed earlier, plants grown in any type of container for a season or more become partially *pot bound*. This often causes roots to grow in a circular pattern; ultimately, as the roots enlarge in diameter, a girdle root condition results.

In the early days of container production of nursery stock, pot-bound plants received some corrective measures quite by accident. The plants were mostly grown in straight-sided metal cans (egg cans and large food cans). In order to get the plant out of the can, it was necessary to cut the side in two or more places. Special can cutters were developed for this purpose. In the process of cutting the can, the roots on the outside of the ball were wounded (scored). This promoted root development outside of the pot-bound root ball and less girdle root occurred.

More modern containers are made of fiber or plastic. They have sloped, smooth sides and the root ball can be slipped out easily. Unless scoring of the root ball is done deliberately with a sharp knife, the roots frequently remain tightly wound in the original ball and girdled root ultimately occurs. Scoring of roots of a pot-bound plant is highly recommended, but must be done quickly lest the roots themselves dry up. Using a sharp knife, vertically score about ⅛ inch deep, about every 2 to 3 inches around the circumference. The split-ball method may also be employed for plants grown in soilless mixes as described earlier.

If large, woody roots are already encircling the ball, carefully "tease" them away from the ball and attempt to straighten them. If necessary, cut away a portion of roots already beginning to girdle.

Plants in Wire Baskets

Wire baskets pose a different problem than containers do, although the effect on the plant is similar. Wire does not deteriorate readily in soils. The corrosive action of the soil will produce a layer on the surface of the wire, but further corrosion seems to be halted or significantly reduced thereafter. As a result, roots that grow between the wire mesh may ultimately become partially restricted (figs. 4-5 and 4-6).

Obviously, the smaller the mesh, the more roots will be restricted. Chicken and rabbit wire will restrict more roots than will 2- by 4-inch or 4- by 4-inch mesh, common in machine-dug trees. What is not always obvious, however, is that regardless of the mesh size, the time required for root restriction is the same. As roots grow out of the original ball, regardless of whether the mesh size is 1 inch or 6 inches, some encounter

Figure 4-5. Root restriction from wire mesh. Severe stunting of the tree resulted. (Courtesy Eugene B. Eyerly, Eyerly & Associates)

the wire immediately. If a root is adjacent to a wire, it will become partially girdled as it enlarges in diameter (fig. 4-7). Often, only partial restriction occurs, and the tree succumbs to stress during a drought or falls prey to bark engraver or wood-boring insects.

Wire mesh of any kind must be removed from around the root ball. This is best done after the tree is placed in the planting pit. If wire removal appears to result in breaking of the soil ball, backfill and firm one-third to stabilize the ball, then remove the wire down to the top of the backfill. Leave the wire near the bottom of the ball. A special angle-bladed bolt cutter made for this purpose is now available for easy and quick wire removal.

If removal of any wire results in disintegration of the soil ball, you have a tree that is already too loose in the ball because of poor digging or handling. Such trees should be rejected.

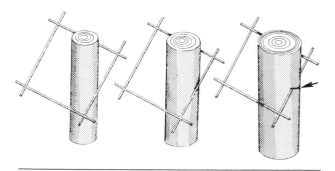

Figure 4-7. Stages of partial root constriction caused by buried wire mesh. Root tissue does not rejoin after closure over wire (arrow).

PLANTING IN PAVED AREAS

Urban situations frequently call for plantings in paved areas. Such locations are usually harsh from the standpoint of environment for plant growth. Paved areas reflect considerable heat, often shed excess water into plantings pits, or may shed water away from plant roots. Air exchange into the soil, needed for proper root growth, may also be severely limited.

Asphalt-paved Areas

When planting into asphalt-paved sites, a contractor should be wary of possible soil-contaminating chemicals. Many paving companies, as a matter of routine, apply soil sterilant chemicals prior to paving to prevent damage from perennial weeds such as bindweed (*Convolvulus arvensis*) and quackgrass (*Agropyron repens*). Most chemicals used, such as bromacil (Hyvar), picloram (Tordon), prometon, and sodium borate are long-lasting under pavement. Plantings have died from sterilant-contaminated soils even when the planting was done eight or ten years after application of the chemicals. Chapter 8 contains information on testing for possible soil contamination.

If the original grade is such that surplus (runoff) water tends to flow into planting pits, make sure that the grade in the planting area is elevated to reduce chances of flooding during heavy rains. Plants should be elevated at least 4 inches above the surrounding pavement.

Figure 4-6. Nylon ropes have partially girdled this tree. The buried wire basket (arrow) will also restrict deeper roots. (Courtesy Eugene B. Eyerly, Eyerly & Associates)

Concrete-paved Areas

Soil-sterilizing chemicals are not usually applied prior to paving with concrete or similar hard surfaces. As with asphalt-paved sites, however, it is necessary to check the grade and flow of runoff to make sure that excess water does not move into planting pits. Raise the final grade for the plantings at least 4 inches above adjacent pavement. This is especially important where pavement surrounds the entire planting pit.

Pedestrian Traffic Areas

In pedestrian traffic areas, it is usually necessary to cover the top of the root ball with a grate or pavers to avoid accidents. Breakaway metal grates are available for this purpose; even better are dry-laid pavers because they conform better to the slight grade change from pavement up to the plant base. They are also easier to remove as the plant increases in diameter.

Where specifications insist on a level grade, the top of the root ball will need to be several inches below

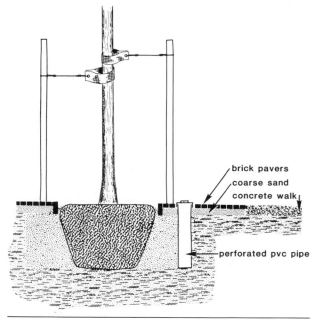

Figure 4-8. A method of planting in pedestrian traffic areas. Perforated PVC pipe is used to check water accumulation.

the surrounding pavement. This is less desirable and ultimately more costly. In this type of situation, one or more vertical PVC pipes (4 to 6 inches in diameter) should be installed just outside the root ball to monitor water accumulation. The pipe should extend from the surface to the bottom of the planting pit and have a removable cap. If pavers are used instead of metal grates, lay coarse sand (not mortar sand) on top of the root ball to level pavers with surrounding concrete (fig. 4-8).

This type of planting requires frequent monitoring of water collection, particularly during rainy periods. A simple dip stick can be used to determine if water is collecting at the bottom of the pit. A small submersible pump can be used to remove the excess water.

Where metal grates are used, periodic checks should be made to ensure that the recessed area below the grate is not filling with silt and debris.

Avoid using solid precast-concrete "lids" to cover tree wells. They are difficult and costly to remove and cannot be easily reduced in size to accommodate tree growth.

COMMON PRACTICES TO IMPROVE SURVIVAL OF TRANSPLANTED TREES AND SHRUBS

Several practices have been used over the years to increase the survival chances of transplanted trees and shrubs. These include use of hydraulic soil needles, staking and guying, wrapping with various materials, spraying with antitranspirants, and top pruning.

Hydraulic Soil Needles

The use of hydraulic needles, especially with newly transplanted trees, has aroused some controversy. Obviously, if water is injected under high pressure in a loose backfill, uneven settling could result. This, however, is an improper use of such equipment. Hydraulic soil needles are of value more from the standpoint of providing aeration to the heavier soils beyond the backfill area than they are in providing water. If used 6 to 12 inches beyond the soil ball, they will not cause problems and can actually provide needed aeration for the development of new roots as the roots grow out of the backfill and into the old soil. An air column left by the device provides a good environment for root growth. Cross sections made through such holes have shown that roots do form in masses in these air columns. In the same way, roots will mass in drain tiles and sewer lines.

Staking and Guying

Staking and guying trees prevents the plant from falling over or leaning from the force of winds until the root system is reestablished enough to do the job. The term *staking* is used when posts, singly or in multiples, are employed. *Guying* refers to the use of ropes or wires inclined at an angle from the tree to ground anchors. Both methods are commonly used in new landscape plantings, even in the same installation.

Not every tree that is planted needs to be staked or guyed. Common sense and past experiences with similar kinds of stock can help landscape managers decide if some support is needed in particular situations. Most bare-root trees should be staked at least for the first season. Container-grown, balled and burlapped, and spade-dug trees often do not need staking, especially if they have a adequate root-ball size in proportion to caliper. Densely branched trees, especially evergreens and trees that appear top heavy, are likely candidates for staking.

Stake and guy systems should not be left in place for more than two growing seasons.

Securing Cables or Guy Wires

An age-old method of securing a tree to stakes or guy wires is to run a wire through old pieces of garden hose wrapped around the tree. Although this practice was thought to prevent damage to the bark of the tree, *using wire and garden hose should be avoided.* This method may prevent cutting of the wire into the bark, but the hose does not distribute the pressure created by tension on the wire. This, in turn, causes restriction of the phloem, cambial area, and new xylem in the vicinity of the wire (fig. 4-9).

The proper method to secure cables or guy wires is to use webbing and/or strips of indoor-outdoor carpet through which metal grommets have been inserted. The strapping should be at least 3 inches wide. The

Figure 4-9. Pressure from wire is not relieved with a rubber hose: (*top*) hose and wire in normal position; (*bottom*) hoses moved to show indentations in bark from wire. This constriction occurred in the first year of guying. (Courtesy Eugene B. Eyerly, Eyerly & Associates)

Figure 4-10. Webbing results in less constriction of a tree than do hose and wire. Webbing will allow flexibility of guys if not wired too tightly.

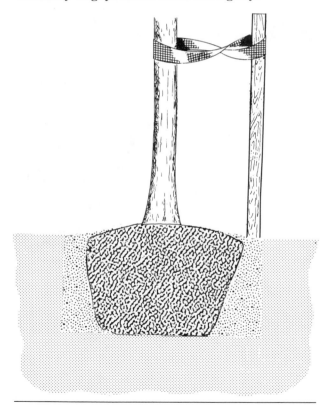

Figure 4-11. Staking a tree with a single strap. The strap can be secured with a staple or tack on a wooden stake.

strapping is placed around the tree, and the cables are threaded through the grommets, as shown in figure 4-10. When trees are secured to stakes rather than guy wires, the same strapping can be used, except no grommets are needed. In this case, the strap is placed around the tree, crossed over and then around the stake or post, as shown in figure 4-11. If wood posts are used (2- by 2-inch clear pine is a common choice), the straps can be tacked or stapled on the out-facing side of the stake.

Whether guyed or staked, trees must not be held too rigidly. A certain amount of natural sway is needed. Research by Harris, Leiser, and Davis (1976) has shown that trees guyed or staked too rigidly fail to develop strong roots, have poor trunk taper, and become weakened. Such trees tend to lean when ties are later removed (fig. 4-12).

Anchor stakes in guyed trees should be driven *at the same angle* as the guy wire unless commercial tree anchors are used. If driven at a 90-degree angle to the wire, as is commonly done, the stakes will be levered back and forth under pressure from gusty winds. The stakes will loosen and soon pull out. Where soils are too sandy to hold anchor stakes firmly, it is best to employ staking methods using posts, as illustrated in figure 4-8. This method is also preferable when securing trees in public areas or where foot traffic, playing children, and sports activities are anticipated. Guy wires can become "trip" or "hang" wires and can result in serious injuries.

Single Versus Multiple Staking

Whether a single stake or guy wire or several (two, three, or four) are used depends mostly on the size of the tree. As a general rule, trees with less than a 3-inch caliper need only one stake placed on the windward side. Trees having greater than 3-inch calipers are best staked or guyed in two or three directions. The three-way method is best on trees requiring high wind resistance.

Height of Attachment

The point at which guy wires or other tree braces are attached varies from tree to tree. Some natural sway

Figure 4-12. The tree at left, which had been staked, fell over when ties were removed. The tree at right had never been staked. Improperly staked trees may be weakened by staking. (From Harris 1983)

is desirable, and attachment too high will reduce this sway. Therefore, attachments should be as low as possible on the trunk yet still prevent the tree from falling over.

Vertical stakes can usually be attached lower to trees than guy wires can. Guy wires require a sharp angle of ascent from the anchors to the tree to prevent them from slipping. As a result, higher attachments are required.

Wrapping Young Trees

Tree wrap is used to prevent sudden temperature fluctuation. Commercial crepe wraps are scientifically designed to insulate against temperature drop and reflect heat. Alternatives to tree wrap include painting with white latex paints, shading of the bark with boards, and allowing lower limbs to remain on trunks (avoid "limbing up") until the plant is established. The latter is the best method for the tree.

Some nurserymen and arborists use strips of burlap or other cloth material to wrap trees. This practice is not recommended because burlap does not reflect heat and, once wet, will conduct heat. Burlap and other cloth materials also are more likely to harbor disease organisms and insects than are commercial crepe wraps.

Latex paints, while somewhat effective, are aesthetically undesirable. Latex is more commonly used in orchards, where aesthetics are not as important as in landscapes.

Wrapping Procedure

Trees should be wrapped from the base upward to the second scaffold branch (fig. 4-13). Wrap is overlapped so that it will shed moisture. Do not wrap from the top downward, as this will leave water-catching seams. To secure the last turn of the wrap, use a *single* staple or waterproof tape.

Trees should be wrapped in the fall, and the wrap removed in spring. Tree wrap left on during the growing season can harbor disease organisms and insects, such as earwigs and various borers. Wrapping for two winters is usually sufficient.

Trees to Wrap

Young, thin-barked trees should be wrapped. These include honeylocust, green ash, mountain ash, plum,

Figure 4-13. Apply tree wrap from the bottom upward. Wrap should be overlapped to shed water.

Japanese pagodatree, most oak, maple, and many others. Trees that do not need wrapping include birch, aspen, and bur oak. These trees have insulative bark even in very young plants. Any tree with corky, mature bark does not need to be wrapped.

In some instances tree wrap should not be applied even if the tree is thin-barked. For example, trees with recent bruises and mechanical abrasions and trees that have existing bark cankers such as *Cytospora* should not be wrapped. Unfortunately, tree wraps are often used to hide such flaws. A buyer, unaware of the damages, finds out too late that mechanical damage and cankers are present. The discovery usually is not made until the tree declines as the disease organisms proliferate in the ideal environment under the tree wrap.

To avoid this problem, do not allow trees to be delivered to a planting site with tree wrap already on the trunks, or remove wrap and inspect the trees before final acceptance. Where possible, inspect the trees both at the nursery where they have been grown and at the planting site.

Some nurseries claim that tree wrap protects the bark during shipment. While some protection may be afforded, tree wraps do little to cushion against abrasion and mechanical wounds. Wraps also hide bruises incurred during shipments. Trees with tender bark, such as honeylocust, maple, ash, and birch, should have corrugated cardboard cylinders or other protective cover around the trunks during transport. Several layers of burlap, especially where trunks of trees will rub during transport, are effective in reducing bark damage.

Trees with fresh mechanical wounds and active cankers should be rejected or, if deemed salvageable, treated to reduce further damages. After treatment, usually with a fungicide, the southwest side of the trunk should be shaded with boards to prevent sun scald rather than being wrapped.

Antitranspirants

Antitranspirants (antidesiccants), when properly used, can be helpful in reducing water loss from the foliage of transplanted trees and shrubs. They have also proved helpful in some areas of the United States for reducing winter desiccation of established evergreens. Recent studies have shown that certain antitranspirant materials can also increase fruit size in peaches and apples.

There are basically three types of antitranspirants: film formers; chemicals that interfere with the opening of the stomates; and materials that cause a reflection of incoming radiation away from the leaves, thereby reducing temperatures and subsequent water vaporization. The most common antitranspirants in commercial use today are the film-forming types. These include various waxes, wax–oil emulsions, plastics, silicones, latexes, and resins. The function of a film-forming antitranspirant is simply to coat the leaf, including the stomates, thereby reducing transpiration.

The ideal antitranspirant should be nontoxic to the plant, resist breakdown or decomposition, and allow the admittance of the essential wavelengths of light; it should not interfere with photosynthesis and respiration. Such a material, to be economically practical, should also be inexpensive and easy to apply without gumming up a sprayer. No antitranspirant on the market today meets all of these requirements.

Most of the film-forming antitranspirants available interfere with photosynthesis by preventing the assimilation of carbon dioxide. If applied too heavily, they can result in a suppression of growth. Some of the antidesiccants on the market, particularly silicone and latex formulations, may prevent the passage of carbon dioxide more than they prevent water loss.

On the other hand, some antitranspirants may be too efficient in reducing water loss. This may affect other growth processes in the plant, including the production of food for sound root growth. Fortunately, the rate at which antitranspirants are applied and the usual methods of application make it difficult to apply a coating sufficient to cause problems. The stomates on most leaves of broad-leaved plants are usually greater in number on the lower leaf surface than on the upper. Unless a tree is immersed in an antitranspirant solution, complete coverage of all leaf surfaces is almost impossible.

Another problem with some antitranspirants is that they may not stick firmly to the leaf upon drying. Plastic-based materials frequently have this fault. They may also form an unsightly crust on the leaves.

Contrary to popular belief, antitranspirants do not cause a drastic increase in leaf temperature, at least when the plant is under normal growing conditions. It was once thought that leaves cooled themselves by water evaporation. It is now known that transpiration has only a partial effect on the cooling of leaves and that most of the heat is dissipated by direct thermal emission from the surface of the cells.

It is now generally accepted that antitranspirants are beneficial when transplanting trees in full leaf, provided the correct dilution mixture and the proper equipment are used to apply the material. Their benefits, however, are fewer in arid areas than in more humid climates. One of the biggest reasons for failure to achieve reduced water loss through the use of antitranspirants is improper application. If the application equipment produces poor coverage of the liquid, poor results will be obtained. For example, a nozzle delivering large droplets provides poorer coverage of material than a nozzle that delivers a mist or small, closely spaced droplets. To obtain maximum benefit from antitranspirants in broad-leaved trees, the material should be applied primarily to the lower leaf surface.

Davies and Kozlowski (1974) demonstrated wide variations in the effects of antitranspirants. The effects of most types are of short duration (two weeks or less) from the standpoint of reducing water loss. Those that produce longer-lasting effects may, under certain environmental conditions, cause phytotoxicity and a "suffocation" injury to plants.

Pruning after Planting

It has long been common to prune a portion of the tops of trees and shrubs after planting. This practice was based on the belief that top pruning would compensate for root loss and maintain a balance between the two. A common recommendation is to remove one-third of the top, especially in bare-root stock. It is also a common practice to leave container-grown plants and balled-and-burlapped plants unpruned, because fewer roots are disturbed. Collected pines are usually not pruned at all, yet the root system lost may be as much as 98 percent.

The problem with trying to prune tops to compensate for root loss is in determining exactly how much root damage or loss has occurred. It can vary from plant to plant even in the same lot of nursery stock. It has also been shown through research that top pruning of transplanted stock does not help to ensure plant survival and can even be damaging by removing potential carbohydrate production, thus reducing the chances of root regeneration.

Richardson (1958) found that removal of the terminal buds of sugar maple seedlings delayed the initiation of root growth until another bud developed. In a six-species test of bare-root stock, Whitcomb et al. (1979) found that nearly all trees survived post-plant pruning, but none benefited from it. Furthermore, those pruned 30 to 45 percent did not reestablish a natural growth form.

Current recommendations are to prune only dead, dying, or weak branches and to avoid pruning tips and small branches (suckers) along the trunk until after the plant is reestablished.

REFERENCES

Davies, W. J., and Kozlowski, T. T. 1974. Short- and long-term effects of antitranspirants on water relations and photosynthesis of woody plants. J. Am. Soc. Hort. Sci. 99(4):297–304.

Gouin, F. 1983. Girdling by roots and ropes. J. Environ. Hort. 1(2):48–50.

Harris, R. W. 1983. Arboriculture: Care of Trees, Shrubs and Vines in the Landscape. Englewood Cliffs, NJ: Prentice-Hall.

Harris, R. W., Leiser, A. T., and Davis, W. B. 1976. Staking landscape trees. Univ. Calif. Agric. Ext. Leaflet 2576.

Richardson, D. S. 1958. Bud dormancy and root development in *Acer saccharinum*. *In* The Physiology of Trees, K. V. Thimann (ed.), New York: Ronald Press.

Schulte, J., and Whitcomb, C. E. 1975. Effects of soil amendments and fertilizer levels on the establishment of silver maple. J. Arboriculture 1:192–95.

Watson, G. W. 1985. Tree size affects root regeneration and top growth after transplanting. J. Arboriculture 11(2):37–40.

Watson, G. W., and Himelick, E. B. 1983. Root regeneration of shade trees following transplanting. J. Environ. Hort. 1(2):50–52.

———. 1982. Root distribution of nursery trees and its relationship to transplanting success. J. Arboriculture 8:225–29.

Whitcomb, C. E., Byrnes, R. L., and Ward, J. D. 1979. Factors affecting the establishment of urban trees. J. Arboriculture 5(10):217–19.

———. 1976. What is a $5 planting hole? Am. Nurseryman 144(5):16.

5. 🌿

Pruning and Wound Care

Pruning is a practice that dates back to ancient times. It is even mentioned in the Bible with reference to grapes. Pruning is also a natural process, more correctly called *shedding*. Shedding involves both branches and roots in trees and shrubs. It is part of the natural survival system inherent in plants. While shedding occurs in all plants, herbaceous or woody, the discussion in this chapter will deal primarily with pruning of woody plants.

As ancient as pruning is, until recently few had observed how shedding occurs under natural conditions. As a result, most advice on pruning has been incorrect because the defensive mechanisms built into woody plants have been overlooked. Traditionally, pruning has been, and in many cases still is, a matter of removing plant parts to accomplish aesthetic affects, increase quality of fruit, repair mechanical damage, or correct improper placement of plants in a landscape. However, little attention has been paid to pruning as a science and to the plant's reaction to cutting away its parts.

PLANT DEFENSES

One of the unique structural features of woody plants is the way they develop into orderly compartments. As described in chapter 1, a woody plant increases annually in length through growth of meristematic areas of shoots and roots and in diameter through special meristematic cells called the cambium. The cambium forms carbohydrate-conducting tissues on the exterior (phloem) and water- and mineral-conducting tissues on the interior (xylem). Connecting both radially are special living cells in groups called rays. Ray cells serve to transport food materials back and forth as sugars for utilization in growth. Stored food is in the form of starches, fats, and lipids. Each layer of cell groups in the xylem, or wood, thus forms more or less wedge-shaped compartments. The ends of cells up and down also tend to form compartments. The compartment structure of a tree is illustrated in figure 5-1.

The significance of these compartments has been only vaguely understood, even though they were described about 100 years ago by R. Hartig in Germany. The exhaustive research of Dr. Alex Shigo of the U.S. Forest Service first demonstrated the importance of compartments in trees during the past two decades (Shigo and Marx 1977). This research, which has been supported by many others, has shown conclusively that the compartments in a woody plant serve as effective natural boundaries that make it difficult for pathogens (disease organisms) to spread. In this way, woody plants resist spread of infectious microorganisms

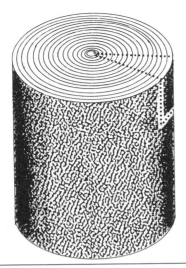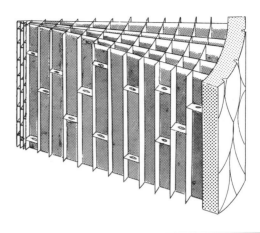

Figure 5-1. The compartmentalization of a tree. The three-dimensional view at right shows twelve years' growth rings. The basic compartment is a single cell; groups of cells in rings or radially as rays form other compartments. The weakest areas are the ends of single cells.

throughout all parts of the plant (see Shigo 1986 for a more thorough discussion of how trees resist infectious organisms).

The boundaries formed by rays and annual xylem layers are stronger than those formed by ends of cell walls (vessels, tracheids, and fibers). This is why infections that do occur will usually spread up and down (mostly down) and tend to be stopped radially and tangentially (toward the interior). Thus, a woody plant defends itself in all three dimensions by compartmentalizing infection (fig. 5-2).

Responses to Wounding

With regard to wounding, compartmentalization in woody plants needs to be understood as a two-part process. Part 1 involves the formation of built-in chemical *reaction zones* that strengthen the structural boundaries just described; part 2 is the formation of *barrier zones* by the cambium that separate the tissues present at time of wounding from those formed after wounding.

Reaction Zones

The reaction zone is a region in sapwood in which antimicrobial substances produced by living cells (wood

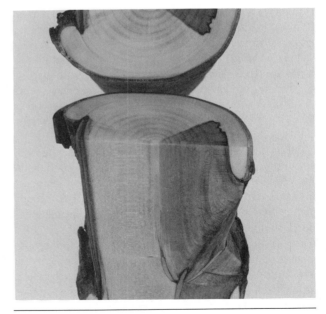

Figure 5-2. Compartmentalization following the wounding of a red maple. Note how a deep wound at a branch union on the right caused discoloration in a three-dimensional wedge. Surface wound on the left side resulted in discoloration of the last growth increment only. (Courtesy Kenneth R. Dudzik, N.E. Forest Experiment Station)

parenchyma) accumulate at the edge of an infection (fig. 5-3). These zones retard longitudinal and inward movement of infections that develop after wounding or branch infection. While the chemistry of reaction zones is not completely understood, some of the known reactions include the development of phenolic compounds, such as tannin in deciduous plants and terpenes in conifers. These chemicals are effective antimicrobial substances.

Under natural conditions, reaction zones are not static; that is, they may be constantly broken down by microbial action and new zones formed in advance of an organism's attack. The resistance to breakdown of barriers in plants varies from species to species and even within the same species, depending upon genetic makeup as well as the general health of a given plant. Trees can compartmentalize themselves to death. Repeat injuries followed by walling off of the injury may use up all the energy within the tree and decrease storage space for energy reserves (Shigo and Tippett 1981). Such is the case with Dutch elm disease (Shigo 1982).

Barrier Zones

When wounding occurs, the cambium in woody plants develops a barrier, or wall, of nonconductive tissue, which provides a strong defense against invading pathogens. In oaks, Pearce and Rutherford (1981) found suberin in the cell walls, which tends to strengthen the cell. In much the same way, a potato tuber will *suberize* when cut and exposed to air for a day or so. In conifers the barrier zone may include proliferation of resin ducts forming cell layers highly resistant to organism encroachment (Schuck 1982; Tippett and Shigo 1981). A more detailed discussion on barrier zones in relationship to diseases is presented in chapter 7.

Wound Closure

When the cambium is totally destroyed by wounding, the tree develops *wound callus* from cambial cells adjacent to the injured area. This process is called *wound closure.*

The term *wound healing* is so ingrained and commonly used that it is unlikely to be replaced with the more correct *wound closure.* Nonetheless, arborists, nurserymen, and landscape managers should understand that when the term *healing* is used, the actual process is *closure.*

Wound closure in woody plants has been misunderstood for centuries, partly because humans have tended to compare formation of wound callus in plants with healing of wounds in animals. The two processes, however, are distinctly different. In animals, damaged tissue is replaced in the same spatial position as the damage. In plants, damaged tissue is not repaired, but more tissue is generated in a new spatial area. Thus, plants do not heal wounds in the sense of regeneration or restoration; rather they close over defects and compartmentalize them in layers of new tissue (fig. 5-4).

The term *wound healing* is so ingrained and commonly used that it is unlikely to be replaced with the more correct *wound closure.* Nonetheless, arborists, nurserymen, and landscape managers should understand that when the term *healing* is used, the actual process is *closure.*

It may seem that the difference between the two

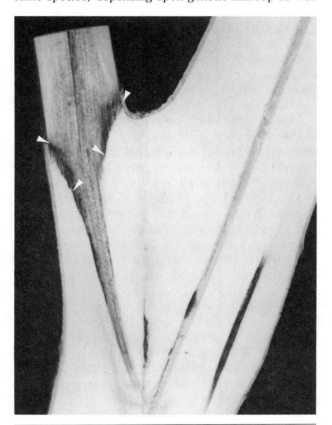

Figure 5-3. The reaction zone in a branch (arrows). This zone provides chemical protection against microorganism invasion. (Courtesy Kenneth R. Dudzik, N.E. Forest Experiment Station)

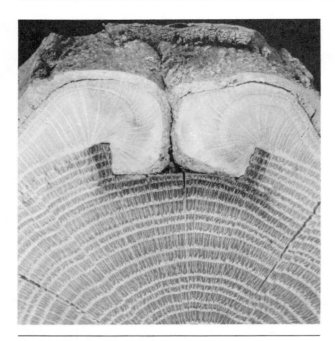

Figure 5-4. Wound closure in white oak. A sample from a tree intentionally wounded three years prior to cutting. Note that healing does not occur. Discoloration is merely compartmentalized by new growth. (Courtesy Kenneth R. Dudzik, N.E. Forest Experiment Station)

terms is not sufficient to be important. Yet, the misunderstanding of how woody plants respond to wounding has led to horticultural practices that are futile. Foremost of these practices is the use of wound dressings or paints.

Wound Dressings

The practice of painting wounds in trees has been common for centuries. In spite of research showing that wound dressings are of limited benefit in wound closure and of no value at all in infection abatement, many types are in common use. Collins (1934), Marshall (1950), Shigo and Wilson (1977), Mercer (1979), and Dooley (1980) have shown conclusively that tree wound dressings, regardless of type, do not prevent decay in woody plants. Thorough reviews of wound dressing research by Shigo and Shortle (1983) and Ossenbruggen (1985) summarized years of studies comparing more

than a dozen treatments and combinations. Included were common tree paints used in the past, such as orange shellac, and more modern materials, such as water-emulsifiable asphalts. Their exhaustive work should put to rest the controversy over wound dressings.

The tendency to use tree wound dressings is a natural one because, as explained earlier, we often equate plants with animals. A wound dressing on a tree is thus thought of as an antiseptic and bandage. An antiseptic on a wound may stop infection in animals and may even temporarily help plant wounds in some cases. A bandage over a wound in animals helps to reduce further infection. However, as anyone who has left a bandage on too long knows, a bandage will eventually aid infection because it provides a protected, moist environment that is ideal for growth of organisms.

Wound dressings on woody plants essentially do the same. A wound on a woody plant is better kept dry than wet. Dry tissues cannot support growth of microorganisms. Complete wound closure may take several years to occur, depending upon wound size, tree vigor, and tree type.

All wound dressings available today eventually crack and weather away. Few last more than one year. In the meantime, microorganisms can get a foothold under the dressing. Thus, painting wounds is a waste of time and effort. If you have clients (or a boss) who insist on it out of ignorance or old habits, then apply a thin coat. Apply just enough to change the color of the wound surface, no more. This is what I call, "psychological wound dressing." It probably will do no harm and definitely will do no good, but it appeases the eye, making one think they are doing a good thing for the tree.

LOCATION OF PRUNING CUT

Once a thorough understanding of a plant's response to wounding is gained, selection of where to make a pruning cut becomes more obvious.

Before discussing the mechanics of pruning, however, it is necessary to review how branches are attached to stems (trunks). As described in chapter 1, the branch of a woody plant is not joined to the stem as a continuous sheath of wood, but rather is joined only at the underside of a branch. The stem then forms a collar *over* the branch (see figs. 1-6–1-10). The important thing to remember when pruning a plant is that branch removal must be done in such a way that the branch collar is not injured. A cut into the collar will destroy natural defensive mechanisms in the tree and open the tree to infection. Thus, the traditional practice of flush-cut pruning should *never* be done because it invariably removes this natural protective zone (fig. 5-5).

Since it is not possible to see the actual protective zone in a woody plant, external guidelines are needed to determine where a cut should be made. This is described by Shigo (1982) as "natural target pruning." The procedure to use is as follows:

1. Locate the ridge of bark formed above a branch at the union, or crotch, of stem and branch.
2. Locate the stem collar surrounding the branch. This is usually a slight swelling near the main stem or trunk.
3. Remove the branch by making a cut *outside* of both branch bark ridge and collar (fig. 5-6).
4. Where an obvious swelling or collar is not present, cut *outside* of the branch bark ridge and at an angle opposite that formed by the ridge (fig. 5-7).
5. Limbs over 1 inch in diameter or long, heavy branches should be removed by the three-step method illustrated in figure 5-8. Otherwise, bark will be stripped before the branch has been completely removed.

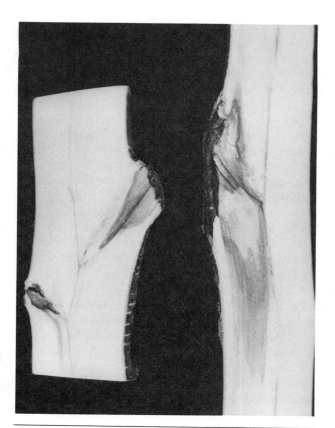

Figure 5-5. Reaction by a tree to proper branch removal (*left*) and to flush-cut pruning (*right*). Note the large area of discoloration in flush-cut sample. (Courtesy Kenneth R. Dudzik, N.E. Forest Experiment Station)

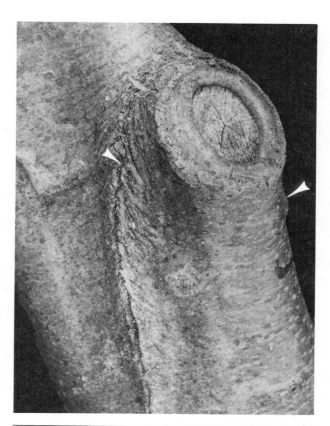

Figure 5-6. Wound closure after proper branch removal. The cut was made outside of the branch bark ridge (*left arrow*) and the branch collar (*right arrow*).

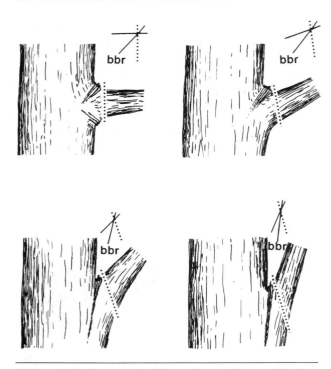

Figure 5-7. Removal of branches where a distinct collar is not present. Angle of cut (dotted line) should be equal and opposite the angle of the branch bark ridge (bbr).

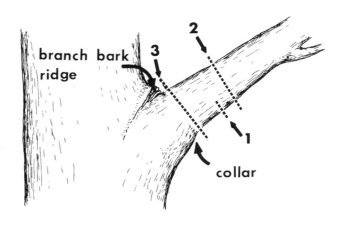

Figure 5-8. Removal of heavy limbs by the three-cut method. Final cut should be outside of the collar and branch bark ridge.

TOPPING TREES AND SHRUBS

The practice of topping trees and shrubs to reduce plant height should be avoided where possible. Topping exposes large openings in stem or trunk tissues, which become easy access points for microorganisms. Topping also removes large amounts of leaf-bearing shoots, which produce carbohydrates needed for callus formation. Foliage removal also reduces the amount of chemical inhibitors (hormones) that discourage weak sprouts arising from epicormic growth.

Epicormic growth results from the removal of inhibitory chemicals that normally suppress buds previously formed during shoot development. These are referred to as *latent* or *buried latent* buds. Epicormic growth can also occur adventitiously from meristematic cells at the ends of rays.

Shoots arising from epicormic growth are always weaker than those from normal, unsuppressed buds because the attachment of the shoot to stem consists only of a thin thread of vascular tissue. Suppressed buds elongate at their bases as new xylem is formed, keeping pace with the diametric growth. The suppressed buds, however, do not increase in diameter. Consequently, when such a bud does "awaken" and grow out, its attachment is no deeper than the bark and much smaller in diameter than the shoot produced (fig. 5-9). Subsequent growth of the stem or trunk will tend to overgrow the base of the epicormic shoot. This results in a sort of ball-and-socket attachment (fig. 5-10). Such growths should be avoided in trees for the sake of safety, as epicormic branches are the first to break in wind storms and under heavy snow loads.

If topping a tree is necessary, all cuts should be made outside a branch bark ridge and parallel with the remaining branches or leader. This is called *drop-crotching* (fig. 5-11). The branch remaining should be as large as possible and should *not* be pruned. It is important that ample foliage be retained for suppression of epicormic growth, as well as carbohydrate production for callus formation. On vigorous trees, such as poplar, willow, Siberian elm, and soft maple (silver maple), leave a leader that has a stem diameter at least half the size of the branch or stem removed. With less vigorous trees, the leader should be at least one-third the diameter of the one removed.

Trees severely damaged by wind, snow, and ice storms may require removal of more top than desired. Often there is little choice. In these situations, follow the drop-crotch method as closely as possible, removing no more foliage-bearing branches than necessary. Avoid the tendency to reshape the tree to create a more aesthetic balance. Overpruning invariably occurs, and abundant epicormic growth results. Reshaping should wait a season or two or until the tree has regained a more normal balance of foliage on its own. Gradual, selective branch removal can then be performed to return the tree to a more natural form.

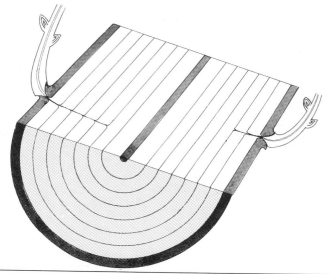

Figure 5-9. A section through a stem with epicormic shoots. Both shoots grew the same year, but the one on the left formed from a latent bud five years earlier; on the right, two years earlier.

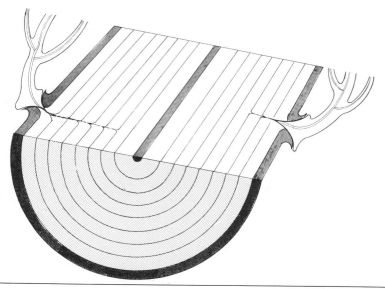

Figure 5-10. Epicormic shoots in figure 5-9 a year later. Note the weak ball-and-socket shoot attachment.

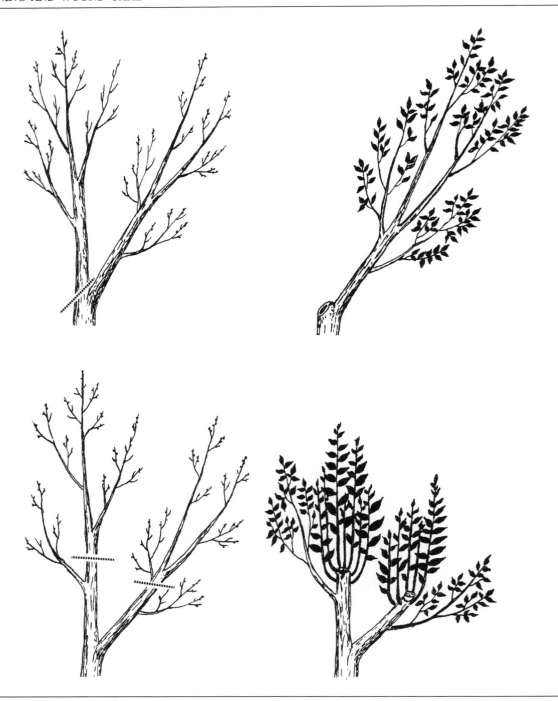

Figure 5-11. Proper (*top*) and improper (*bottom*) top removal of a tree. Note response on the right in each case. Topping in the bottom example results in weak, epicormic growth.

PRUNING OLD STUBS

Where old stubs occur in trees as a result of previous unrepaired storm damage or poor pruning methods, check the stub base carefully. Callus tissues may be forming near the stub base from the surrounding collar of stem or trunk cambium (fig. 5-12). Avoid damage to this callus. Make the cut just outside the callus (fig. 5-13). Removal of the callus will destroy a strong protective barrier against invading organisms. The result will be the spread of any decay organisms present in the branch stub into previously healthy tissues.

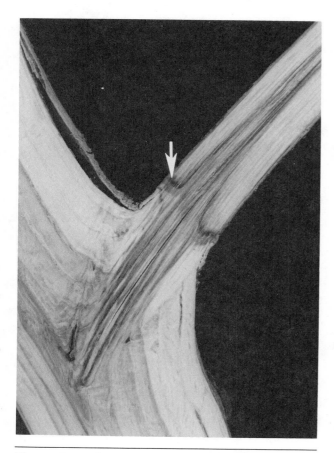

Figure 5-12. The protection zone (arrow) following natural branch dieback. The zone forms outside of the branch bark ridge and branch collar. Proper branch removal should be done just right of arrow. (Courtesy Kenneth R. Dudzik, N.E. Forest Experiment Station)

TRAINING YOUNG TREES

Young or newly planted trees need to be trained by selective branch removal. The general method employed will depend somewhat on the end result desired. Trees in street-side plantings or those where there is pedestrian traffic will need eventual clearance of the lowest limbs by 8 to 15 feet. Trees in nontraffic areas can be allowed lower limb development, unless turf is desired beneath them. Whatever ultimate result is desired, early training of a tree is important. If training is done incorrectly while a tree is young, it becomes difficult, if not impossible, to achieve the desired effect as the tree becomes older, at least not without injurious effects.

The primary objective in training a tree is to achieve strong scaffold branches. These form the primary structure. Selection of branches to remove is based on the objective of achieving good spacing up and down the main trunk, as well as radially around the trunk. It is undesirable from a structural standpoint to have several branches arising from the same radial plane, except in the case of pine, spruce, and other conifers that naturally have whorled branches.

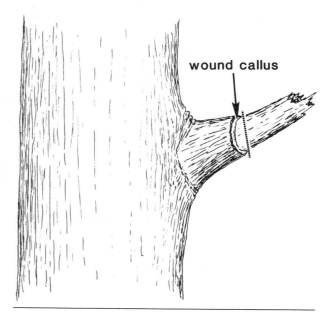

Figure 5-13. Proper removal of an old stub. Make a cut outside of the wound callus, as damaging the callus will open the tree to infection.

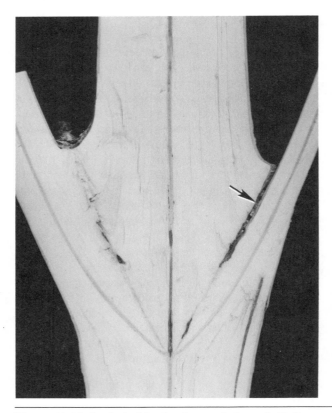 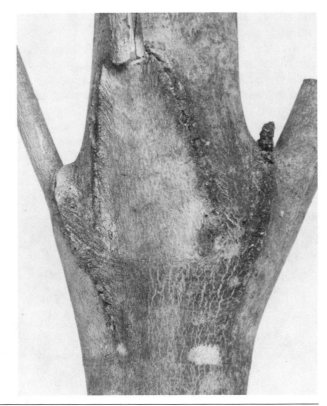

Figure 5-14. Included bark of a weak branch (*left, arrow*). The exterior of the same section, from a red maple, is shown at right. (Courtesy Kenneth R. Dudzik, N.E. Forest Experiment Station)

Branches that are on a collision course with others, those that are rubbing together, and those showing weak crotch characteristics also are candidates for removal. Branches that have narrow crotches (very upright branch habit) are likely to have included (in-growing) bark in the crotch (fig. 5-14). Sometimes included bark can be found even on wide crotches. If allowed to remain, such branches may eventually break in a storm or become entry points for disease organisms.

The amount of training required depends upon the size and age of the tree and any prior pruning it received in a nursery. Trees may be unbranched whips or well-branched saplings. If time is of no concern, it is preferable to start with an unbranched whip, so that the tree can be custom-trained to the site in which it is to be grown.

In today's landscape plantings, however, whips are rarely, if ever, planted; generally larger and well-branched nursery-grown specimens are used. Trees properly trained in the nursery may need little, if any, additional training. Unfortunately, few nursery-grown trees are trained for perfect branch spacing, and thus some corrective pruning is usually required.

Training Unbranched Whips

Trees started from unbranched whips or those with very few branches are usually forced to branch from lateral buds by cutting back the top shortly after planting (fig. 5-15). This causes lateral shoot development. It is best to wait until after the first growing season to begin selective removal of side shoots because removal of growth the first year tends to rob the tree of carbohydrates needed for root growth.

At the beginning of the second year, remove branches

that appear crowded but resist limbing the tree up from the base. Some branches low on the trunk should be retained to provide carbohydrates for stem diameter growth. Trees limbed up too soon will tend to develop weak trunks and poor taper (Harris et al. 1976).

In late winter or early spring of the third year, final selection is made of branches to be retained and undesirable lower limbs to be removed for needed clearance or aesthetic considerations. *Avoid tip pruning* of branches, except for minor shaping or to remove damaged growth.

Training Well-Branched Young Trees

Newly planted trees, regardless of size, should be given only minimal pruning until the root system is established. At time of planting, remove only dead, diseased, or very weak and broken branches. As with whips, avoid removing lower shoots on the trunk and also tips of branches. As discussed in chapter 4, some nurseries still follow the old practice of removing one-third of the top. This usually overprunes the tree, removing valuable sources of carbohydrates for root growth and development of trunk caliper. It also tends to destroy the natural shape of a tree and invariably forces weak epicormic branches. Selection of the strongest, best-spaced scaffold branches should be done in the second year after planting (fig. 5-16). Even then, it is wise to avoid removing all the branches that ultimately need to be taken out. Wait at least until late winter of the third growing season to do the final selection of scaffold branches and lower limb removal where desired.

As the tree grows, other limbs must be removed, especially where traffic clearance is required, such as along a street or sidewalk. If properly trained from the beginning, however, the amount of pruning needed later will be minimal and the tree will be structurally sound.

Codominant Stems

During the growth of trees, leading shoots usually dominate over lateral branches. Sometimes, however, a branch may grow equally with a leading shoot forming "twin" stems of nearly equal size, which are referred

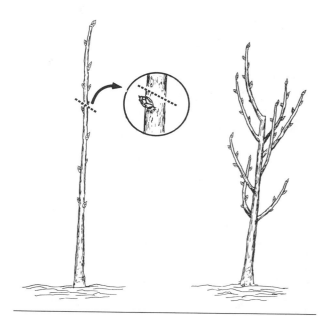

Figure 5-15. Training a young tree from a whip. Cutback above a bud (*left*) forces branching (*right*).

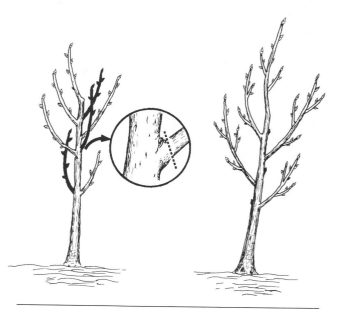

Figure 5-16. Selection of scaffold branches after the second year. At left, branches in black are removed because they interfere or are weak. Subsequent growth in the third year is shown at right.

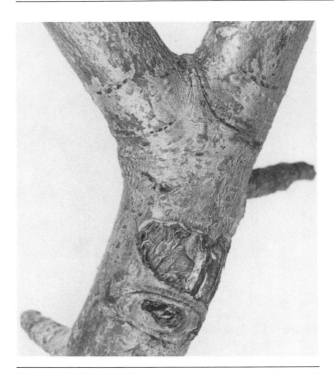

Figure 5-17. Codominant stems—stems of nearly equal size—can result in problems to a tree later. Removal of one when the tree is young is recommended. (Courtesy Kenneth R. Dudzik, N.E. Forest Experiment Station)

to as *codominant stems* (fig. 5-17). This phenomenon can occur as a result of injury to the leading shoot, pruning, or storm damage; it also is genetically inherent in certain species, such as American elm, aspen, Carolina poplar, red maple, and silver maple.

Codominant stems in trees are undesirable. Usually the crotch area is weak due to included bark, but even worse, any damage that occurs to one of the stems can move into the trunk or stem portion below the union of the two stems. If one stem dies, discoloration and decay can then affect as much as 50 percent of the stem below the crotch. This severely reduces space in the tree for stored food energy.

When training young trees, strive to prevent codominant stem growth through selective pruning. Remove one of a pair of stems having equal size while young. To wait until the tree is older results in permanent damage.

PRUNING SHRUBS

In some ways, the reason for pruning shrubs is opposite to that for pruning trees. In trees, pruning is performed to avoid production of epicormic sprouts. In shrubs, epicormic sprouts are encouraged when extensive thinning of canes is performed. Cutback of the entire shrub may also be desired, thus forcing a new plant entirely from epicormic buds.

Pruning in shrubs can be classified into two basic categories: *thinning* and *heading back*. Thinning is the preferred practice because it helps to renew the plant on a gradual basis. Heading back often results in a sheared look and a loss of natural shape.

Renewal Pruning by Thinning

Shrubs allowed to grow unpruned usually thin themselves by shading out weaker canes. This usually causes the shrub to become leggy. In a landscape situation, this is unsightly. To avoid shading out and legginess, periodic thinning of shrubs should be performed. If done on a regular basis, shrubs can be made to retain dense foliage, quality flowers, and a healthy, natural appearance (fig. 5-18).

Thinning is best done in the dormant season, preferably just a few weeks before growth resumes in early spring. To thin a shrub, first remove all dead canes and then very large, oversized ones. Finally, remove weak, spindly growth. Make cuts as close to the ground as possible. Remove cut canes from the shrub as gently as possible to avoid damaging buds on the remaining shoots. It is usually best to pull cut growth from the top upward and outward rather than up from the base.

When selecting canes to be thinned, look for heavy infestations of insects, such as borers and scale. Also check closely for canes with discolored stems caused by canker diseases. Those that are heavily damaged by pests should be removed.

Shrubs with colorful canes, such as some of the shrub dogwoods (*Cornus sericea, C. alba,* and others), are best thinned on an annual basis after the shrub is about four years old. This is because the canes lose their brilliant coloration upon aging. Renewal thinning maintains the attractive color. Thinning frequency on

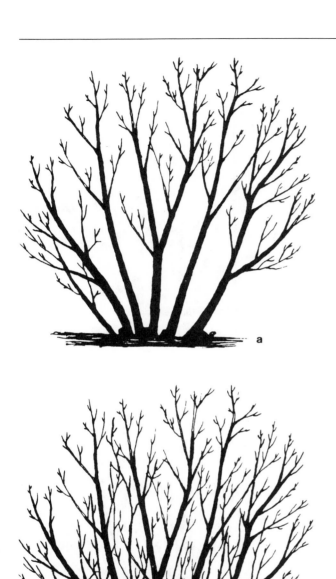

Figure 5-18. Renewal thinning of a shrub: (a) older canes and interfering stems have been removed near the ground; (b) replacement of new growth one season later.

most other shrub types will vary with the vigor of the plant, proneness to pest problems, and space allowed for growth.

Heading Back

Heading back of shrubs is a common practice. All too often, however, it is done with hedge shears and results in a formal, unnatural shape. Legginess also results because the shearing forces abundant side shoot development near the exterior of the shrub. This causes the growth near the base and in the interior to become shaded out (fig. 5-19).

Heading back should be performed only to remove unwanted shoot growth (for example, growth that interferes with access along sidewalks, porches, and driveways or blocks a view or window) and growth that tends to destroy the natural shape. Plants that need constant pruning to keep them "in bounds" are either planted in the wrong place or are the wrong type for the location. If maintenance costs are a concern, removal and replacement of plants needing frequent pruning should be considered. In the long run, it is less expensive to correct a plant placement error than to try to correct it with pruning.

To head back a shrub, simply drop-crotch prune as you would branches on a tree (fig. 5-20). Always leave a leading shoot and avoid stubs. If heading back is done to reduce the size of the plant, remove some branches deep and others shallow into the plant. This will avoid a sheared look and retain a more natural form.

Pruning Treelike Shrubs

Some shrubs develop into treelike forms having one or more large canes that become a permanent part of the structure. Examples include blackhaw viburnum (*Viburnum prunifolium*), snowball viburnum (*V. opulus roseum*), and European euonymus (*Euonymus europaea*). Thinning of old canes in such species is not needed. Some thinning of inside branches may occasionally be necessary to promote a more full-foliaged appearance (fig. 5-21). Avoid heading back except to remove interfering branches as already described. Treelike shrubs should be pruned in the same way as a tree, avoiding flush cuts and leaving stubs.

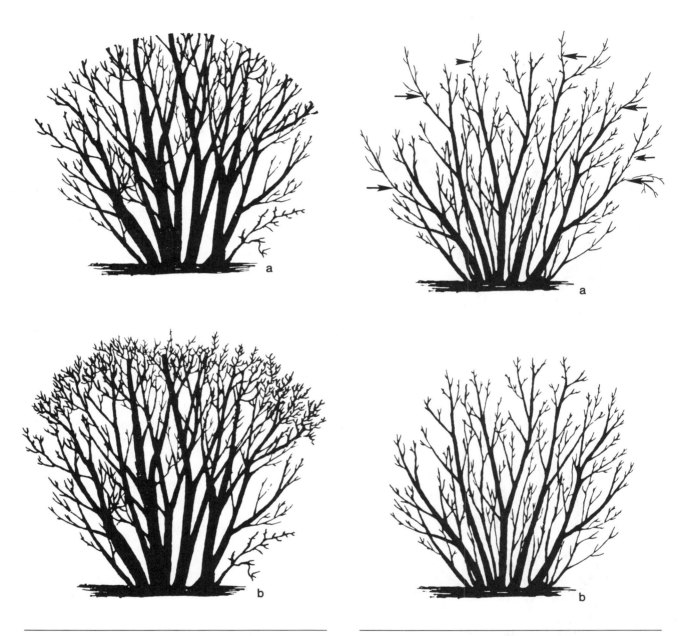

Figure 5-19. Shearing a shrub: (*a*) shrub after shearing; (*b*) dense peripheral growth a year later results in shading out of the shrub interior.

Figure 5-20. Heading back a shrub: (*a*) removal of selected branches (arrows); (*b*) shrub after heading back. This method is preferable to shearing.

Figure 5-21. Thinning of shrubs that have single, dominant stems: (*a*) before thinning; (*b*) after thinning. Thin from outside, not outer periphery.

Rejuvenation Pruning

Large, overgrown shrubs and most summer-flowering types can be rejuvenated by starting the shrub all over from basal sprouts. This is a drastic measure and generally should be avoided on spring-flowering species.

This treatment is not truly pruning, but rather a shearing practice. All top growth is cut away, preferably in late winter or early spring. New growth develops from epicormic buds present on the basal stubs that remain.

Most summer-flowering shrubs, such as orange-eye butterflybush (*Buddeia davidi*) and Froebel's spirea (*Spiraea bumalda* 'Froebel'), respond well to this treatment. It is often the most practical way to remove dead and weak canes. Flowering shoots are also the strongest from basal sprouts induced by severe cutback.

Spring-flowering shrubs vary greatly in response to rejuvenation pruning. Much depends upon the health and vigor of the plant. Shrubs that are in poor vigor and have been neglected for several years may respond poorly. In any case, this treatment will result in a delay of at least one growing season before flowering shoots develop in spring-flowering species. The practice should never be performed on rhododendron and grafted clones of lilac. Rhododendrons do not respond well to severe cutback. Grafted lilacs may lose the grafted clone, being replaced with sprouts of privet or common lilac, depending on the rootstock used.

PRUNING EVERGREENS

Evergreen trees, such as pine, spruce, and fir, rarely need to be pruned except to remove occasional dead branches or growth that is interfering with traffic areas or structures. Evergreen shrubs, such as juniper, may require more frequent pruning than trees because they are commonly planted in close masses and in restrictive locations close to walks, buildings, and driveways. With the exception of pines, pruning methods for evergreens are no different than those described already for deciduous trees and shrubs.

Pines: A Special Case

Pines do not form lateral buds along the shoot, only as a whorl at the base of the terminal bud (fig. 5-22). Therefore, any tip pruning of shoots will remove all shoot meristems. Some pines may respond by producing shoots from needle fascicles, which are actually short shoots or spurs, but this usually takes at least two growing seasons. Growth from needle fascicles is usually weak and can be equated to the epicormic growth of deciduous plants.

If more dense growth is desired in pines, as might be the case in a production nursery or with shrub types like mugo pine, side branching can be forced by removing a portion of new shoots before new buds have fully formed. The growth stage when this is done is commonly referred to as the *candling stage* (fig. 5-23). The time

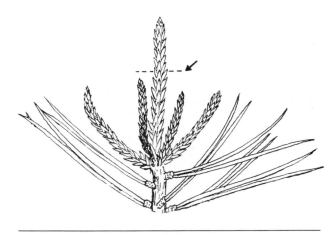

Figure 5-23. Snapping new growth (candles) in pine. New buds form near severed shoots by mid-summer.

Figure 5-22. A terminal bud cluster in a pine (arrows). Cutting below the arrows will remove shoot growth and may result in dieback.

to do this varies from one species to another and according to climate. When candles snap cleanly without stringy fibers, they are ready to be removed.

Rather than remove candles with pruning shears, a better practice is to snap or whip them off. This reduces wounding of young needles present on the shoots, which would later result in a brownish haze as wounded ends of needles become dry. In nurseries, hand-snapping of candles is not practical. Whipping with a large-bladed knife is common and much more practical even though some aesthetic damage temporarily results.

It is important to leave a portion of the stem. Near the cut on the stem new buds will form. These result in side shoots the following season.

MAINTAINING HEDGES AND SCREEN PLANTINGS

Hedges and screen plantings serve as living fences or barriers to delineate different parts of a landscape or to screen off an undesirable view. Some may also serve as sound barriers along high-traffic areas or as windbreaks. Hedges and screens may be maintained as formal or informal plantings.

Formal hedges are labor-intensive and should be avoided unless a budget is allowed for their proper maintenance. Informal hedges, used often as a visual screen, while less costly to maintain than formal hedges, still require more maintenance than individual plantings, at least in the first two or three growing seasons after planting.

Shearing Hedges

Whether formal or informal, hedges need to be trained into dense masses while young. To do this requires severe cutback soon after planting in order to force lateral shoot development. Normally, a hedge is sheared at least three times the first season after planting and twice per season thereafter. To prevent shading out, always shear the hedge so that the base is 6 to 10 inches wider than the top. Hedges oriented in an east–west direction should be sloped more on the north-facing side to compensate for lower light.

Informal hedges and screens should be treated the same way. After the third growing season, however, they should be allowed to grow unsheared. Only occasional light pruning may be needed thereafter.

Almost any tree or large shrub can be made into an informal screen or hedge. It is best, however, to pick species that do not have known diseases that spread by root-graft. Species prone to verticillium wilt, oak wilt, and Dutch elm disease should be avoided. Included are maples, oak, sumac, elm, and Russian olive. Wilt diseases will travel from plant to plant and can quickly destroy the whole hedge.

For formal hedges, fine-leaved species are best. Good choices are privet, spirea, flowering quince, currant, and purple osier willow. If flowering is desired, choose species that form flower buds laterally on shoots rather than terminally. Some examples are forsythia, flowering quince, and flowering almond.

Rejuvenating an Old Hedge

Hedges or screens that have become too tall or shaded out and leggy can be rejuvenated. This is a drastic practice involving severe cutback, and may permit stem cankers and decay organisms to gain easy access. Nevertheless, rejuvenation pruning may be employed as a last resort, particularly if replanting is not economically feasible.

Remove all large canes and weak, spindly growth as close to the ground as possible. Retain smaller, healthy shoots but cut these back about two-thirds. Retrain into a properly shaped hedge as new growth develops in the same way as a newly planted hedge. It usually takes a minimum of three years to attain a satisfactory hedge after rejuvenation pruning.

CARE OF WOUNDS

Injuries often occur to trees and other plants in spite of the best precautions. The most important treatment factor is *prompt action*. Unfortunately, workmen often are reluctant to report an injury caused by a machine or tool they were using, as they are afraid of being accused of negligence. Even if it was their fault, the supervisor should commend them for a prompt report and immediately send a qualified person to make a repair.

Storms and severe winds may also cause injury by breaking branches and even uprooting trees. While these are most prevalent during the summer, they can occur in any season. A survey should be made to determine any injury as soon as the storm has abated. Prompt treatment should follow.

Bark may be destroyed by rabbits or mice during the winter. Sunscald may kill the bark on the trunk or branch crotches in late winter. Large animals such as horses, cattle, and deer may occasionally rub off the bark. Children may hack at trees or scar them with various contrivances. Trees may be injured in many ways.

Treatment of Bark Injuries

If a piece of bark has merely been knocked off the trunk or a large branch and the cambium has not been injured *and is still moist* (which indicates it is active), the bark should be reattached to the exposed cambium. This can be done by nailing or by using strips of elastic material (rubber or plastic) to hold the bark firmly against the cambium. *Do not* apply wound dressings. An alternative treatment is to wrap about 2 inches of moist, clean sphagnum moss over the bark after nailing and then cover the area with white polyethylene. The plastic may be sealed against the trunk at the top and bottom with asphalt paint to prevent moisture loss. The plastic and sphagnum should be removed in two to three weeks.

If the bark is too dry or dirty to replace, clean the cambium with a spray of clean water, apply moist sphagnum, and place a cylinder of poultry wire over the sphagnum to hold it in place. Cover the wire with white polyethylene or other material to shade the wound. A barrier zone of nonconductive tissues will form from the cells of uninjured cambium. Remove the sphagnum and plastic in two to three weeks.

When the cambium is injured or the wound is old, the damaged area should be cleaned and dead or loose bark removed from the edges. Avoid cutting into healthy tissue. Callus will develop from the sides of the wound. Complete closure, however, will take months or years depending upon tree health, species, and exposure.

BRACING AND CABLING

Bracing is the installation of bolts or threaded rods to support or strengthen two sections of *sound* wood (fig. 5-24). Bracing is often done in combination with cabling to join weak or split crotches to ensure safety. In the past, bracing was also used to support cavities before filling, but this practice is no longer recommended because it can damage the compartmental walls as described earlier. The practice of inserting steel rods through split halves *below* a crotch to add additional support is termed *lip bolting* (fig. 5-24).

Cabling is used to support two or more limbs where storm damage has already caused splitting or to prevent splitting. It is particularly important in trees near buildings or in public areas where breakage could be injurious to people. It is a good insurance policy where public liability is concerned. Lawsuits in the many thousands of dollars could have been averted by installation of cables where needed.

Managers of public areas, such as park and recreation sites, should be especially aware of such potential liability and take preventive measures. Cabling, while sometimes costly, is worthwhile if a tree is valuable enough and in good condition. Trees that are in poor condition and have considerable internal decay should be removed rather than braced or cabled.

Both bracing and cabling are *permanent* installations. No attempt should ever be made to remove rods, hooks, or bolts, as this will cause extensive damage to a tree. In addition, once a tree is supported artificially, it becomes dependent on this support. Wood structure formed after installing cables and rods is not as strong as it would be under normal conditions. Trees relieved of the artificial supports will usually break with the added weight of leaves or snow or in the slightest breeze.

Bracing can be done any time of year, but late winter is best. This is when cambial activity starts and rapid callus development occurs. Cabling, however, should be done only during the dormant period, except for emergency repairs, as cables applied in the growing season will become slack in the fall when defoliation occurs.

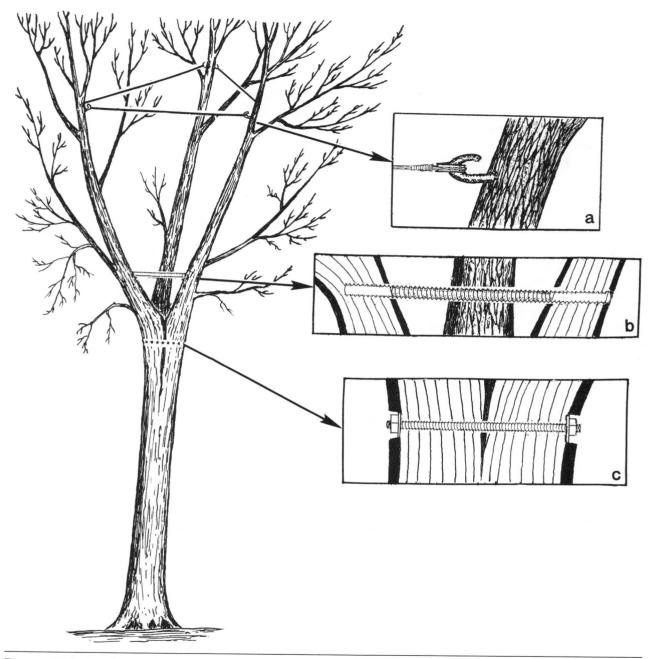

Figure 5-24. Bracing and cabling a tree. Enlarged views at right show: (*a*) hook and thimble assembly; (*b*) rigid brace; and (*c*) lip bolt with countersunk washers and nuts.

Equipment

Special equipment is required to install braces and cables. For bracing, a heavy-duty electric drill is recommended. The drill should have at least a 1-hp capacity and be reversible. For drilling straight holes in large-diameter trees, a "ship auger" type bit should be used. These wood bits are available in various lengths from arboricultural supply houses. The bit diameter should be $\frac{1}{16}$ inch smaller than the diameter of the rod or bolt used. Threaded rods and bolts with lag-size threads are best. Machine-threaded rods can be used but will take more time to turn into the holes. See table 5-1 for recommended rod sizes.

Also needed for bracing are a "power pull" or block and tackle to pull split portions together, a large wrench (crescent or closed-end type), and a dead nut. The dead nut is a nut that fits the rod used and is closed at one end. (An alternative is to use a pipe wrench to turn the rod into the tree and cut off the surplus.)

For cabling, some of the same equipment is required, such as a drill and power pull, but the following additional hardware also is needed:

- Lag-threaded hooks
- Seven-strand galvanized cable
- Galvanized thimbles
- Drill bits $\frac{1}{16}$ inch smaller in diameter than hook thread
- Steel rod or heavy-duty screwdriver (to use as leverage to turn in hooks)
- Hacksaw with metal-cutting blade and hammer
- Climbing and safety gear

Recommended sizes for anchor units and cable for different limb or tree loads are listed in table 5-1.

Installing Rigid Braces

Trees that have split or are in danger of splitting should be braced (lip-bolted) as well as cabled. The first step is to attach a *comealong* (power pull) in the crotch of the tree to pull the two sections together. Use several layers of burlap around branches where the device is attached to prevent damage to the bark.

Once the sections are pulled together, drill holes through both sections with a ship's auger or, in cases

Table 5-1. Recommended Anchor Unit and Cable Sizes for Estimated Limb or Tree Load[a]

Estimated Load (lb)	Limb Diameter (in.)	Anchor unit size (in.)			Cable size (in.)	
		Lag Screw	Eye Bolt (bent hook)	Eye Bolt (drop forged)	7-strand Galvanized	7-strand Copper
100	1½– 2	¼			³⁄₁₆	
200	2½– 3½	⁵⁄₁₆			³⁄₁₆	
300	3½– 5	⅜			³⁄₁₆	
500	6 – 8	½			¼	
600	6 – 8	½	½		⁵⁄₁₆	
900	8 –15	⅝	⅝		⁵⁄₁₆	
1000	8 –15		⅝		⁵⁄₁₆	
1200	10 –18		⅝		⅜	
1400	10 –20		¾	⅜	½	⁵⁄₁₆
2200	14 –24			½	½	¹¹⁄₃₂
3000	15 –28			⅝		⁷⁄₁₆

Source: Parr (1970).

a. Rigid braces recommended include ⅝-inch lag-threaded rods for trees up to 10 inches in diameter; ⅞-inch rods for trees 10 to 30 inches in diameter; and 1-inch rods for trees over 30 inches in diameter.

where the distance is great, through one section and at least one-half of the other. The number of holes needed will depend upon the size of the tree. In large-diameter trees, the holes are placed parallel with each other at about the same height. Usually two rods through the tree below the crotch and two above are sufficient.

Thread rods into holes using crescent or pipe wrench and dead nut, as described earlier. Score the rod as close to the bark as possible with a hacksaw and break rod surplus off with a hammer. If washers and nuts are used (machine-threaded rods), always countersink the washer *below* the bark (fig. 5-24). Apply nuts to the rod ends and cut flush with the nuts.

Installing Cables

To cable, relocate the comealong higher into the tree (slightly above two-thirds distance between crotch and branch tips). Pull the branches to be cabled toward each other slightly more than normal. **Caution: Do not overpull.** This will cause permanent damage to the vascular system.

Select the proper hooks and cable sizes for the load (see table 5-1). Select a drill bit $\frac{1}{16}$ inch smaller in diameter than the thread diameter.

Drill pilot holes for the hooks on the inside of branches to be cabled, approximately two-thirds the distance from the crotch to the tip of limbs. Turn the hooks into the tree until the open end of the hook is close enough to the bark so that the thimble can be barely slipped on. Measure the distance between hooks accurately and prepare cable with thimbles accordingly. Place the cable over the hooks and turn the hooks *one turn* so that the open end is facing upward. Carefully release tension from the power pull.

Some professionals can prepare and splice cables with thimbles in the tree without having to measure. Use of cable clamps rather than hand-splicing is not recommended because fluctuating temperatures will tend to loosen clamps. A typical hook, thimble, and cable assembly is shown in fig. 5-25.

CAVITY FILLING

The once-common practice of filling cavities with layers of cement, brick, or rubber blocks is of little use today.

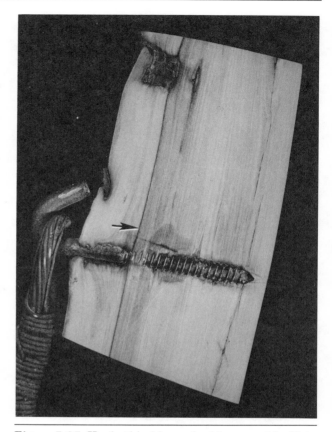

Figure 5-25. Hook, thimble, and cable assembly. Note the barrier zone (arrow) formed after hook insertion. (Courtesy Alex L. Shigo [ret.], N.E. Forest Experiment Station)

Cost of labor is a major deterrent, but an even more valid reason to discontinue the practice is that cavity fills rarely, if ever, add structural support to a tree. The practice of including cross-braces actually increases decay spread to otherwise sound wood (fig. 5-26).

Many different materials have been used to fill tree cavities including layers of cement separated by roofing paper, bricks, rubber blocks, polyurethane foams, and sand and asphalt mix. All are costly in terms of material and labor. None of them reduces or prevents decay, and few add significant structural support. In some cases, cavity fill materials such as brick or cement provide too rigid a support and may act as a fulcrum, so that trees break off above the cavity fill during a severe wind storm.

Figure 5-26. Decay following cavity fill in a tree. (Courtesy Alex L. Shigo (ret.), N.E. Forest Experiment Station)

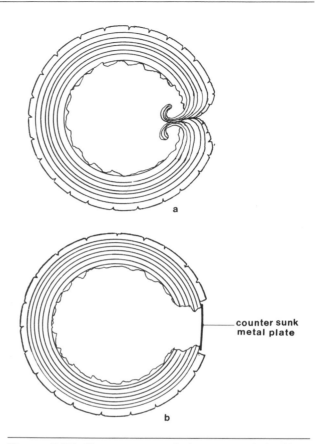

counter sunk metal plate

Figure 5-27. To prevent ram's horn growth inside a cavity (*a*), countersink a metal plate, over which wound callus will grow (*b*).

The only reason a cavity should be treated is to prevent callus growth from forming a coil (*ram's horn*) inside the cavity (fig. 5-27*a*). The growth can ultimately result in damaging internal pressure. To prevent this, simply install a metal plate over the wound, countersunk to allow for callus to form over the plate surface (fig. 5-27*b*). The tree will compartmentalize its own cavity, as discussed earlier. Any attempt to clean out the cavity to sound wood will result in spread of the decay. It is therefore best to leave decayed material in the tree.

It was once thought that leaving water trapped in a decay cavity promoted more decay. A common practice was to drill drain holes in the cavity base and insert a pipe to prevent water collection. Water in tree cavities does tend to be a breeding place for insects, but drilling a hole to drain the water rapidly spreads more decay. Leave the water in the cavity and simply cover the cavity opening with a countersunk plate.

PRUNING TOOLS

Good tools are essential to perform efficiently the ongoing tasks of pruning in a landscape management operation. Inferior, inexpensive tools can be purchased, but in the long run such tools cost more than they save in frustration and time spent for repair. Cheap tools will not hold up under continuous use. Good tools can last a lifetime.

There are many brands of pruning equipment. The

best are usually sold through arboricultural supply companies or directly from tool manufacturers. Manufacturers who specialize in pruning equipment usually have the best available. A few guidelines for selecting pruning shears and saws are presented in the remainder of this chapter.

Hand Pruners

Select tools made from hardened drop-forged steel. Avoid cast-iron and aluminum shears; although the blades may be steel, the handles are either of brittle iron or soft aluminum and do not hold up well.

Hand pruners should be constructed in two solid steel halves with an adjustable, lock-nut center pivot. Avoid pruners that have rivets or screws attaching various parts, such as handles. Also avoid pruners that have an open coil spring. The closed, strap-type spring steel coil is better. An open coil spring will jam with twigs and debris, causing frustration and delay.

Blade-and-anvil-type shears also should be avoided. While suitable for light work, the blade usually becomes sprung and out of alignment. This type of pruner cannot be satisfactorily sharpened. Sharpening removes some metal from the blade edge, resulting in a gap between the blade and anvil except at the very tip.

Choose shears to fit the hand of the user. If vinyl grips are included, make sure they are the dipped type, which conform to the handles and do not come off. Removable sleeve-type grips soon twist or fall off.

Long-Handled Loppers

Lopping shears should have the same basic construction and quality steel as hand pruners. In addition, good loppers have a soft rubber shock absorber near the pivot.

Both hand pruners and loppers should be easily taken apart so that the cutting blades can be sharpened on a honing stone. Never use a file or high-speed grindstone to sharpen pruner blades.

Hand Saws

Curved tempered steel blades are a must for pruning saws. The teeth should point toward the handle so that cutting is done when pulling (the best mechanical advantage) and cleaning out when pushing.

A good test of the steel in a saw blade is to hold each end and flex (bend) sharply. Release tension, then sight down the top edge. The cheaper blades will not spring back to perfect alignment.

The best handles are made of highly finished hardwood and riveted on. Those with bolts soon become loosened through vibration. A protective scabbard (sheath) is recommended to protect the blade from damage and prevent injury to the operator or others when the saw is not in use.

Chain Saw

There are many brands of chain saws on the market. Individual preference is often based upon past experiences with a particular type. Qualities that are important to look for include:

- lightest weight for the task at hand
- ease of servicing (disassembly–assembly)
- ease of chain tension adjustment
- safety features
- availability of parts

It is important to keep chains sharp. Dull chain saws not only do a jagged and slow cutting job but their motors also wear out more quickly. A dull chain saw, like a dull knife, can also be more dangerous than a sharp one because more effort is required to control the equipment when making a cut.

Follow all servicing and safety standards recommended by the saw manufacturer.

REFERENCES

Collins, J. F. 1934. Treatment and care of tree wounds. USDA Farmers' Bull. 1726.

Dooley, H. L. 1980. Methods for evaluating fungal inhibition and barrier action of tree wound points. Plant Dis. 64:465–67.

Harris, R. W., Leiser, A. T., and Davis, W. B. 1976. Staking landscape trees. Davis, CA: University of California, Univ. Calif. Agric. Ext. Leaflet 2576.

Marshall, R. P. 1950. Care of damaged shade trees. USDA Farmers' Bull. 1896.

Mercer, P. C. 1979. Attitudes to pruning wounds. J. Arboriculture 5:457–65.

Ossenbruggen, S. 1985. Tree wounds: To paint or not to paint? *Grounds Maintenance*, June:46.

Parr, F. L. 1970. Bracing, cabling and guying standards for shade trees. McLean, VA: National Arborist Assoc. Standards Committee.

Pearce, R. B., and Rutherford, J. 1981. A wound-associated suberized barrier to the spread of decay in sapwood of oak (*Quercus robur* L.). Physiol. Plant Pathol. 19:359–69.

Schuck, H. J. 1982. The chemical composition of the monoterpene reaction in wounded wood of *Picea abies* and its significance for the resistance against wound infecting fungi. Eur. J. For. Pathol. 12:175–81.

Shigo, A. L. 1982. Tree health. J. Arboriculture 8:311–16.

———. 1986. A New Tree Biology. Durham, NH: Shigo and Trees Assoc.

Shigo, A. L., and Marx, H. G. 1977. Compartmentalization of decay in trees. USDA For. Serv. Inf. Bull. 405.

Shigo, A. L., and Shortle, W. C. 1983. Wound dressings: Results of studies over 13 years. J. Arboriculture 9:317–29.

Shigo, A. L., and Tippett, J. T. 1981. Compartmentalization of American elm tissues infected by *Ceratocystis ulmi*. Plant Dis. 65:715–18.

Shigo, A. L., and Wilson, C. L. 1977. Wound dressings on red maple and American elm: Effectiveness after five years. J. Arboriculture 3:81–87.

Tippett, J. T., and Shigo, A. L. 1981. Barriers to decay in conifer roots. Eur. J. For. Pathol. 11:51–59.

6.

Identification and Management of Insects and Related Pests

The most dominant group of animals on earth is the insects. They occur in almost every part of the world and surpass all other land animals in number. Entomologists have described several hundred thousand insect species. Indeed, insects constitute more than three-fourths of *all* the known animal species. It is possible to find at least one thousand kinds of insects in a fair-sized backyard, and more than one million may be present in an acre of landscape.

Despite all the various types of insects, only a few are considered pests; these are the ones that cause man the biggest problems and will probably continue to do so as long as man and insects exist together. The conflict between people and pests was probably stated best by Forbes (1915), a USDA entomologist:

The struggle between man and insects began long before the dawn of civilization, has continued without cessation to the present time, and will continue, no doubt, as long as the human race endures. We commonly think of ourselves as the lords and conquerors of nature. But insects had thoroughly mastered the world and taken full possession of it before man began the attempt. They had, consequently, all the advantage of possession of the field when the contest began, and they have disputed every step of our invasion of their original domain so persistently and successfully that we can even yet scarcely flatter ourselves that we

have gained any very important advantage over them. If they want our crops, they still help themselves to them. If they wish the blood of our domestic animals, they pump it out of the veins of our cattle and our horses at their leisure and under our very eyes. If they choose to take up their abode with us, we cannot wholly keep them out of the houses we live in. We cannot even protect our very persons from their annoying and pestiferous attacks, and since the world began, we have never yet exterminated— we probably shall never exterminate—so much as a single insect species.

Even though that statement was made early in the twentieth century, it is probably still true today, despite the fact that man has developed all kinds of chemical pesticides. Many insects have responded to what really is overexposure to some pesticides and, through a process of elimination, become immune—only the most resistant insects survive. There are certain pesticides— generally organic compounds—that insects have not been able to cope with. Yet, some insect species have developed some resistance even to very potent organic formulations.

To understand how this can happen, one must realize that insects reproduce at fantastic rates and by shear volume are able to overcome almost any control method that man has been able to develop. An example is the

Oriental fruit fly, *Drosophila*. Under ideal conditions, this insect can reproduce twenty-five generations in a single year. Each female lays about 100 eggs, and of that number approximately 50 percent will be female. It has been calculated that if a single pair of these flies, enjoying ideal conditions, produced twenty-five generations per year and if all the young were used to form a ball, containing 1000 insects per cubic inch, the compressed ball would be 96 million miles in diameter, or almost as large as the distance between the earth and the moon. Incidently, in only the seventh generation, the populations from a single pair of fruit flies would be one trillion, 562 billion, 500 million (1,562,500,000,000)!

It has also been said that if all the insects in the world that died did not decompose, their bodies would cover the face of the earth, including the highest mountain peaks.

ANATOMY AND LIFE CYCLE OF INSECTS

Insects differ from other forms of animal life primarily in that they possess an exoskeleton. This is the hard, bony structure that supports the body. It is on the exterior and is segmented, including the legs. The segments are grouped into three distinct regions: the head, thorax, and abdomen. The head bears the eyes, antennae, and mouth parts; the thorax bears the legs and wings if they are present; and the abdomen bears the spiracles and reproductive organs (fig. 6-1).

Spiracles are also unique to insects. These are breathing pores that connect directly to a series of tracheal tubes within the body; thus, it is possible for an insect to "breathe" even with its head under water. The spiracles can be closed to survive loss of moisture during hot weather, or to prevent injury to the insect when it comes into the presence of a poisonous gas such as might be produced by a pesticide. Insects can survive a long time with very little air by controlling their spiracles so as to slow their metabolism and reduce their use of energy. This is probably why insects have outsurvived all other animal life and can survive in so many different places.

In order to control insects, it is important to understand how they feed and their life cycles. With few exceptions, insects are more vulnerable in the mid-

stages of life (nymphs or larvae). This is because these stages are the most active and do the most feeding. Adult stages of an insect are more difficult to control because they tend to migrate from place to place and feed very little; they may not feed at all. The egg stage of an insect is the most difficult to kill with chemical pesticides. Not only is the protective covering of the egg impervious to most chemicals, but the metabolism of the egg is generally so low that even suffocation

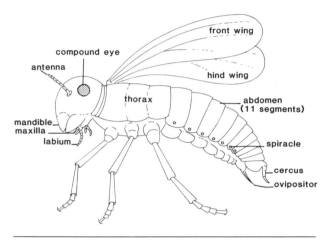

Figure 6-1. Representative chewing-type insect and its parts.

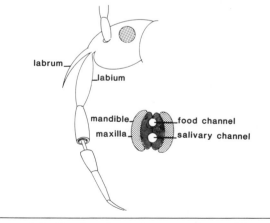

Figure 6-2. Head and mouth parts of a sucking-type insect. Section through the labium shows food and salivary channels.

becomes difficult. An exception to this are scale insect eggs, which, under proper conditions, can be successfully smothered with dormant oil.

Types of Mouth Parts

Whether an insect has chewing mouth parts (fig. 6-1) or piercing and sucking mouth parts (fig. 6-2) influences the type of insecticide that is most effective against it.

An insect such as the grasshopper, which has only chewing mouth parts, is probably better controlled chemically with stomach posions. These are pesticides that must be ingested by the insect in order to be effective. Aphids, on the other hand, have only piercing and sucking mouth parts and would not be readily controlled with a stomach posion except by way of a systemic insecticide, which renders the plant sap poisonous. Aphids and similar insects are best controlled with contact insecticides. In this case, the chemical used for control enters through the spiracles and, in a sense, causes suffocation. Some pesticides act as both contact and stomach poisons.

Life Cycles

All insects develop from eggs. Most are oviparous; that is, the young hatch from eggs after they have been laid. A few insects can give birth to young from eggs that develop and hatch within the body of the female (viviparous). This is the case with aphids.

During the growing season, when food is ample, aphids will bear living young and the young will remain wingless. When food supplies begin to shorten, the living young that are produced will have wings. The winged form can then fly to a better food supply and will lay eggs before they produce a generation by again bearing their young alive. The last generation before freezing weather will also produce eggs in some types rather than bear live young. The eggs then become the overwintering form.

Molting

Because insects have an exoskeleton, they must undergo various stages of *molting* in order to increase in size. These molting stages are referred to as *instar* stages. Some insects may only molt two or three times before they reach the adult size; others may undergo a dozen or more moltings. Sometimes the first instar stage of an insect will not look anything like the final or adult stage. This may lead to confusion as to the identity of an insect. Occasionally this has resulted in unnecessary spraying of an insect that later turns out to be a beneficial one. A good example of this is the ladybug.

Metamorphosis

There are two principal types of metamorphosis in insects—simple and complete. In simple metamorphosis, the young hatch from eggs and are called *nymphs*. They very closely resemble the adult but are smaller in size and are usually a different color. Nymphs are normally wingless, whereas most of the adults possess wings. Examples of insects with simple metamorphosis are the aphid and the grasshopper (fig. 6-3).

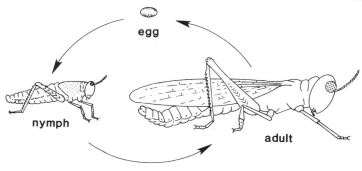

egg

nymph

adult

Figure 6-3. Simple metamorphosis illustrated by the grasshopper's life cycle.

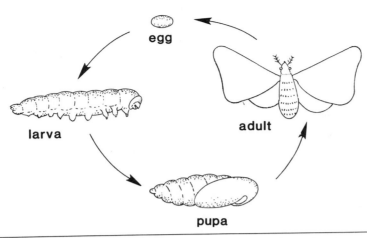

Figure 6-4. Complete metamorphosis illustrated by the moth's life cycle.

In complete metamorphosis, the mature and adult stages of the insect are usually quite different in form and have different types of habitats. Butterflies, moths, and flies are good examples. A typical cycle would include the egg, larva, pupation, and emergence as an adult as shown in figure 6-4.

IDENTIFYING INSECT PESTS

Proper identification of insects and related pests is essential to the selection of timely and appropriate control. It is not enough to just know that the pest is a beetle, bug, aphid, or mite. The *exact* species must be known because life cycles vary considerably even within similar insect groups. Knowing the precise life cycle of the pest helps in selecting the best method of control and in determining the proper timing of application.

It is not the intent of this chapter to present a detailed description and life cycle of the insect pests that might be encountered in a landscape situation. This would require volumes. Local sources of information on insect pests should be consulted. Sources include Cooperative Extension Service offices, state and county pest control agencies, commercial arborists, and books on insect pests written for the area of concern. A list of suggested information sources is given in the references section.

The following procedure is helpful in determining the identity of an insect or related pest *if the pest apparently causing the damage is present:*

1. Collect samples, placing them in small containers with tight-fitting lids. Soft-bodied insects, such as larvae (caterpillars and grubs, for example) are best put directly into alcohol. Household isopropyl alcohol will do. Hard-bodied insects, such as adult stages of beetles and flies, should be put into a container with a small amount of killing agent. An effective killing agent is rubber cement. Smear a small amount on the inside of a jar lid and close tightly. The fumes from the rubber cement will kill the pest quickly.

2. Examine pests and compare with available local literature. Knowing the host plant and common pests of the host will often, through elimination, permit identification of the pest in question.

3. If identity is not certain, send pest samples along with background information to the local Extension Service office or the entomology department of a state university offering identification services. The land-grant universities in most states usually offer this service free or for a nominal charge. Information accompanying the sample should include host plant, date of collection, degree of infestation (if known), and the part or parts of the host plant affected by the pest.

4. Select control measures, if warranted, based upon available literature or advice from an entomologist.

If damage is evident, but no apparent pest is present, collect samples of *damaged and undamaged* plant tissue. Try to identify the problem using the key presented in the next section, or send the sample to one of the agencies suggested above for possible identification of the pest. In cases where no pest is present, control measures are not usually warranted. It is helpful, however, to know what caused the damage so that steps can be taken in the future to prevent a recurrence. While it is not always possible to identify the exact pest causing injury from feeding damage alone, the *general* pest type can usually be determined.

Key for Identifying Pests Based on Feeding Damage

The following key is helpful in arriving at the general pest type based upon feeding damage. Start by selecting 1a, 1b, or 1c, as appropriate, and then proceed to numbered pairs as instructed. Identified pests are in boldface type.

1a. Leaves with damage—*see* #2
1b. Twigs or bark with damage—*see* #10
1c. Roots with damage—*see* #15
2a. Leaves appearing chewed or skeletonized with tissue between veins on lower side missing (fig. 6-5)—*see* #3
2b. Leaves not chewed; either off-color and appearing "stippled" or silvery (fig. 6-6) or having galls or swollen tissues (fig. 6-7)—*see* #5
3a. Leaves chewed mostly along margins—*see* #4
3b. Leaves chewed mostly underneath, appearing skeletonized (veins remaining): **leaf beetles; pear "slug"** (a wasp larva)
4a. Chewed leaf margins semicircular and smooth; not jagged (fig. 6-8): **cutter bee** (common on roses); **blackvine weevil** (common on euonymus)
4b. Chewed leaf margins jagged and irregular; not smooth and semicircular (fig. 6-9): **grasshoppers; caterpillars** (many types); **Japanese beetle**
5a. Leaves with swellings or galls—*see* #9
5b. Leaves without swellings or galls, but stippled or silvery—*see* #6
6a. Leaves silvery in irregular pattern when viewed from above: **thrips** (common in privet and chokecherry)
6b. Leaves stippled, sometimes appearing grainy or mealy beneath—*see* #7

7a. Fine webbing present; leaves mealy beneath: **spider mites**
7b. No webbing present; leaves not mealy beneath; stippled yellow or brown—*see* #8
8a. Stippled leaves also curled or distorted (fig. 6-10); use caution here—some herbicides cause similar symptoms: **eriophyid mites; leafhoppers; plant bugs; some aphids**
8b. Stippled leaves not curled or distorted: **many aphid species**
9a. Swelling or galls nipplelike on leaf surface: **psyllids** (common on hackberry); **eriophyid mites** (gall mites)
9b. Swellings variously shaped, but not nipplelike; sometimes on leaf petiole: **gall wasps; spindle midges; gall midges**
10a. Damage on twigs or buds only, not on main branches or tree trunks—*see* #12
10b. Damage on main branches or trunks—*see* #11
11a. Bark partially or completely chewed down to the wood: **rodents** (squirrels, mice); **grasshoppers** (in heavy infestations where food supply is short)
11b. Bark with circular or D-shaped holes; may be oozing sap, or pitch or frass ("sawdust") may be present: **borers** (larvae of beetles, moths, wasps, and flies); **bark engravers** (larvae of beetles)
12a. Twigs or buds forming galls or swollen areas—*see* #13
12b. Twigs or buds without galls; twigs with holes or central pith with channels (fig. 6-11)—*see* #14
13a. Galls in buds: **gall-forming eriophyid mites**
13b. Galls in twigs: **gall midges**
14a. Twigs with holes; pith not channeled: **borers; bark engravers; weevils**
14b. Twigs with channeled pith: **shoot-tip borers** (larvae of moths); **pith borers; cane borers**
15a. Young roots with gall-like swellings (*caution:* some plants such as those in the pea family have nitrogen-fixing nodules on thir roots, which may look similar; these are beneficial): **nematodes**
15b. Roots chewed or with holes—*see* #16
16a. Roots chewed: **rodents; insect grubs** (beetle and moth larvae)
16b. Roots with holes: **root borers; weevils** (often these insects are secondary to roots undergoing decay from fungi)

Figure 6-5. Leaves skeletonized by leaf beetle larvae. (Courtesy Kenneth R. Dudzik, N.E. Forest Experiment Station)

Figure 6-7. Insect galls on leaves. (Courtesy Kenneth R. Dudzik, N.E. Forest Experiment Station)

Figure 6-6. Leaves stippled by sucking insects. (Courtesy Kenneth R. Dudzik, N.E. Forest Experiment Station)

Figure 6-8. Chewing-insect damage to leaf margins: (*left*) black vine weevil on euonymus; (*right*) leaf cutter bee on rose leaflet. (Courtesy Kenneth R. Dudzik, N.E. Forest Experiment Station)

Figure 6-9. Leaves chewed by caterpillars (larvae of moths or butterflies). (Courtesy Kenneth R. Dudzik, N.E. Forest Experiment Station)

Figure 6-11. Typical wood-boring insect larva. Channels often contain "sawdust," or frass (arrow). (Courtesy Alex L. Shigo [ret.], N.E. Forest Experiment Station)

Figure 6-10. Witches broom distortion of honeysuckle caused by the aphid *Hyadaphis tataricae*. Secretions by the insect during feeding cause distortion of leaves and shoots. The insect is commonly called Russian aphid because of its origin.

BENEFICIAL INSECTS

A landscape manager should not only know and be able to identify destructive pests, but also should be acquainted with the major insects and related arachnids that are beneficial. Beneficial insects are usually more numerous than pests and often keep destructive pests in check. Unnecessary or untimely pesticide applications can reduce or eliminate the effectiveness of beneficial insects. Learn to recognize the major beneficial insects in your area. Know the different stages of their life cycle.

Often, what may appear to be a pest, is actually a beneficial insect. An example is the ladybug (lady beetle). Most people know what the adult stage looks like (shiny orange with black spots), but few can recognize the larval and pupal stages. The spiny, gray wormlike larval stage of the ladybug may be mistaken for an unwanted pest. In addition to the lady beetle, some of the more common beneficial insects that should be recognized include lacewings, syrphid flies (hover fly), and parasitic wasps. Some examples are shown in figure 6-12.

Many beneficial wasps are so tiny that they may resemble gnats or black flies if not examined closely (fig. 6-13). They are also commonly in close association with some pests because they are largely parasitic on egg or larval stages. This makes them especially vulnerable to pesticide applications.

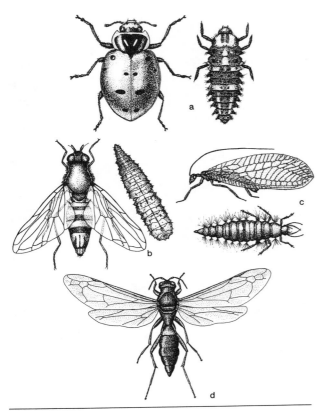

Figure 6-12. Beneficial insects: (*a*) ladybird beetle adult and larva; (*b*) larva and adult of a hover fly (Syrphid); (*c*) green lacewing adult and larva; (*d*) polistes wasp adult. (Drawings by T. J. Weissling, Colorado State University)

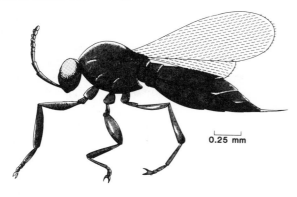

Figure 6-13. Tiny beneficial wasp (*Platygaster* sp.) resembles a pesky black gnat or fly.

MAJOR INSECT PESTS

In this section, major insect groups containing the most serious pests are briefly described.

Aphids, Leafhopper, Scale, Whitefly (Homoptera)

The order Homoptera contains a rather diverse group of insects, some of which have extremely complex life cycles. In this group are some of the most destructive pests of landscape plants, including scale, leafhoppers, whitefly, and aphids. Mouth parts are similar to those of true bugs, but the beak arises from the back of the head rather than from the front, as in true bugs. These insects have four wings. The front wings are usually similar to the hind wings, and both pairs are membranous. Rather than the wings resting flat on the abdomen, as in true bugs, they usually rest in a rooflike fashion over the body. Several types of Homoptera have wingless females, with only the male being winged. In other cases, as in aphids, the entire population may be wingless females, with no males present. These wingless females are capable of reproducing young alive (viviparous reproduction).

Butterflies, Moths (Lepidoptera)

Butterflies and moths are among the best known of insects. There are approximately 11,000 species in the United States and Canada. The larval stage causes the most damage. The larvae have chewing mouth parts, whereas the adults have sucking mouth parts. Many of the adult forms do not feed at all. The life cycle of a lepidoptera is complete metamorphosis, going from egg to larva to pupa or cocoon (called a chrysalis in butterflies) and then changing into an adult moth or butterfly (see fig. 6-4).

Among the most serious pests in this group are the tent caterpillar, leaf roller, gypsy moth, sod webworm, tussock moth, and similar defoliators. They can often be confused in the larval stage with the larvae of pests in other orders such as the sawfly, which is actually the larva of a wasp (fig. 6-14). The larvae of elm leaf beetles look much like butterfly larvae. The principal difference is the way in which the legs of the larva are

Figure 6-14. Larvae of redheaded pine sawfly (*Neodiprion lecontie*). Though the larvae of a wasp, they resemble caterpillars of moths and butterflies. (Courtesy Kenneth R. Dudzik, N.E. Forest Experiment Station)

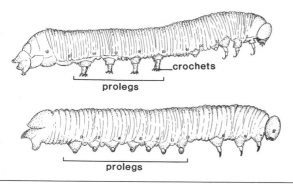

Figure 6-15. Comparison of larva from a butterfly or moth (Lepidoptera) (*top*) with larva of a sawfly (Hymenoptera) (*bottom*). Hooklike crochets are lacking on the more numerous prolegs of the sawfly larva.

formed. In a butterfly or moth larva, there are three pairs of true legs, one pair for each of the three segments behind the head. There may be as many as five pairs of prolegs or other segments toward the posterior. The prolegs are simple appendages that help in crawling but structurally are not true legs. The prolegs of Lepidoptera larvae have a pair of tiny hooks called crochets at the tip. Sawfly larvae, which usually have more than five pairs of prolegs, do not have crochets on their prolegs (fig. 6-15).

Grasshopper, Cockroach, Cricket (Orthoptera)

The order Orthoptera contains many well-known insects, both destructive and beneficial. It is a relatively primitive order and includes household insects, such as the cockroach. Cockroaches, which are very primitive, are one of the most difficult pests to eliminate.

Insects in this order may be winged or wingless. The winged form has four wings, with the front wings generally longer than the rear wings and somewhat thicker, providing a protective cover for the membranous wings underneath. The typical structure of insects in this order is represented by the grasshopper. Metamorphosis is simple.

Beetles (Coleoptera)

The Coleoptera is the largest order of insects, containing about 40 percent of the known insect types. Over a quarter of a million beetle species have been described, and more than 26,000 of these are found in the United States. Beetles can be found almost everywhere. The soil is inhabited by many that are serious pests. Others live in the wood of trees. Beetles vary in length from less than $\frac{1}{16}$ inch to up to 5 inches. A few tropical ones, such as the rhinocerous beetle, may even exceed 5 inches. Beetles are distinctive in structure in that the front wings are shell-like coverings that usually meet in a straight line down the middle of the back. The front wings cover the membranous hind wings. The front wings of a beetle, called *elytra,* are one of the primary features used in identifying the species.

The larval stage of many beetles is destructive, but some adult beetles are equally destructive. Both stages have chewing mouth parts. Beetles undergo a complete metamorphosis, the larvae varying considerably from the adult. Among the more serious beetles in landscape plantings are the wood borers and leaf beetles. The order also includes aquatic forms that have special adaptations, such as the diving beetles and the waterboat oarman. These are predaceous. The order also includes a number of scavenger beetles, such as the carrion beetle, and predaceous types, such as the lady beetle, that are beneficial.

Termites (Isoptera)

Termites are social insects that live in large, well-organized colonies. Both winged and wingless individuals form a colony. Termites are sometimes called white ants. Ants, however, belong to the order Hymenoptera. Unlike ants, termites have soft bodies rather than hard exoskeletons. Their wings are longer than those of ants and are held flat over the abdomen while at rest. Ants have smaller hind wings than termites, and the wings of ants are usually held above the body while at rest. Another difference between ants and termites is that the abdomen in the termite is joined to the thorax broadly, while in ants it is constricted to a thin waist.

Metamorphosis in termites is simple. Mouth parts are of the chewing type. While termites are rarely seen attacking healthy trees, they occasionally will colonize

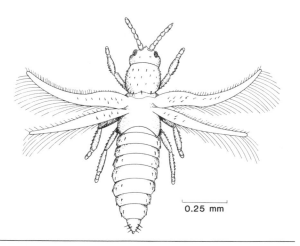

Figure 6-16. Adult greenhouse thrips. These thrips are difficult to see with the unaided eye.

in a tree that has been damaged or that is beginning to decay.

Thrips (Thysanoptera)

Thrips are very tiny insects ranging in size from 0.5 to 5 millimeters in length. Exceptions are some tropical species, which may be as long as 0.5 inch. The wings are primarily a fringe of hairs, thus the name of the order: *thysano* = fringe and *ptera* = wings (fig. 6-16). The mouth parts are the sucking type. Metamorphosis is intermediate, between simple and complete. The first instar stage has no wings externally and is called the larval stage. Following the larval stage, there is a quiescent or pupal stage, sometimes involving a cocoonlike structure. From this emerges the adult, which is usually winged.

Thrips are a serious problem, particularly in flowers such as roses, because they often infest the bud stage and cause internal damage resulting in distorted flowers. Some thrips feed on leaves. One of the more common types causes considerable stippling damage to the foliage of privet, ash, and chokecherry. Some thrips are even considered beneficial, feeding on other smaller insects. A few are known to cause irritating bites to man.

Earwigs (Dermaptera)

Earwigs are long, slender insects resembling beetles, but they have a large, forceplike appendage, known as a *cerci*, at the tip of the abdomen (fig. 6-17). Adults have four wings. The front are short, leathery, and veinless; the hind wings are membranous and radiating with veins. When at rest the rear wings are folded up under the front wings. Mouth parts are the chewing type. Metamorphosis is simple. Only one species is a problem in the United States, the European earwig.

Earwigs are usually nocturnal, hiding during the day in cracks and crevices. While they are usually scavengers and feed on decaying materials, they can also cause damage to plants, particularly to flowers and silks of corn. Because they tend to colonize in wounds of trees, they may also irritate wounds, slowing or preventing callus formation. The name earwig comes from an old superstition that they entered people's ears. However, earwigs are quite harmless to man.

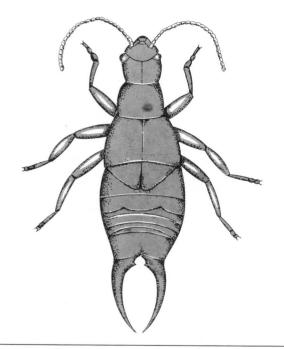

Figure 6-17. European earwig (*Forficula auricularia*). Earwigs are often found in tree wounds and under loose bark.

Springtails (Collembola)

Springtails are tiny insects rarely exceeding 5 to 6 millimeters in length. They get their name from the fact that the last segment of the abdomen, the *furcula,* is folded under the forward section and can be used as a spring, making them capable of jumping 3 to 4 inches.

Springtails have a combination of chewing and piercing mouth parts. Most feed on fungi, but some species cause damage to pot plants and mushrooms. They are normally found in moist locations.

INSECT GROUPS THAT ARE MOSTLY BENEFICIAL
Antlions, Lacewings (Neuroptera)

The order Neuroptera includes antlions, lacewings (see fig. 6-12*c*), and several aquatic forms such as alderflies.

They are characterized by having four large, lacy wings. Sometimes they are confused with the dragonfly, but unlike the dragonfly, their wings lay in rooflike fashion over the back when at rest. The egg stages of some Neuroptera are distinctive in that they are attached to a long filament and often appear like spores of a fungus. Lacewings can be purchased in the egg stage for biological control and have been used in orchards and other areas with a concentrated crop.

Bees, Wasps, Ants (Hymenoptera)

Hymenoptera insects are highly advanced and are known for their complex social organization. Very few species are considered pests, generally because of interference with man's social life. The sting of bees, wasps, hornets, and fire ants can be painful, even fatal.

From the standpoint of plants, Hymenoptera insects are beneficial in providing cross pollination and, in many cases, act as predators or parasites on destructive insects. Many wasps are parasitic on the egg or larval stages of destructive moths, midges, and beetles.

Only two important insects of this order can be considered damaging to landscape plants: the cutter bee and the sawfly. The bee cuts semicircular pieces from the edges of leaves, particularly roses (see fig. 6-8); this damage is usually slight, however. Sawflies are serious defoliators, especially on pine (fig. 6-14).

True Bugs (Hemiptera)

The term "bug" is used by most people as vernacular to refer to most any insect. The order Hemiptera, however, includes species that are correctly classified as true bugs. The name is of Latin origin (*hemi* = half and *ptera* = wings), referring to the characteristic of the front pair of wings, which is partially leathery and partially membranous. The hind wings are always shorter and entirely membranous. When at rest the wings are held flat over the abdomen with the membranous tips of the front wings overlapping (fig. 6-18). Mouth parts of bugs are of the piercing-sucking type, consisting of a slender segmented beak arising from the front part of the head. This beak usually extends back along the ventral (lower) part of the body.

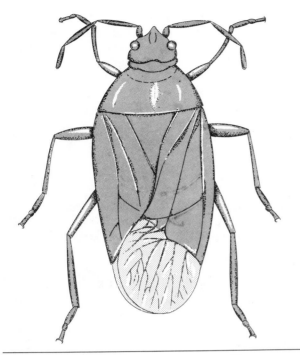

Figure 6-18. A true bug (Hemiptera). The common boxelder bug was used as the model for this illustration.

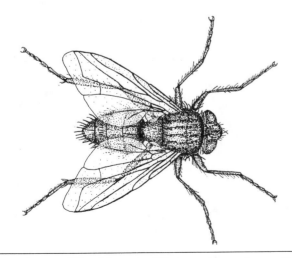

Figure 6-19. Though resembling a common house fly, this tachinid fly is beneficial. (Drawing by T. J. Weissling, Colorado State University)

The segmented beak encases four piercing stylets used in feeding. The true bugs resemble closely those in the Homoptera order but are usually distinguished, in addition to the half wing, by the fact that the front legs are usually modified into grasping structures. Typical are the numerous types of leaf bugs, the ambush bug, and the assassin bug. A few are damaging to plants, but a large majority are beneficial, being predaceous on other insects.

Flies (Diptera)

The order Diptera is second in size to Coleoptera. Flies are distinctive in that they have a functionally developed pair of membranous front wings, but the rear wings are reduced to knobby structures called halteres (fig. 6-19). These apparently function as balancing organs and are not used for flight. The haltere is often so reduced that it takes a hand lens to see it. Mouth parts of flies vary; mosquitoes, for example, have piercing-sucking types, while the biting fly has a modified chewing-sucking-piercing mouth part. Diptera undergo complete metamorphosis. The larvae are called *maggots* and are distinguished from most other larvae in that they are legless and wormlike.

Many species of flies are beneficial, being predaceous on other insects, but a few can be serious pests, such as the apple maggot, the horse fly, and the mosquito.

MAJOR ARACHNID PESTS

Mites, spiders, ticks, and scorpions belong to the class Arachnida. Like the insects, arachnids have segmented bodies, and most have exoskeletons. They differ from insects in having only two, rather than three, body regions and two or four, rather than three, pairs of legs. Spider mites and eriophyid mites can be significant pests in landscape settings.

Spider Mites

Spider mites are tiny, eight-legged arachnids common on a large variety of landscape plants. A hand lens is necessary to see them in any detail because they rarely exceed 0.04 inch. Mites in immature stages have only three pairs of legs and could be mistaken for insects.

As they mature, however, the normal four pairs of legs appear.

Many mites are host-specific, feeding only on a single type of plant. An example is the honeylocust mite (*Eotetranychus multidigituli*). Others, such as the two-spotted mite (*Tetranychus telarias*), feed on a wide variety of plants.

The presence of mites on plants is detected more often by their characteristic feeding injury rather than by observation of the mites themselves. In some cases, a film of webbing on the leaves and stems aids in detection. Feeding injury to plants from mites usually is evident as a stippled appearance on the leaves. Severe infestations cause leaves to turn yellow or bronze, followed by defoliation.

Adult mites appear in late spring. Females lay fifty or more eggs, which hatch within a week. Many cycles can occur in a growing season with major population buildup during hot, dry weather.

Many insects and mites are predatory on destructive mites. Indiscriminant pesticide application can often result in increased mite populations as predators are eliminated.

Eriophyid Mites

When one begins to study eriophyid mites, the first difficulty encountered is actually seeing the mites. Because eriophyid mites average only about one-fifth the size of spider mites, they are not easily seen even with a ten-power hand lens. For observation of eriophyid mites on leaves, it is necessary to scan with at least 30X lens. The easiest to observe are those present in galls, such as the woody bud galls of the cottonwood (poplar gall mite, *Aceria parapopuli*) or those found in the flower galls in ash.

The presence of eriophyid mites on landscape plants is most readily detected by the plant deformations they produce. The most common eriophyids cause leaf deformation similar to that produced by the herbicide 2,4-D. Such is the case with the leaf vagrants found on Siberian elm, American elm, American linden, green ash, elder, forsythia, and several other species. Some eriophyids also cause a reddish or white velvetlike fuzz on leaf surfaces. Aspen, mountain maple (*Acer glabrum*), and boxelder are common hosts of these types of mites. Still other species produce cone-shaped projections ("spindles") on leaves of specific plants. Among the more common are the spindle galls on chokecherry. For color illustrations of eriophyid mite injuries to woody plants, refer to Kiefer et al. (1982).

The life cycle of most eriophyids is rather simple in that they pass through two nymphal instar stages, the second of which produces the adult after a brief resting period. In the resting stage, the genitalia form and protrude through the body wall. Growth from the egg to the adult takes from about ten days to two weeks. Not all eriophyids have this simple life cycle. Kiefer (1952) described a condition known as *deuterogyny*, present in certain groups of eriophyids. In this type, there are two distinct stages. In the first, the female resembles the male and exists only on the leaves of the host plant. In the second stage, the female transforms into a specialized form for hibernation. This form usually overwinters in bark crevices or at the bases of buds. In the spring, the second stage comes out of hibernation and lays eggs on the new leaves as they unfold. The leaf vagrant found on Siberian elm is an example of the deuterogyny type.

Little is known about how eriophyid mites cause deformation in plants. It is known that the mouth parts of eriophyid mites are so small that they can penetrate plant cells without causing damage or death of the cells. Thus, unlike spider mites, no typical leaf stippling occurs. Some evidence indicates that the modifications caused by the mites result from secretions of hormonelike materials. In fact, some of these materials chemically resemble 2,4-D. This explains the typical herbicidelike deformations of foliage caused by leaf vagrant eriophyid mites.

CHEMICAL INSECTICIDES

At the beginning of World War II, research in chemical control of insects was dramatically increased. This eventually resulted in a huge arsenal of potent, long-lasting chemicals, some of which are still in use. Gradually, traditional nonchemical insect control methods were abandoned or used only in limited ways. In time, near total reliance was placed on synthetic chemicals for insect control, an unfortunate situation with several serious consequences.

Heavy reliance on chemical insecticides is likely to

cause detrimental side effects to nontarget pests and contamination of the environment. Headline reports of insecticide contamination had become alarmingly commonplace by the 1960s and 1970s.

Heavy dependence upon chemical control has also resulted in strong resistance in some serious insect pests. This has led to the development of even more potent chemicals. For example, it was found that 75 percent of the most serious agricultural insect pests in California had developed resistance to one or more insecticides. In some cases, the most effective chemicals caused resistant pest populations to grow faster (Harris 1983).

Traditionally, the goal of chemical pest control has been to eliminate *all* pests in a given population. Such an approach, however, has only served to destroy natural pest controls and, as already mentioned, to strengthen some pest populations.

Control of pests, whether insects, rodents, diseases, or weeds, is better approached with the goal of holding pests to tolerable populations rather than eliminating them. This means using suitable combinations of control methods in an effective balance while reducing undesirable side effects. Though this concept is not at all new, it has regained popularity in a form known as *integrated pest management* (IPM).

INTEGRATED PEST MANAGEMENT

While IPM is practiced for both disease and weed control, it is described in this chapter on insect pests because of its major practical implications for landscape plantings.

Key elements in an IPM program include:

1. Proper identification of the pest and knowledge of its life cycle.
2. Close monitoring of the pest's activity and population.
3. Application of appropriate controls that are most effective in reducing the pest population, while causing the least damage to nontarget organisms and the environment.
4. Adjustment of control measures to avoid injuring nontarget organisms and the environment.

Economic Versus Aesthetic Thresholds

The economic value of cash crops such as wheat, potatoes, beans, and corn can be readily measured. Thus, the economic threshold, or level, at which a pest population must be controlled before monetary losses occur is relatively easy to determine. In landscape situations, measurement of economic threshold levels is more difficult because much of the value is in less definable, aesthetic terms.

Loss of aesthetic value to a landscape as a result of pest damage can be expressed in monetary terms based on appraisal of total property value loss. Even this approach, however, can have its pitfalls because pest damage in a landscape may only temporarily affect the aesthetic value. For instance, a defoliating caterpillar may create an ugly landscape scene in June, but by August the pest ceases activity and new growth of the plants returns the site to its original attractiveness. The long-range effects of insect damage on plant health are extremely difficult to measure in monetary terms.

The allowable level of insect damage will vary from one landscape site to another, sometimes even within the same site. For instance, a garden of prize-winning roses may understandably be assigned a low threshold of pest damage, whereas a screen planting or windbreak of trees on the same property might easily have a higher threshold. A landscape manager should try to make decisions of what is allowable pest damage based on the use and "value" of each area being managed. In this way, pest control measures can be directed to the more critical areas rather than being applied uniformly to an entire site. In a public park, for instance, low pest damage levels would be desirable near heavily used areas, such as picnic grounds, tennis courts, and display gardens. Higher pest damage would normally be acceptable in outlying, or fringe, areas and along nature trails.

Commercial arborists usually have to establish low allowable pest tolerance levels because of the expectations of their clients. Client education and consultation by the arborist, however, can result in arriving at a "threshold plan" that maintains pest levels acceptable to the client and reduces pesticide applications. Many commercial arborists are now including consultation services for a fee as a regular part of their pest management programs for clients. Monitoring the pests on an individual site basis is also becoming more common.

IPM in Urban Areas

The very demographics of urban areas and the close habitation and diversity of inhabitants demand the stability of the environment that IPM can effectively create through deliberate, planned, and intelligently implemented combinations of pest control strategies. These strategies have been shown to reduce reliance on pesticides and to encourage suitable alternatives, thus substantially minimizing human or other nontarget exposure to toxic chemicals.

By their very nature, IPM programs emphasize the need for harmony between pest management practices and the environment. Implementation of an IPM program often makes it possible to reduce pesticide usage; when pesticides are necessary in specific situations, careful attention is paid to the timing and dosages used, so as to achieve effective control with the least detrimental side effects. This type of approach results in sound urban environmental management. The reduction in pesticide usage also reduces the need for storage and disposal sites, a problem that is usually more critical in crowded city areas than in rural communities.

The effectiveness of integrated pest management has been amply demonstrated in large and small cities throughout the United States. A case in point is pandemic Dutch elm disease. Sanitation measures, combined with selective pesticide application and careful street-by-street scouting, have resulted in a significant decrease of tree mortality. At the same time, this approach maintains an acceptable aesthetic and economic threshold. In addition, a valuable benefit of IPM programs in cities combatting problems such as Dutch elm disease has been greater community awareness of the importance of a tree canopy in improving environmental conditions for human life. There is every reason to believe that other community-wide pest problems can be successfully managed in a similar way through IPM programs.

Research in Urban IPM

A great deal of research is currently underway to suppress pest populations in urban situations safely. While it is not realistic to expect rapid replacement of pesticides with alternative measures, public pressure and an increased awareness of environmental factors affecting human health are beginning to force change. Fortunately, recent gains in the understanding of insect physiology, behavior, and communication have opened up new directions for pest control research.

Sex pheromones and juvenile hormones are two of the many promising areas receiving increased research emphasis. As a result, it is already practical to use pheromone traps to determine the presence of certain pests of urban landscapes, such as lilac and ash borers. In addition, such traps help to establish the best timing of pesticide applications when necessary. This, in turn results in substantially reduced pesticide use and exposure. Research on cultural control of pests also is receiving more emphasis than in the past because of the relatively low cost of such methods compared with chemical and biological methods. Cultural methods have wide public appeal because they do not involve the danger of pesticide exposure.

Future Developments

As urban IPM programs are accepted and their value is proven, a shift of emphasis and practice to more professional consulting services and less spray application can be expected by commercial pest control operators (PCOs), such as arborists and structural pest control firms. IPM programs require that PCOs have a good understanding of pest life cycles, natural and cultural controls, and the interactions of various control methods. Current EPA certification training programs have already created more awareness and have resulted in some changes, changing the classification of PCOs from "spraymen" to "professional pest control consultants."

The benefits of an urban IPM program can be realized in several ways: (1) savings on pesticide costs, which have spiraled along with oil, the primary pesticide source; (2) reduced needs for disposal and storage sites for waste chemicals; (3) increased public acceptance of control measures that tolerate some pest damage but cause less environmental contamination; and (4) public discussion of pest management, giving the public an alternative, that has wide appeal. In the future, PCOs in urban areas probably will be in demand for a wide range of consulting and education services as communities begin to appreciate the options available in pest control. Simply pulling a chemical from the shelf and loading up the spray equipment is no longer sufficient.

IPM in Landscapes

Implementing an IPM program in individual landscape areas is generally more difficult than in a forest, orchard, or field crop because of the wide diversity of plants, pests, and microclimates. Cultural practices that can be effective, however, include sanitation such as the removal of debris that tends to harbor pests, proper pruning to remove insect-infested branches, and prompt care of wounds to trees.

Biological control is usually less effective in landscapes than other methods, although careful timing and discretionary use of pesticides can allow natural controls to keep certain pests in check. Lady beetles, lacewings, and several other insects are effective in reducing some aphid populations. Predatory mites will keep populations of two-spotted and spruce mites at low levels.

Recent introduction of insecticidal soaps (potassium salts of fatty acids) show promise in controlling many soft-bodied insects, including aphids, mealybug, whitefly, and some scale insects.

Knowing *when* to apply a control measure is the real key to an IPM program. This requires monitoring of pests on a regular basis. As an aid to monitoring insects, attractants have been developed. Light traps for night-flying insects have been used for many years. The list of available chemical lures (pheromones) is growing. Pheromone-baited traps promise to be one of the most useful ways for the landscape manager to monitor pests. It is now possible to detect the exact time of adult activity of several insect pests of landscape plants. Knowing the adult flight time permits timely application of controls. Some pests of landscape plants for which pheromone traps are available are:

- Lilac/ash borer (*Podosesia syringae*)
- Oak borer (*Paranthrene similans*)
- Peach tree borer (*Synanthedon exitiosa*)
- Codling moth (*Laspeyresia pomonella*)
- Fall armyworm (*Spodoptera frugiperda*)
- Fruit tree leafroller (*Archips argyrospilus*)
- Gypsy moth (*Lymantria dispar*)
- Nantucket pine tip moth (*Rhyacionia frustrana*)

REFERENCES
Pest Identification

Anderson, R. F. 1960. Forest and Shade Tree Entomology. New York: John Wiley and Sons.

Johnson, W. T., and Lyon, H. H. 1976. Insects That Feed on Trees and Shrubs: An Illustrated Practical Guide. Ithaca, NY: Comstock Publishing Assoc.

Kiefer, H. H. 1952. Eriophyid mites of California. Davis, CA: University of California, Calif. Insect Survey Bull. 2 (1).

Kiefer, H. H., Baker, E. W., Kono, T., Delfinando, M., and Styer, W. E. 1982. An illustrated guide to plant abnormalities caused by eriophyid mites in North America. USDA Agric. Res. Serv. Handb. 573.

Smith, M. D. 1982. Ortho Problem Solver. San Francisco: Ortho Books.

Pest Management

Bowen, R. W., Gibeault, V. A., Ohr, H. D., and Thomason, I. J. 1979. Integrated pest management: A system whose time has come. Golf Course Mgmt. 47(2):16–23.

Brewer, J. W. 1971. Biology of the pinyon stunt needle midge. Ann. Entomol. Soc. Am. 64(5):1099–1102.

Davis, D. W. 1979. Biological control and insect pest management. Davis, CA: University of California, Agric. Sci. Publ. 4096.

Evans, B. R. 1981. Urban integrated pest management. A report of the Extension Committee on Organization and Policy. Athens, GA: Cooperative Extension Service, University of Georgia.

Forbes, S. A. 1915. The insect, the farmer, the teacher, the citizen and the state. Bull. Ill. State Lab. Nat. History.

Harris, R. W. 1983. Arboriculture. Care of Trees, Shrubs and Vines in the Landscape. Englewood Cliffs, NJ: Prentice-Hall.

Hock, W. K. 1984. IPM—Is it for the arborist? J. Arboriculture 10(1):1–4.

7.

Disease Management

Prior to the middle of the nineteenth century, plant pathology was shrouded in mystery, with crop maladies blamed mostly upon spontaneous generation. This concept of the cause of plant disease was even supported by certain experiments. For example, in an experiment in 1748, Needham, an English clergyman and naturalist, boiled meat in flasks, corked them, and soon thereafter found that the meat had spoiled because of microorganisms. Eventually, other workers showed that this apparently spontaneous generation was brought about through faulty techniques, which led to contamination from the air. Despite this, the cause of diseases continued to be attributed to "evil fogs," wind, excess moisture, nutrition, insects, or other factors.

Even after Prevost, a Swiss professor of philosophy, clearly demonstrated the pathogenic nature of microorganisms in 1807, a committee of the French Academy rejected his conclusions as unsound. It took another forty years before other scientists confirmed and adopted Prevost's work. Pasteur, in 1860, finally furnished irrefutable evidence that microorganisms found in diseased or decaying tissues arise from living entities.

By 1900, bacteria had finally been accepted as plant pathogens. Viruses also were recognized as "infectious maladies," but little was learned about their structure until the invention of the electron microscope. Some still question the validity of calling viruses living organisms because they cannot reproduce on their own. Fungi also were recognized as disease-causing agents and by the early 1900s had been classified into many types by mycologists.

Most of the real strides in plant pathology have occurred since World War II. New classes of organisms have been discovered, for example, mycoplasmas, which cause a fatal disease in elms called phloem necrosis. More recently, scientists discovered a viruslike organism in chrysanthemums, calling it a viroid. A viroid differs from a virus in that it lacks the protein shell that normally surrounds the nucleic core of a virus.

Undoubtedly even smaller organisms will be discovered eventually, just as nuclear physicists have continued to discover smaller and smaller particles of nonliving matter.

DEFINITION OF DISEASE

In the strictest sense of the word, a plant disease is any abnormal change in the structure or physiological processes of a plant. Such changes may be brought about by environmental conditions unfavorable for optimum plant growth, such as cold, heat, poorly aerated soil, lack of moisture, or by a parasitic organism.

The difficulty with this or any other definition of a plant disease is that no clearly defined line separates normal and diseased plants. The definition also seems to include all plant maladies whether caused by environmental factors, chemical spray injuries, insects, or microorganisms. This leads to the classification of plant diseases into two basic types, *abiotic* and *biotic*.

Abiotic or Nonpathogenic Diseases

Abiotic diseases are plant maladies incited by conditions of the environment alone. At least two factors are needed: a host plant and unfavorable environmental conditions for that plant. Abiotic diseases may result from unfavorable temperatures, soil atmospheric conditions, or soil moisture; air pollutants; mineral excesses or deficiencies; lightning; and chemical spray burn.

Biotic or Pathogenic Diseases

Biotic diseases are maladies incited by the combination of three factors: a host plant, a parasitic organism, and environmental conditions that favor the development of the parasite. A biotic disease cannot develop without all three factors being present (fig. 7-1). For instance,

it is well established that the spores of many infectious disease organisms are present in the air, in soil, and on plants throughout the year. These spores, however, will not result in disease until the proper environmental conditions exist, such as high humidity and warm temperatures. Even then a diseased condition cannot occur unless the organism develops on or in the proper host plant.

It is primarily because of environmental conditions that the incidence of parasitic diseases in trees, shrubs, and garden flowers is relatively low in the arid western states and fairly high in the more humid and moist climates of coastal and southern states.

DIAGNOSING DISEASES
Symptoms

Whether a plant has a biotic or abiotic disease, diagnosis is usually based upon changes in the plant that are visible to the naked eye. Such changes are called symptoms. Common symptoms are spots on the leaves, loss of chlorophyll, discoloration of the bark, dieback of twigs, and curling or cupping of foliage.

The difficulty in diagnosing a disease problem is that symptoms may have more than one cause. For instance,

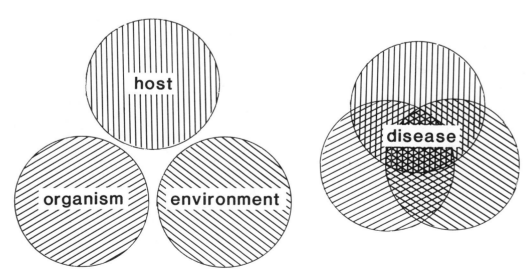

Figure 7-1. The three factors required for a biotic disease (*left*). Disease will occur only when all three factors are present (*right*) and the environmental conditions are unfavorable for the host but favorable for the organism.

browning (necrosis) of leaf margins is a symptom of drought injury, high salts in the soil, potassium deficiency, some pathogenic diseases, and certain air pollutants. It may also resemble spray injury. In order to diagnose a problem based on symptoms, it is important to consider the environmental conditions that exist at the time the symptoms appear, as well as conditions occurring prior to the appearance of the symptoms.

For example, if a plant is showing browning and it is growing in an alkaline, clay soil, potassium deficiency would be unlikely because it would be rare to find such a soil deficient in potassium. It would be more likely in sandy or acid soils. Even though potassium deficiency could be eliminated as a cause in this case, several other possible causes exist. Arriving at the most likely cause is done through a process of elimination. To continue this example, if rainfall or irrigation has been adequate, scorch or drought injury would not be likely. The next possibilities are pathogenic disease or spray burn. Records on spraying should be checked. If the conclusion is that a disease organism is the cause, a tissue sample should be submitted to a laboratory. After the sample is cultured in an agar medium, the causal agent or pathogen can be identified under a microscope.

Signs of Biotic Diseases

Sometimes it is possible to identify a biotic disease easily if there are signs of the disease along with symptoms. A sign is any actual visible evidence of the disease organism, for example, spore bodies or mycelium (strands of growth of a fungus). Mushrooms are a familiar sign of decay organisms (fig. 7-2). Such cases are simple to diagnose. Unfortunately, the signs of a disease are not always present and are, in fact, only present under certain conditions brought about by rather exacting environmental factors.

Diagnosis of Abiotic Diseases

The most difficult conditions to diagnose are the abiotic diseases caused by too much water, too little water, nutrient deficiency, and other similar factors, which usually have external causes. Furthermore, many biotic diseases are only the end result of a condition that started with an abiotic problem. For instance, a plant that is growing in a tight, oxygen-starved soil may ultimately fall prey to a pathogen or even an insect. Diagnosing such conditions in order to arrive at an appropriate corrective measure sometimes requires detective work. The steps in arriving at the most likely causes are discussed in the next section.

Key to Plant Abnormalities

The following key, while not all-inclusive, can help to determine the probable cause or causes of many plant abnormalities. Once the general type of problem is identified, its exact nature or the specific causative organism can be determined from local literature or a plant disease laboratory. In the case of biotic diseases, the causal agent often is fairly host specific and can usually be determined if the general type of problem and the identity of the host plant are known. The following key should be used only as a guide to identification. Always follow up with further investigation.

Figure 7-2. Mushrooms are signs of a decay organism. (Courtesy Alex L. Shigo [ret.], N.E. Forest Experiment Station)

To use this key, first select statement 1a, 1b, 1c, or 1d, depending on which is most true of the problem being diagnosed. Then proceed to the numbered pairs of statements as indicated. Probable causative agents are in boldface type.

1a. Symptoms mostly on or in foliage—*see #2*

1b. Symptoms mostly on or in young twigs—*see #13*

1c. Symptoms mostly on or in main branches or trunk—*see #17*

1d. Symptoms mostly on or in roots—*see #20*

2a. Leaves of normal size but off-color or with spots, holes, or off-colored margins—*see #5*

2b. Leaves smaller than normal or wilted; not discolored or spotted—*see #3*

3a. Leaves wilted or drooping—*see #4*

3b. Leaves not wilted, but smaller than normal: **cold injury; drought; viruses; mildews**

4a. Stems not showing stain (cut stem with clean knife, as stain can result from residue on the knife blade): **soil too wet or too dry**

4b. Stems with distinct stain in sapwood (cut diagonally with clean, sharp knife): **wilt disease (Dutch elm disease, verticillium wilt, etc.)**

5a. Leaves with white or gray cast: **powdery mildew fungus**

5b. Leaves with spots or blotches—*see #6*

6a. Scattered spots or blotches on one or both leaf surfaces or circular holes in leaves (fig. 7-3)—*see #11*

6b. Leaves not spotted but with yellow or brown margins, sometimes extending between veins—*see #7*

7a. Margin of leaves brown (fig. 7-4)—*see #8*

7b. Margin of leaves yellowish, usually also between veins (fig. 7-5): **check soil for Fe, Zn, or Mn deficiency or soil sterilants**

8a. Weather conditions have been hot and dry: **drought scorch or high salts**

8b. Weather conditions have not been hot and dry—*see #9*

9a. Soils in area very acid *or* very sandy: **test soil for potassium deficiency**

9b. Soils *not* particularly acid or sandy—*see #10*

10a. Weather conditions have been moist, humid: **anthracnose and similar leafspot diseases**

10b. Weather conditions not moist or humid: **check for soil sterilants; air pollution also possible**

11a. Leaves with relatively uniform holes; margins of holes brown or reddish (caution: some insects can cause similar damage): **shothole fungus or xanthomonas caterium**

11b. Leaves without holes, but with spots or blotches—*see #12*

12a. Leaves irregularly blotched; no particular pattern; sometimes of several colors: **spray damage** (check records); if blotches red or white and "velvety," probably **eriophyid mites**

12b. Leaves with relatively uniform spots (brown bordered by yellow, red, or light green); usually most evident on upper surface: **leafspot fungi**

13a. Young twigs with raised pimplelike structures—*see #16*

13b. Young twigs dying back—*see #14*

14a. Dieback of twigs with buds that failed to open in spring: **winter injury**

14b. Young twigs dying back after buds open in spring—*see #15*

15a. New growth black or brown, curled backward: **tipblight fungus; fireblight bacterium; frost injury**

15b. New growth still greenish but shriveled; or if brown, leaves still attached: **drought injury; transplant shock; spray injury**

16a. Raised structures orange or black; orange ooze or black powder may be present: **fungus cankers such as Cytospora and Nectria**

16b. Raised structures tan or usually lighter than surrounding bark; oval, round, or lens-shaped; regular in shape: **normal lenticels in bark**

17a. Main branches or trunk with localized sunken areas—*see #19*

17b. Main branches or trunk raised or swollen structures—*see #18*

18a. Structures raised are like orange, reddish, or black pimples: **fungus cankers such as Cytospora, Nectria, and Thyronectria**

18b. Structures are swollen stem or trunk parts; fissures in bark may have orange powder: **stem rusts**

19a. Sunken area discolored, cracked, and usually in a streak on the southwest side of trunk: **sunscald**

19b. Sunken area irregular, on any exposure, and often

near base of trees: **mechanical impact bruises or cankers**

20a. Symptoms at base of tree trunks in flare of roots— *see #21*

20b. Symptoms in smaller roots—*see #22*

21a. Bark loose; wood beneath soft and punky when probed: **root rot** (often follows overwatering in compacted soils)

21b. Tumorlike growth from bark: **crown gall bacterium**

22a. Roots with small pealike swellings: **root knot nematode or normal nodules of nitrifying bacteria** (legumes and buffaloberry)

22b. Fine roots (feeder roots) slimy, dark-colored; sometimes with sewerlike odor: *many causes;* **oxygen starvation most common in landscape plantings**

Figure 7-4. Brown leaf margins, as in this maple leaf, are a common symptom of drought scorch. (Courtesy Kenneth R. Dudzik, N.E. Forest Experiment Station)

Figure 7-3. Examples of leafspot-infected leaves. (Courtesy Kenneth R. Dudzik, N.E. Forest Experiment Station)

Figure 7-5. Comparison of normal (*left*) and chlorotic (*right*) leaves of red-osier dogwood. Many different conditions can cause chlorosis, including mineral deficiencies and soil sterilants. (Courtesy Kenneth R. Dudzik, N.E. Forest Experiment Station)

DISEASE CONTROL

The control of plant disease usually involves a combination of measures, most of which are preventive in nature. Control measures can be classified into several basic types.

Exclusion refers to any measure designed to prevent introduction of an organism into an area where it did not previously exist. Such measures are generally conducted on a county, state, or national level. The most common way to achieve exclusion is by quarantines, which are normally controlled by the government and require a legal document to establish. Plants coming into the United States from another country must go through quarantine measures. The Arnold Arboretum in Jamaica Plains, Mass., and the U.S. Arboretum in Washington, D.C., are two locations among several that act as quarantine areas for introduced plants. Using the exclusion method on a local level with landscape plants is usually not practical.

Resistance is usually developed through breeding and selection practices and is most common in field crops and other annual types of plants. Breeding and selection programs in landscape plants have increased since the 1970s, and it is now possible to obtain disease-resistant types of some trees. For example, several cultivars of crabapple are now available that resist infection by bacterial fireblight. A number of selections of elms show some resistance to both phloem necrosis and Dutch elm disease. It is also possible to purchase many garden annuals that are resistant to certain types of mosaic viruses. In fact, using resistant strains is about the only practical method for controlling virus infection, because there are no chemical means known to stop a virus infection in plants.

Elimination of a pathogen or a host from an area is accomplished by *eradication* of specific host plants. Like a quarantine, eradication measures usually require a legal document to implement. An example is the attempt, beginning in the 1930s, to eradicate the European barberry (*Berberis vulgaris*) and related barberries that acted as the alternate host for black stem rust in wheat. Eradication programs are usually very expensive and remain effective only when governmental funds are adequate. Few such programs exist today.

Chemical protection is the most common method cur-

rently in use for controlling plant diseases. Preventive control involves application to a plant of a chemical that forms a chemical barrier to the development of a disease organism. Some systemic fungicides have been developed that not only provide preventive control but also a degree of postinfection protection.

Cleaning up waste vegetation—*sanitation*—and discouraging disease development by *environmental manipulation* are two very effective methods of disease control. For example, the incidence of disease redevelopment in blackspot of rose can be reduced significantly by destroying infected leaves and reducing frequency of overhead watering. In turfgrasses, less frequent applications of irrigation water can help reduce the severity of some diseases.

Maintaining plant health is an important aspect of disease control because, with few exceptions, a plant in good health will rarely fall prey to serious disease problems. Maintaining optimum nutrition, proper soil aeration, and adequate water is a better preventive practice than any chemical method known. Experience and a good ability to detect even subtle changes in plant appearance are important in employing this type of control. Maintaining a healthy plant also includes judicious and correct pruning, as well as wound prevention practices.

Nonchemical Control

Over 90 percent of all plant diseases can be controlled or avoided without the use of chemicals. Effective nonchemical control may require the integration of two or more nonchemical control methods. (Review discussion on integrated pest management in chapter 6; the basic principles apply to disease control as well as insect control.)

As mentioned previously, resistant strains are becoming more widely available as plant breeders develop more and more cultivars that are relatively resistant to a variety of diseases. In certain plants it is also possible to buy certified, disease-free seed, which is produced under controlled conditions. This is an effective way to prevent some of the more serious seedborne diseases.

Practicing good sanitation can be highly effective in controlling certain diseases. Many microorganisms will overwinter in debris, and some may be found harboring on some of the weeds in a nearby field. Destroying debris and controlling weeds in adjacent areas will often keep the incidence of disease to a tolerable level. Sanitation also includes disinfecting tools and other equipment used in pruning, harvesting, or cultivating plants. This is particularly important with diseases, such as fireblight, known to be easily transmitted on pruning tools and other equipment. Sanitation also includes the control of insect vectors. Some insects, such as leaf hoppers, are known to carry virus diseases. Thus, the control of an insect will often reduce or prevent the spread of a disease.

A more difficult control method is modification of the environment in an urban landscape situation. It is often possible, however, to reduce the incidence of disease by altering watering practices. Avoiding overhead irrigation and frequent, light waterings will tend to discourage leafspot diseases and mildews.

Wound Prevention—A Key to Disease Control

Wounds in plants permit access to pathogens—the first step in the process that leads to infection and eventual decline or decay. A leading source of wounding in urban landscapes is mechanical abrasion from lawn mowing and trimming equipment. One abrasion wound to the bark of a tree may not result in noticeable decline, but repeated injuries caused by weekly mowing activities will. Mowing crews must understand the seriousness of mechanical abrasion by equipment. They need to know how a tree responds to damage through barrier zone formation and how this zone, through repeated injury, will eventually give way to invasion by microorganisms.

Barrier Zones in Trees

Barrier zones in trees were first defined by Shigo and Larson (1969) as distinctive layers of specialized parenchyma cells produced by the cambium after physical injury (fig. 7-6). Distinctive bands of parenchyma that formed in trees after invasion by certain infectious organisms were also recognized as barrier zones by Tippett and Shigo (1981). These zones not only function as physical barriers to invading organisms but have been

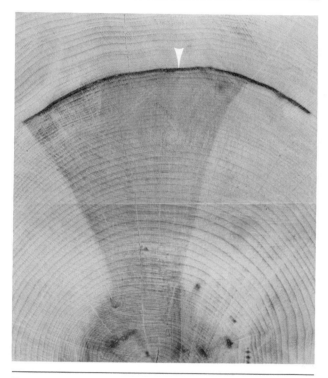

Figure 7-6. Barrier zone formed after wounding (arrow). Note the wedge-shaped discoloration of wood. (Courtesy Alex L. Shigo (ret.), N.E. Forest Experiment Station)

shown by many researchers to contain chemicals such as phenols that impart some disease resistance (Green et al. 1981; Sharon 1973; Shain 1968, 1971; Shigo 1986; Shigo and Wilson 1982; Shortle and Cowling 1978).

It was previously thought that barrier zones were misaligned, defective tissues. It is now known that they are highly specialized cell groups that form in response to both wounding and microorganism invasion. The strength of the zone varies from one species to another, as well as the general health of a given tree.

Trees can survive invasion by vascular organisms, such as those causing Dutch elm disease and verticillium wilt in maple, if the barrier zone is successful in walling off the invasion. The barrier zone protects the cambium from total destruction, allowing the tree to recover. This may be why some trees, even within the same species, can survive repeated infections while others cannot. However, even trees that have strong barriers will succumb to invasion if bombarded with frequent impact wounds, improper pruning, and adverse environmental conditions.

Suggested Measures to Prevent Wounding

Trees in urban landscape situations undergo many more stresses than those in natural forests. In addition to the vagaries of climate, soil, and natural pests, they are exposed to unnatural conditions such as heat radiation from pavement and structures; air and soil contaminants; oxygen starvation to roots by compaction, pavement, and plastic weed barriers; overwatering; overfertilizing; restricted roots; and mechanical abrasions to the bark. A landscape manager can do much to prevent such stresses, so that the tree's natural boundaries to invasion by microorganisms are given a fair chance to wall off the problem.

Wound prevention should be a top priority of a landscape management program. This management activity, more than any other, will go a long way in reducing future problems to trees and shrubs. Remember that wounds begin the sequence of invasion, discoloration, and decay in woody plants. Common preventive measures include the following:

- Design properly from the start, so that the trees and shrubs are isolated from turfgrass areas.
- Remove a ring of turf from around the base of existing trees.
- Use grass-killing chemicals to discourage turf near trees. Glyphosate is safe if used cautiously near thin-barked trees. Avoid wetting the bark of any tree with herbicides.
- Use temporary metal or plastic shields to prevent damage from string-type weed cutters. Where possible, avoid using string-type weed cutters near tree and shrub bases.
- Instruct maintenance crews on the importance of wound prevention to trees and the consequences of carelessness.

Many landscape managers have devised various shields, "bumpers," or mower guards to be placed more or less permanently around trees. This practice, however, is not helpful in preventing wounds to trees; in many cases, trees "protected" by such devices suffer greater injury than unprotected trees, for three reasons.

First, any type of impact guard, whether rubber hose, high-impact plastic, corrugated plastic pipe, or even foam rubber, will not cushion the impact from mowing equipment. In most cases the shields will tend to spread the damage over a wider surface area than would occur in the absence of the shields. Although shields may help on a temporary basis to reduce damage from string-type weed cutters, they do not in any way prevent mower-impact injury (fig. 7-7). Unfortunately, appearances are deceiving in the case of these devices. They may reduce surface abrasion or visible damage to the bark, thus appearing to give protection. Unseen is the internal bruising and crushing of vital cells and tissues.

Figure 7-7. Corrugated plastic pipe used to protect trees from string grass-cutter equipment. The pipe does not protect from mower impact.

The second reason that mower guards should not be used is purely psychological in nature. Mower guards create a false sense of security. Mower crews, therefore, tend to become complacent about hitting trees with the equipment. Some have been found to hit trees all the harder!

A third reason why mower guards are undesirable is that trees tend to overgrow most types. Girdling of the tree trunk results.

In addition to the damage they may cause, mower guards are aesthetically unpleasant and detract from the natural appearance of a landscape.

Chemical Control

Although there is a general tendency to try to find a chemical to control every plant disease problem, less than 10 percent of the diseases need chemical control. Most can usually be kept in check by the nonchemical methods already discussed. With few exceptions, chemical fungicides are effective *only* as preventive measures and have no ability whatsoever to actually stop a disease organism that is already active in the plant.

Preventive fungicides can be likened to preemergent herbicides, such as crabgrass killers, in that they are applied to the surface of the plant as a barrier. For example, when the spores of a fungus begin to grow on a treated plant, the radical (fungus root) comes in contact with the chemical, which is toxic to the organism. This prevents it from penetrating the host plant. In recent years, however, some systemic fungicides have been developed. When applied to a plant in the proper way, they move throughout certain plant parts and control the disease from within. So far, such materials have been effective only to a limited degree with fungi on certain types of plants. Benomyl (Benlate) is known to have certain systemic qualities. Its soluble form, Lignasan BLP, shows promise in the control of Dutch elm disease. Its actual effect within a plant is to stop the progress of the organism. The chemical does not kill the organism. Therefore, this and similar chemicals are more correctly called *fungistats* rather than *fungicides*. Many more systemic materials will undoubtedly be developed in the future.

Preventive chemical controls are generally classified into four basic types: fumigants, soil drenches, foliar treatments, and antibiotics.

Examples of *fumigants* are Vapam and methyl bromide. These chemicals are applied either in liquid or gaseous form to the soil, but it is the gaseous stage that generally penetrates and kills most organisms. Use of most of these chemicals is practical only on a small scale (as in greenhouses). All of them are dangerous to the user. Methyl bromide is usually purchased in a pressurized canister. These canisters also contain a small amount of tear gas, which acts as a warning device should the user get too close or spray so much into an area that the concentration of methyl bromide can be injurious.

Soil drenches are used to control soilborne organisms, such as rhizoctonia and verticillium fungi. An example is PCNB (Terraclor).

Foliar treatments are by far the most commonly used and include such chemicals as Maneb, Zineb, sulfur, and fixed copper. Benomyl, classed as a systemic, is also used as a foliar treatment because it can act as a barrier, as well as somewhat systemically.

Antibiotics include agricultural grades of streptomycin, which is sold under brand names such as Agri-Strep and Agrimycin. They are primarily used in landscape horticulture in the control of fireblight disease but must be applied at a specific time, namely in the flowering stage of the host plant, in order to be effective at all.

When using chemicals to control biotic plant diseases, keep in mind that none is effective in the absence of other appropriate measures, such as reducing irrigation, avoiding crowding of plants, using sound pruning practices, and avoiding overfertilization. Few plant diseases are ever stopped once started unless the conditions favorable for disease are reduced or eliminated. Unless this principle is clearly understood and implemented in practice, effective disease control is impossible.

REFERENCES

Green, D. J., Shortle, W. C., and Shigo, A. L. 1981. Compartmentalization of discolored and decayed wood in red maple branch stubs. For. Sci. 27(3):519–22.

Shain, L. 1968. Resistance of sapwood in stems of loblolly pine to infection by *Fomes annosus*. Phytopathology 58: 1493–98.

————. 1971. The response to sapwood of Norway spruce to infection by *Fomes annosus*. Phytopathology 61:301–7.

Sharon, E. M. 1973. Some histological features of *Acer saccharum* wood after wounding. Can. J. For. Res. 3:83–89.

Shigo, A. L. 1986. A New Tree Biology. Durham, NH: Shigo and Trees Assoc.

Shigo, A. L., and Larson, E. H. 1969. A photoguide to the patterns of discoloration and decay in living northern hardwood trees. USDA Agric. Forest Service Rep. NE 127.

Shigo, A. L., and Wilson, C. L. 1982. Wounds in peach. Plant Dis. 66:895–97.

Shortle, W. C., and Cowling, E. B. 1978. Interaction of live sapwood and fungi commonly found in discolored and decayed wood. Phytopathology 68:617–23.

Smith, M. D. 1982. The Ortho Problem Solver. San Francisco: Ortho Books.

Tattar, T. A. 1978. Diseases of Shade Trees. New York: Academic Press.

Tippett, J. T., and Shigo, A. L. 1981. Barrier zone formation: A mechanism of tree defense against vascular pathogens. Int. Assoc. of Wood Anatomists Bull. 2(4):163–68.

8. 🌿

Weed, Brush, and Root Management

Control of weeds in landscape plantings is a major pest management activity. The control methods used will vary with the type of weeds, time of year, and the specific type of landscape plantings. There are four basic methods employed in weed control:

1. *Mechanical*—physical removal of weeds by hand-pulling, digging, or cultivation
2. *Exclusion*—maintenance of dense stands of desirable plants that will successfully compete with weeds through shading out and/or water and nutrient demands; natural and artificial mulches can also help to exclude weeds
3. *Chemical*—application of chemicals that can prevent or stop the growth of weeds through toxic activity in weeds or soil
4. *Biological*—use of specific insects or diseases to control weeds

As a general rule, weed control in turf areas involves chemical and exclusion (cultural) techniques. By maintaining turf in good vigor through appropriate fertilizer applications, watering, and mowing, weeds can be effectively excluded. In nonturf areas, mechanical, chemical, and exclusion methods are used. Exclusion by competition, however, is generally ineffective except in very dense plantings of ground covers. Use of mulches and fabric barriers to exclude weeds is becoming a popular practice in nonturf areas. In both turf and nonturf areas, biological control of weeds has potential, but little is known to date on this subject.

MECHANICAL CONTROL

As defined earlier, mechanical control is physical removal of weeds by pulling, digging, or cultivating. A distinct advantage of this method is that the weeds are taken from the planting site, resulting in an immediate improvement of the appearance of an area. This method also does not involve toxic chemicals, which can harm desirable plants or the worker.

A disadvantage of mechanical control, obvious to anyone who has hoed or pulled weeds all day, is the amount of time it can take and the physical energy required. Another disadvantage is that with some weeds, mechanical removal may actually spread the problem and/or propagate the weeds. Removal of weeds at a time when they have ripe seed may distribute the weeds over a larger area than before. This is usually the case with some winter annuals, such as cheatgrass (*Bromus tectorum*), and early mustards, such as pepperweed (*Lepidium campestre*). Grassy weeds such as

Figure 8-1. Both the turfgrass and the low-growing juniper in the park reduce weeds by exclusion. (Courtesy Alan Rollinger, landscape designer)

quackgrass (*Agropyron repens*) and broadleaf weeds like purslane (*Portulaca oleracea*) also are often propagated by mechanical weed control methods because they can regenerate new plants from small fragments of stem or rhizome.

In spite of some disadvantages, mechanical weed control remains one of the best alternatives to chemical methods.

EXCLUSION

Weeds can be controlled simply by excluding them through competition with desirable plants or by using mulches (fig. 8-1). Keeping a turf area in good vigor, as previously mentioned, is a good example of excluding weeds through competition. However, it is usually easier to keep weeds under control in turf than in shrub borders or flower beds because if weeds do appear in turf they can be selectively and easily removed with herbicides (fig. 8-2). In nonturf areas, weeds that manage to overcome the ground cover or grow through the mulch may have to be removed mechanically; if chemical methods are employed in such areas, great care is needed to prevent damage to adjacent plants. Ground covers that develop good density and are thus generally effective in weed control include creeping junipers, ajuga, English ivy, pachysandra, Santolina, winter-creeper euonymus, creeping mahonia, and cranberry cotoneaster.

Figure 8-2. Grassy weeds (arrows) in this broadleaved ground cover can be controlled with selective grass killers.

Mulches

Using mulches to exclude weeds is becoming more and more popular in the home landscape. There are two basic types of mulches, organic and inorganic. Organic mulches include wood and bark chips, straw, grass clippings, and seed hulls. Inorganic (inert) mulches include polyethylene film, landscape fabrics, fiber mats, and gravel.

The ideal mulch does not compact readily. It does not retard water and air movement into the soil, is not a fire hazard, and breaks down slowly. In addition, the ideal mulch is uniform in color, weed free and attractive, and will not blow away.

Selecting a Mulch

The selection of a mulch depends upon its intended use. If improvement of appearance is the main goal, inorganic mulches may be the best choice. If soil improvement is the major goal, an organic mulch that breaks down gradually should be considered.

The size of the area in relation to the cost of material and availability also must be considered.

Another factor influencing the type of mulch selected is the type of plant to be mulched. If the area is used primarily for annual flowers, it is usually most practical to use a temporary organic mulch, which can be turned under each fall. The advantages and disadvantages of various mulch materials are summarized in table 8-1.

When to Apply Mulches

Mulches used to enhance appearance and control weeds may be applied at any time.

Mulches used to protect fall transplants should be applied immediately after planting. Organic mulches up to 5 inches deep will help delay deep frost penetration. This allows more time for root growth before extremely cold temperatures occur.

If the mulch is to be used to reduce frost heave and delay spring growth, it should be applied after the ground has frozen. This type of mulch is often used to protect small bulbs, such as squill and crocus, and to prevent early emergence of the shoots.

Inorganic (Inert) Mulches

Plastic films: Polyethylene film covered with gravel or bark is one of the most common mulches in home landscapes. This is unfortunate because plastic mulches, while excellent for weed control, reduce air and water penetration into the soil. If polyethylene film is used, it should be layed in overlapping strips no wider than 18 inches and no thicker than 4 mil. This procedure improves air and water penetration but may reduce the weed control value of the film because weeds will tend to emerge along the seams.

Another problem with plastic film is the creation of an environment that promotes shallow root development. It is not uncommon to find roots creeping on top of the soil in the interface area between soil and plastic. Plants under such conditions encounter severe stress from both heat and cold. The same problem can result if organic mulches are applied deeper than about 5 inches.

Landscape fabrics and fiberglass mats: Woven plastic fabrics and fiberglass mats have proven to be useful in weed suppression. These materials, while more costly than most plastic films, allow water and air penetration yet exclude weed growth. One type resembles plastic burlap; another resembles thin fiberglass insulation.

Table 8-1. Characteristics of Various Mulch Materials

Type	Advantages	Disadvantages	General Comments
Organic Mulches			
Cocoa bean	Long-lasting; dark brown color	Tends to compact and form a crusty surface; relatively expensive	Molds may form on surface; this is harmless if stirred to break crust
Crushed corncobs	Uniform in color	May retain too much moisture at surface; may compact if kept wet	Cobs dyed various colors available
Grass clippings	Readily available	Must be applied loosely and in thin layers to reduce matting	Allow grass to dry before applying as a mulch
Hops	Attractive color; nonflammable	Disagreeable odor until dry	May be available from local brewery
Leaves (composted)	Readily available	Not very attractive; may become matted	Good soil amendment
Leaves (fresh dried)	Readily available	Not very attractive; may blow; fire hazard; wet leaves compact into slimy mats	Most appropriate use is in "naturalized" gardens or shrub masses
Manure (strawy)	Usually available	Unpleasant odor; may contain weed seeds	A better soil amendment than a mulch; should be aged and/or heat-treated
Peat (mountain type)	Available in bulk amounts	May crust on surface	Best used as a soil amendment, not as a mulch
Peat (sphagnum)	Usually available in bulk amounts	May crust on surface or may blow away	An acid-forming peat, but even this is variable with source; best used as a soil amendment, not as a mulch
Pine needles	Attractive; do not become compacted	Difficult to obtain in quantity; somewhat of a fire hazard	One of the best for winter protection of fall-transplanted material
Salt hay	Inexpensive	Unattractive; fire hazard	Used as temporary seed cover in eastern coastal states
Sawdust	Attractive; usually available	Fine sawdust may crust; some sources such as walnut produce toxic substances	Addition of nitrogen is usually necessary
Shredded bark (also includes bark chips or "chunk bark")	Long-lasting and attractive; chips or "chunks" more attractive than fine shreds	Cost relatively high; shredded bark may compact	Use for informal walkways
Straw	Readily available	Blows easily; highly flammable; weed seeds often present	Best used as a temporary mulch around plants needing protection in winter; anchor with wire mesh, asphalt, plastic net, or "tackifier"
Wood chips and shavings	Long-lasting; readily available; rustic but usually attractive in appearance; will not compact readily	Variable in texture and color, thus sometimes not uniform in appearance	Chips of 3-inch size are least likely to compact

Table 8-1, *continued.*

Type	Advantages	Disadvantages	General Comments
Inorganic (Inert) Mulches			
Clay aggregates (heat-treated)	Attractive gray and brown colors available; lighter weight than gravel, thus easier to transport; weed free	Relatively expensive	Brands available include Turface and Terragreen; Idealite for use in lightweight cement is similar
Fiberglass mats	Available in rolls or sheets; easy to apply	Becomes matted when wet; fiberglass particles are irritating to the skin; must be pegged down	Recommended only for small areas
Gravel, stone	Readily available in colors to match or complement the architecture; inexpensive	Will not prevent growth of some weedy grasses	Use landscape fabrics beneath to prevent weeds
Polyethylene film (black plastic)	Suppresses weeds well; inexpensive on cost per square foot basis; readily available; useful between vegetable rows	Used by itself, it must be anchored on all edges; becomes brittle with age; easy to puncture; excludes air and water to plant roots	Avoid using beneath trees and shrubs
Landscape fabrics	Long-lasting; resists tearing; allows water and air movement	Initial cost high; some types break down when exposed to sunlight	Most can also be used for slope stabilization

These materials are long lasting and are used not only for weed control but also for stabilization of steep slopes. Other advantages of these mulches over plastic film are their durability when exposed to extreme temperatures. They are also resistant to puncture or tearing when rock or other hard substances are used as a decorative top cover (fig. 8-3).

Organic Mulches

As indicated in table 8-1, many materials have been used as organic mulches. Most should be applied to a depth of 3–4 inches. However, straw, dried leaves, and similar materials need to be applied to a depth of at least 6 inches; a week or two after application these materials will settle to a depth of 3 to 4 inches.

The areas covered to various depths by one cubic yard of organic mulch are listed in table 8-2. The amount of material required to cover other areas, or to other depths, can be obtained by calculation. For example, to cover 40 square feet to a 4-inch depth would require ½ cubic yard; to cover 320 square feet to a 4-inch depth would require 4 cubic yards.

Some mulches, particularly straw and loose leaves, may harbor rodents. When using these mulches, they should not be placed closer than 6 inches to the base of woody plants. When placed close to plants, rodents

Table 8-2. Area Covered to a Given Depth by 1 Cubic Yard of Organic Mulch

Area Covered (ft²)	Depth of Mulch (in.)
80	4
120	3
160	2
320	1

Figure 8-3. A few inches of gravel on top of a landscape fabric effectively reduce weeds in this attractive business park. (Courtesy Eugene B. Eyerly, Eyerly and Associates)

living in the mulch will chew the bark of the plants, girdling and killing them. Voles, which are small short-tailed mice, are a common problem in organic mulches, particularly in winter.

As organic mulches decompose, some of the soil nitrogen in contact with the mulch is used by breakdown organisms. Consequently, nitrogen deficiency may occur. A sign of nitrogen deficiency is a yellowing, primarily of the lower leaves. When this occurs, nitrogen fertilizers should be added. For every 100 square feet of mulched area, 2 pounds of a complete fertilizer, such as 10-6-4, or ¼ pound of ammonium nitrate should be added. A "weed-and-feed" type of fertilizer should *never* be used in mulched areas.

CHEMICAL CONTROL

Modern weed control involves a myriad of chemicals (herbicides) that can control almost any unwanted plant growth. Some chemicals can selectively remove weeds from desirable plantings; for example, 2,4-D is commonly used in turfgrass to destroy broadleaved weeds. Others, through *selective method of application,* can be used to destroy weeds in desirable broadleaf plantings. Some, by application at certain growth cycles of the weed, can kill weeds without harm to other plants. A large number of herbicides, however, are nonselective and will destroy all vegetation.

There are several mechanisms by which herbicides

act on plants. The major mechanisms and examples of herbicides acting in each way are as follows:

- Interference with amino acid production—phenoxy-type herbicides such as 2,4-D
- Interference with chlorophyll production—traizine-type compounds such as amino-triazole and prometon
- Desiccation caused by damage to cuticle or upper cell layers of leaves—Paraquat
- Destruction of growing points (mitotic tissues)—glyphosate
- Suffocation—some oils and solvents
- Plasmolysis (reverse of osmosis)—some salts and soil sterilants (sodium metaborate, sodium chlorate, etc.)
- Inhibition of roots—many types of pre-emergent herbicides such as trifluralin

For the most part, the activity of a herbicide depends on the rate of growth of the target weed, the temperature of the air and soil, and the structure of the weed itself. Actively growing weeds are usually affected more rapidly by herbicides than dormant weeds are because they metabolize more of the toxin. Herbicides generally work best at warm air or soil temperatures. At very high temperatures, however, their effectiveness may be reduced as a result of volatilization. With some herbicides, such as 2,4-D and trifluralin, the hazard to desirable plants is also increased at high temperatures because their vapors may move from treated areas to nearby desirable vegetation.

Selective Herbicides

A selective herbicide is more toxic to one, or a few, species than to others. The most important factors influencing selectiveness of herbicides are structural differences among plants, absorption of herbicides by the plant, translocation in the plant, and physiological differences in the plant. To avoid misapplication, these factors must be taken into consideration when applying herbicides.

Structural differences permit application of certain herbicides, such as 2,4-D in grasses, without injury. Since grasses have their growing points at the leaf base, which are protected by a sheath or located below ground, the meristematic areas do not come in contact with the herbicide. Broadleaved weeds, which lack this structural protection, are killed by the herbicide. It should be noted, however, that 2,4-D used at high rates can kill grass.

Absorption of chemicals may be rapid by one plant and slow, or nonexistent, by others. This can allow for selectivity even among broadleaved plants. Absorption rate can vary because of differences in the waxy cuticle of the leaf. Plants with a thick, waxy cuticle may shed the herbicide or allow only nontoxic levels to penetrate. For instance, glyphosate has been applied to both grassy and broadleaved weeds in a planting of some ornamental ground covers such as juniper with little injury to the plants. This method, however, carries with it considerable risk of damage. It should be attempted only on a trial basis and only by responsible and knowledgeable persons.

Differences in the translocation of various chemicals within plants can result in some selectivity. Some herbicides, such as dicamba, move upward through roots and thus can be used to control shallow-rooted weeds without harm to deeper-rooted plants provided that the herbicide is not leached into the deeper roots by water. Some herbicides move only through foliage to the roots; these can be selectively applied to the foliage of the undesirable plants only. Glyphosate, 2,4-D, and similar herbicides are often used in this manner in shrub borders and flower beds.

Physiological differences in plants also may result in some selectivity. Atrazine, for example, can be used to control weeds selectively in corn because enzyme systems in corn break down the herbicide to nontoxic substances.

BIOLOGICAL CONTROL

Weed scientists are beginning to take a look at the potential of biological methods for the control of weeds. Under certain circumstances, this approach may be feasible although no methods discovered to date can be considered practical in residential or commercial landscape sites.

Insects with a feeding preference for specific weeds seem to hold the best promise. As of 1980, over eighty-five weed-feeding insect species had been introduced into the United States to control forty-three species of weeds under field crop conditions (Andres 1980).

Recent work with plant pathogens has demonstrated their potential in weed control. For instance, a newly discovered race of the fungus *Verticillium dahliae* has been found to attack seedlings of velvetleaf weed (*Abutilon theophrasti*), prevalent in the Midwest (Harvey 1980).

WEED CONTROL IN NONTURF AREAS

Chemical removal of weed from nonturf areas, such as shrub borders, flower beds, and nursery rows, requires careful selection of the herbicide and precise application. First, *you must know what kind of weeds you are trying to control.* If you are dealing with existing perennial and annual weeds, a combination of cultivation and chemical application is generally required to gain acceptable control. Keep in mind, however, that some weeds (such as quackgrass, bindweed, Canada thistle, and purslane) are readily propagated by cultivation. Therefore, you may wish to use chemical methods alone, or a combination of pre-emergent and post-emergent herbicides might be required.

If the weed problem involves mostly existing annuals, cultivation may be all that is needed, or a contact spray followed by cultivation might give best results. Where annual weeds can be anticipated, pre-emergent herbicides will usually give good control.

Most pre-emergent herbicides cannot be applied as a preplant spray; generally they are recommended only for established plantings. For example, diclobenil provides excellent control of many germinating seeds but must be applied only to flower beds or shrub borders where the plants have become established. It is not possible to "plant through" a preplant herbicide barrier without injury to new transplants because the chemical becomes mixed with the soil and in contact with young roots.

Some herbicides used in nonturf plantings are listed in table 8-3 (pre-emergent) and table 8-4 (postemergent).

Currently, there are no soil sterilants recommended for use in landscaped areas. All last too long in the soil and cause injury at very low residual rates to be safe. Keep in mind that roots of trees and shrubs extend well beyond the "drip point." In established plantings,

roots of desirable trees may be present in virtually every square foot of the property. It is also not safe to use sterilants under asphalt or cement, or in gravel areas. Nor is it safe to use them for spot treatment of weeds growing through perforations in black plastic mulches.

CONTROL OF BRUSH, ROOTS, AND TRUNK SPROUTS

Brush control may be necessary in landscaped areas where gregarious woody plant species encroach upon vehicle or pedestrian accesses, turfgrass areas, and landscape structures. Several methods can be used, either singly or in combination to reduce brush encroachment problems. Common methods are brush cutting, cutting and treatment with sprout suppressants, total vegetation control with herbicides, and below-ground root sucker barriers.

Brush Cutting

Simply removing brush with a chain saw rarely produces acceptable control unless followed with sprout suppression treatment because most woody plants will produce stump sprouts following cutting. Many species such as poplar, sumac, tree of heaven, and English elm produce prolific numbers of root sprouts after cutting of the main plant. If, however, the use of chemical suppressants and herbicides is not desirable or practical, brush will need to be cut at least once a year in a way that removes sprouts. This can be done with flail-type mowers with reasonable success. For best results, sprouts should be mowed while young, before they attain large size and have become woody.

Sprout Suppressants

Sprouts from stumps and those from roots can be suppressed with various growth retardants. Most common are formulations containing maleic hydrazide (MH). Epicormic sprouts that form from trunks after pruning are usually suppressed with emulsifiable asphalt pruning paints containing naphthalene acetic acid (NAA). When used at label rates, these materials will slow, but not eliminate, sprouts. Maleic hydrazide should be considered

Table 8-3. Pre-emergent Herbicides for Use in Nonturf Landscaped Areas

Common Name	Trade Names	Dosage (lb active ing. per acre)	Soil Persistence (months)	Uses and Comments
Bensulide	Betasan, Lescosan	10–12	4–6	Crabgrass, poa annua, bulbs.
Dichlobenil	Casoron, Dyclomec, Norosac	5–6	6–12	Perennial and annual grasses and broadleaved weeds. Use two successive years on bindweed and quackgrass. Causes injury to fir, spruce, cotoneaster, viburnum, and most herbaceous plants.
DCPA	Dacthal	10.5–12	3	Annual grasses and some broadleaved weeds. Does *not* control ragweed or mustards. Safe with most woody plants and many herbaceous.
Napropamide	Devrinol	6–10	1–2	Many trees, shrubs, and ground covers. Injurious to bulbs.
Chloropropham	Furloe	6–10	1–2	Chickweed and other *winter* weeds. Applied in fall.
Simazine	Princep	1–3	12+	A long-term control but injures all herbaceous plants and many woody plants. High rates produce sterilant effects. Sometimes used with Dacthal, Devrinol, or Surflan for fall applications. *Avoid use with tree and shrub plantings.*
Oxadiazon	Ronstar, Pro Grow Ornamental Herbicide	4	3	Annual weeds. Does *not* control chickweed. Avoid applying to wet foliage of desirable plants. *Very* injurious to bulbs. Mostly used for container-grown woody plants.
Oryzalin	Surflan	2–4	3	Annual grasses, chickweed, pigweed, and purslane. No incorporation required. *Use on established plantings only.* Potentilla has been shown to be sensitive at the 4-lb rate.
Trifluralin	Treflan	1–4	9+	Often used as a preplant to control annual weeds. Must be incorporated. Shallow cultivation 3 weeks later increases effectiveness.

Table 8-4. Postemergent Herbicides for Use in Nonturf Landscaped Areas

Common Name	Trade Names	Dosage (lb of active ing. per acre)	Soil Persistence (months)	Uses and Comments
Amino-triazole	Amitrol-T, Weedazol, Cytrol	2–11	12 +	Perennials weeds only. Poison ivy. *Spot treat only;* high rates produce soil sterilant effect.
2,4-D	Many	0.25–2	2	Most common postemergent in use for broadleaved weeds. Use amine or low-volatile ester forms to reduce vapor damage.
Dicamba	Banvel	0.5	3–24	For hard-to-kill broadleaved weeds. Spot treat only if used alone. Very detrimental to trees and shrubs. Safest when used in combination at low rates with 2,4-D and MCPP; this is a trimec formulation with synergistic effects.
Dalapon	Dowpon	10–15	None	For grasses. Used to control cattails and some turfgrasses.
Cacodylic acid	Rad-E-Cat 25, Phytar 560	3 gal/acre	None	Weeds around trees. Lawn renovation. Spot treatment.
Fluazifop-butyl	Fusilade	0.125–0.5	<1	Selectively controls annual and perennial grasses in broadleaved plantings.
Glyphosate	Roundup	1 qt/acre for small weeds; 2–3 qt/acre for thistle; 3–4 qt/acre for bindweed	No soil residual	Avoid contact with desirable vegetation, sucker sprouts, and thin- or green-barked trees.

where root sprouts are from nearby desirable trees. Do not use herbicides such as 2,4-D, glyphosate, and ammonium sulfamate in this situation because they will translocate to the source tree and cause injury or death.

Total Vegetation Control

Where total brush and root sucker control is desired and there are no concerns about injury to adjoining plantings, 2,4-D in combination with dicamba is frequently used. Treatment at label rates should be applied to actively growing shoots. A second or even third treatment may be necessary as new sprouts appear.

For sprouts from roots in lawn areas, spot treat with the 2,4-D and dicamba combination.

In nonturf areas, either glyphosate or ammonium sulfamate is effective. Glyphosate tends to react slowly but has the advantage of leaving no toxic residues in the soil.

Ammonium sulfamate is fast-acting but will cause temporary soil sterilization. It should not be used if planting in the treated area is planned within a three-month period following sprout treatment. Glyphosate would be a better alternative. Neither product should be used on sprouts if there is a likelihood that a biological union of roots (natural root grafts) exists between undesirable and adjacent desirable trees of the same species. The chemicals can move to desirable trees through graft unions.

Resist the temptation to use long-term soil sterilants, such as bromacil, prometon, sodium metabolate, and similar materials. While such sterilants will often eliminate sprouts and prevent resprouting for several years, their tendency to migrate to adjoining desirable vegetation can result in serious, costly problems later. The only exceptions might be in industrial sites, such as oil storage "tank farms," equipment storage yards, and electrical substations. Even in these sites, sterilants should not be used near adjoining properties or along drainage systems where desirable vegetation exists.

Root Barriers

To prevent encroachment of sucker-bearing roots of trees, physical barriers can be installed. This is best done before roots grow into the area where sprouting is not desirable. Once sprouting has occurred, severing of roots will usually stimulate even more vigorous sprouts.

The types of barriers that can be used include metal edging, vinyl strips, heavy-mil polyethylene, neoprene, poured cement, and wood. To be effective against root encroachment, edging must be at least 30 inches deep and extend to the soil surface. This makes wood and metal impractical. Plastic or rubber (vinyl, polyethylene, and neoprene) are generally more practical. Polyethylene of 6- to 8-mil thickness is least expensive of the three but may crack with temperature changes. Neoprene and vinyl are expensive but will last indefinitely.

Poured cement in slit trenches might be considered where a wide edging for a mower strip is desired. Cement, however, in addition to being expensive to install, will soon crack. Expansion joints must also be allowed. Both expansion joints and shrinkage cracks provide easy access for suckering roots.

WEED CONTROL IN ASPHALT-PAVED AREAS
Old Pavement

Weeds often invade old pavement by finding places to grow in cracks. As the weeds proliferate, the cracks may become larger and ultimately destroy the pavement.

Spot treatment with glyphosate is effective on most weeds. If weeds do not respond to glyphosate, use a carefully applied mixture of 2,4-D and banvel. Avoid excessive wetting of pavement near weeds, since rain or irrigation water can wash the mixture into desirable vegetation. This is not a problem with glyphosate, however.

Some prefer to apply solvents as contact weed killers. Number two diesel fuel is commonly used. This will give immediate dieback of weeds in pavement but does not kill deep-rooted perennials. Some solvents may also damage the asphalt or the sealant.

Newly Paved Areas

Some weeds, such as field bindweed (*Convolvulus arvensis*), quackgrass (*Agropyron repens*), and bluebells (*Campanua* spp.), frequently break through newly paved areas if not completely removed before asphalt is applied (fig. 8-4). Bindweed and quackgrass will also quickly invade the edges of a paved area, causing cracking. For these reasons, many paving contractors apply herbicides before laying the asphalt. Unfortunately, it is common for contractors to use long-term soil sterilants, such as bromacil, prometon, and ureabor. This practice should be avoided in landscaped areas because roots of trees will eventually grow into the treated area, resulting in injury or death.

Chemical barriers much safer than sterilants are available and labeled for this purpose. Included are dichlobenil and trifluralin. These herbicides do not translocate into tree roots but do inhibit growth of roots and shoots of weeds. They must be applied shortly before paving to avoid loss of the fumes that act as a barrier to weed growth. To be effective, pavement must be a minimum of 2 inches thick and firmly rolled.

Figure 8-4. **Bindweed (*Convolvulus arvensis*) breaking through this asphalt can be prevented with chemical barriers applied before paving. (Courtesy Eugene B. Eyerly, Eyerly and Associates)**

Where economically feasible, a neoprene or vinyl barrier can also be installed in trenches adjoining pavement. The barrier should be sealed against the pavement with a bituminous material, such as that used to surface-seal asphalt pavement. The barrier depth will vary with the type of weeds involved. For quackgrass and bindweed, a minimum of 30 inches is required. For most other weeds, a 24-inch-deep strip is sufficient.

HERBICIDE ACCIDENTS

Herbicides, more than any other chemicals used in the landscape, have resulted in serious damage to plantings. Much of this is caused by misapplication, improper dilution, and poor handling practices. Most damage from herbicides can be avoided by proper training and supervision of the applicators. Accidents do happen however, and when they do, prompt appropriate action is necessary. The type of action to be taken will depend upon the chemical involved, concentration of the chemical, the nature of the accident, and the type or types of plants involved.

Herbicide accidents usually involve drift onto or accidental overspray of desirable vegetation or spillage or overdose to soil in the root zone of desirable plants.

Drift and Accidental Overspray

In the case of drift or accidental overspray, prompt rinsing of affected plants with water will often reduce or even prevent damage. If the herbicide has an oil base, use some detergent in the water, then rinse thoroughly with plain water.

Contact herbicides, such as Paraquat, petroleum solvents, and oils, will usually produce damage immediately. Rinsing plants with water, therefore, will not prevent all damage. The extent of plant injury will vary with concentration of the chemical and temperature.

Herbicides that translocate into foliage, such as 2,4-D and glyphosate, may not result in damage if foliage is quickly rinsed with water.

Spills or Overdoses to Soil

Areas in which herbicides have been overapplied to the soil or accidentally spilled in concentrated form can be treated in several ways depending upon the chemical type and circumstances.

Small Areas

If a spill occurs in an area less than 100 square feet, prompt removal of the contaminated soil is the best and most economical method to prevent future damage. Soil that is removed should be placed in drums with tight-fitting lids, labeled, and then disposed of according to local codes.

Large Areas

Contaminated areas over 100 square feet are treated according to the type of chemical involved and the proximity of desirable vegetation.

Spillages or overdoses of herbicides, such as 2,4-D in turfgrasses, are usually flushed or diluted with heavy applications of water. If dicamba is being used alone or as a mixture, flushing the soil with water can lead to injury to trees whose roots are present in the turfgrass area. Normal irrigation is advised in this situation rather than attempting to wash the herbicide below the root zone of trees.

Where spillage or overapplication involves soil sterilants *do not apply water*. Water will tend to move the chemical into previously uncontaminated soil and increase potential plant damage.

Obtain information from the chemical manufacturer on steps to follow in solving a particular soil contamination problem. Products that are organically based can often be treated with activated charcoal. The charcoal does not deactivate the chemical but adsorbs it, preventing uptake by plant roots. If the product is an inorganic salt, activated charcoal will not work. Soil removal may be the only alternative.

PLANT INJURY REDUCTION AFTER STERILANT APPLICATIONS

Landscape managers, nurserymen, and landscape contractors are frequently faced with planting in areas previously contaminated with soil sterilants, or they may encounter chemical injuries to trees and shrubs adjacent to areas treated with soil sterilants. The problem, in fact, is more common than might be realized.

Studies by Feucht (1981a, b; 1985) between 1969 and 1984 uncovered over 100 herbicide injury cases in the metropolitan Denver area. The herbicides involved were mostly soil sterilants applied beneath asphalt or on gravel roads. The two most common ingredients were bromacil (Hyvar X and XL) and prometon (Pramitol 25E and Triox). In many cases, the property owner or landscape manager was unaware of the presence of soil sterilants and passed off the problem as drought injury, iron chlorosis, or a pathogenic disease.

When planting in new areas near or through asphalt, be suspicious of possible sterilant contamination of soils beneath asphalt, whether it be a parking lot, driveway, or jogging path. If possible, check records with the paving company to determine when and what kind of chemical might have been used. If a soil sterilant has been used, the following procedure is recommended:

1. Collect soil samples from areas to be planted or adjacent to treated pavement at several depths down to at least 24 inches. This is particularly important when installing tree planting pits in previously paved parking lots.
2. Collect soil samples from adjacent areas not suspected of contamination.
3. Put soil samples in clean 6-inch-diameter pots. Tamp lightly and plant three to five each of ordinary garden bean and corn seeds.
4. Moisten soil in pots, but do not apply so much water that it drains out the bottom.
5. Loosely cover pot surfaces with newspaper and place them in a warm location away from direct sunlight.
6. After five days, check the pots. If sprouts appear, remove paper and move to stronger light. Moisten lightly if needed.
7. Check daily after the fifth day. Seeds may begin to germinate even in strongly contamined soil but will cease activity after another few days to a week. Compare with those in uncontaminated soil.

If beans fail to grow but the corn does, the contaminant may be a triazine-type chemical, such as atrazine. If nothing grows or seedlings become stunted or off-color, the contaminant is more likely to be a total vegetation control chemical—bromacil, ureabor, or a similar product. If soil appears to be contaminated, remove soil from the area to be planted, install barriers around the planting pit as described below, and replace with good soil.

When damage already exists in plants, the following procedure can help to prevent further damage:

1. Dig a slit trench about 30 inches deep between affected plants and area of contamination. This serves to sever roots that may be translocating the injurious chemical.
2. Place a plastic or a neoprene barrier vertically in the trench and backfill with good soil or gravel. If slope is such that the chemical contaminant can move with surface runoff into the planting area, seal the barrier to landscape ties or other suitable edging.
3. Conduct tests as previously described to ascertain identity of the chemical.
4. Avoid heavy irrigation in the area of contamination. If appropriate, apply activated charcoal to soils with widespread surface contamination. (This is particularly helpful at edges of driveways and jogging paths.)

In situations where damage claims are being made either through litigation or an insurance company, laboratory tests will be necessary. The tests are expensive, so it is very important to identify the type of chemical involved, if possible, before testing is done.

REFERENCES

Andres, L. A. 1980. Biological control of weeds. Weeds Today, Spring:3.

Beste, C. E. 1983. Herbicide Handbook. Champaign, IL: Weed Society of America.

Feucht, J. R. 1981a. How to detect soil sterilant damage in ornamental trees and shrubs. Am. Nurseryman 158(2):9.

———. 1981b. Misapplication of soil sterilants can damage desirable plants. Grounds Maint. 16(5):48–50.

———. 1985. Diagnosing damage from landscape chemical use. Am. Nurseryman 162(5):92–96.

Harvey, R. G. 1980. Fungus may control velvetleaf. Agrichemical Age, February:24A.

9.

Starting a Turf

Paying close attention to details when establishing a turf can help to ensure a good-quality lawn that is reasonably easy to keep. A few hours spent on planning before planting can be worth thousands of hours in future maintenance. Essential to getting and keeping a good turf are the choice and use of good grasses, knowledge of the site, and proper soil preparation, planting, and postplanting procedures.

GRASSES FOR LAWNS

The decision on which grass to grow is one of the most important that a grounds manager will make. The future quality of the turf and the amount of care that it will require depends upon the grass planted. Lawn grasses are perennial. Once planted, except for over-seedings, they are in for a lifetime. The great increase in species and cultivars within species available for turfgrass uses has given the professional landscape manager valuable tools but has made decisions on what to use more difficult. Currently, there are about fifty cultivars of Kentucky bluegrass (*Poa pratensis*), perennial ryegrass (*Lolium perenne*), and fine fescue (*Festuca* spp.) commercially available. Some species, such as

buffalograss (*Buchloe dactyloides*) and centipedegrass (*Eremochloa ophiuroides*), have very few cultivars available.

Several characteristics need to be considered when choosing grasses for turf sites. For one site, tolerance to drought, cold, and salt tolerance may be of utmost importance, while for another site, performance at low cut and shade tolerance may be major concerns.

The map of turfgrass zones of adaptation in figure 9-1 shows the general climatic adaptation of some commonly grown turfgrasses. It is not possible to refine the map sufficiently to take into account microclimatic influences of mountains, valleys, and large bodies of water on turfgrass adaptation. Further complications exist because different cultivars of the same grass species have different abilities to adapt to adverse conditions. For example, 'Manhattan' and 'Diplomat' have more cold hardiness than common and 'Linn' perennial ryegrass. Perennial ryegrasses have also performed rather well along the Front Range in Colorado, where it gets quite cold.

Most turfgrasses in the southern United States are warm-season grasses that show maximum growth under warm to hot conditions, the foliage becoming brown during cold weather. Northern or cool-season grasses grow best at cool temperatures, and they remain green until it becomes quite cold. Some exceptions to this are buffalograss and blue grama (*Bouteloua gracilis*),

This chapter was written by Dr. Jack Butler, Professor, Turfgrass, Department of Horticulture, Colorado State University.

■	Cool/Cold	Kentucky Bluegrass
		Perennial Ryegrass
		Fine Fescues
		Tall Fescue
		Bentgrass
▨	Transition	Tall Fescue
		Zoysiagrass
		Bermudagrass
▧	Warm/Hot	Zoysiagrass
		Bermudagrass
		Bahiagrass
		St. Augustinegrass
		Centepedegrass

Figure 9-1. Adaptation zones of common turfgrasses in the United States and southern Canada.

which are warm-season grasses found growing quite far north. Cool-season grasses such as perennial and Italian ryegrass (*Lolium multiflorum*) and rough bluegrass (*Poa trivialis*) are sometimes used for overseeding warm-season grass in the south. The cool-season grasses remain green and growing during cool/cold weather, when the warm-season grasses are dormant and brown.

When selecting grasses, it is wise to go with the predominant turfgrasses grown in an area. To select grasses because of national publicity could lead to difficulties. Selection of grasses to be grown at a particular site is best done by looking at performance data gathered close by and visiting with seed suppliers, garden center operators, extension horticulturists, and other local people who are familiar with turf developments.

Cool-Season Turfgrasses
Kentucky Bluegrass

The most common turfgrasses in the northern, cool regions of the United States are Kentucky bluegrass cultivars. Kentucky bluegrass has underground stems (rhizomes) that form excellent sod (fig. 9-2). It is therefore a favorite with sod growers, since it can be successfully lifted without netting. It will also regrow from rhizomes left after harvest. Some commercial sod fields that are harvested have not been seeded for ten years. As a rule, Kentucky bluegrass tolerates drought well, although it may go dormant and turn brown under extended stress. This grass can, if necessary, be mowed fairly low and still maintain good density.

Many exceptionally high-quality cultivars of Kentucky bluegrass area available. These have been selected and introduced into the trade because of certain outstanding characteristics. Two traits that have been sought have been tolerance to low cut and resistance to diseases, especially melting out. Virtually all of the newer cultivars have good density. There has been a tendency to select cultivars of coarser texture (wider leaves). Color varies greatly among cultivars (genetic difference). Color also can vary greatly with location and management (environmental difference). In the end, satisfaction with different cultivars will depend upon the quality of turf needed and management practices. Planting a cultivar and then mismanaging it will lead to dissatisfaction. For

Figure 9-2. Rhizomes in Kentucky bluegrass form dense, durable sod. (Courtesy O. M. Scott & Sons)

example, 'Merion' requires relatively large amounts of nitrogen to produce a high-quality turf. With poor maintenance, its appearance will likely not be as good as common Kentucky bluegrass.

Fine Fescues

Several different kinds of fescues have fine texture. Those most commonly used for turf are hard, chewings, creeping, and spreading fescues. The former two are bunch grasses, while the latter two spread by rhizomes. In recent years, many cultivars of fine fescue have been introduced. The hard fescues have become important turfgrasses since the early 1970s. Turf-type cultivars available include 'Biljart' and 'Scaldis.' Another, 'Durar,' is used for revegetation of hostile sites.

Fine fescues, as a rule, tolerate poor and droughty soils, cold temperatures, and deep shade quite well. Conversely, they do not tolerate heavy fertilization, overwatering, and wet sites. The fine fescues are seldom planted alone. Normally they are mixed with other, finer-textured, cool-season turfgrasses.

Perennial Ryegrass

For a long time, perennial ryegrasses were considered to be "nurse grasses." That is, they would establish rapidly, to be replaced in a few growing seasons by more permanent grasses, such as Kentucky bluegrass. The lack of longevity, as well as poor mowing quality and lack of good density, still persists in common and a very few of the named cultivars of perennial ryegrass. In order to differentiate between poor- and high-quality cultivars, the term *turf-type* was introduced. Turf-type cultivars generally are better than those not so designated. However, the turf-type designation does not mean that a particular perennial ryegrass cultivar is the best for a particular site.

Perennial ryegrasses are bunch grasses and establish rapidly from seed. With good growing conditions, perennial ryegrass seed requires only a few days to produce a large, vigorous seedling. This grass is quite drought and salt tolerant, and the turf-types can be cut low. A major use of perennial ryegrass has been for renovating existing, but poor-quality, Kentucky bluegrass and annual bluegrass turf. Also, because of their fast, vigorous

start, these grasses are frequently mixed with other grasses to provide fast cover for erosion control.

A major concern with perennial ryegrass is its lack of tolerance to cold temperature. Of the common cool-season turfgrasses grown in the northern United States, perennial ryegrass is the least cold tolerant. In order to offset the lack of good cold tolerance, perennial ryegrasses are usually planted in combination with other, more hardy, cool-season grasses. In more moderate climates, for example, west of the Cascades and in the Bay Area, stands that are predominantly perennial ryegrass are planted.

Annual or Italian Ryegrass

Coarse-textured annual ryegrass is often found as a major component of inexpensive seed mixtures. The name annual ryegrass is, under most conditions, a misnomer, since grasses sold as annual ryegrass may be found growing several years after planting. Because of this, another common name, Italian ryegrass, would generally be a better designator. In some instances Italian ryegrass is seeded to provide quick cover. Since Italian ryegrass is so dominant and frequently persists as a weed in fine-textured turf, it often is better to plant turf-type perennial ryegrass to provide higher-quality quick cover.

Bentgrasses

Creeping bentgrass (*Agrostis palustris*), colonial bentgrass (*Agrostis tenuis*), and redtop (*Agrostis alba*) are sometimes planted for turf. Redtop, once used extensively as a nurse crop for lawns, is now primarily used for revegetation and pasture on acid soils. Creeping bentgrass is widely used for golf course greens, tennis courts, and lawn bowling courts. Colonial bentgrass is occasionally used for home lawns and golf course fairways and tees.

Creeping and colonial bentgrass are stolon-forming grasses and require high maintenance to produce high-quality turf. Winter and summer drought problems, as well as serious pest outbreaks, are common in bentgrass. Seed, stolons, and sod of creeping bentgrass are commercially available. Although seed of creeping and colonial bentgrass are sometimes mixed, they are seldom used with other kinds of cool-season turfgrasses. Under most growing and maintenance conditions, a very low percentage of bentgrass in a mixture will allow it to dominate a stand in a very short time.

Bentgrass golf course greens have been planted farther and farther into the southern United States, primarily because the alternative, bermudagrass (*Cynodon* spp.), is a warm-season grass. The development of pesticides to control certain hot weather diseases, such as pythium blight, and annual grasses, especially goosegrass and crabgrass, has made bentgrass a bit easier to keep under adverse weather conditions.

Tall Fescue

Tall fescue (*Festuca arundinacea*) is widely used for roadsides, pastures, and athletic turf. Tall fescue is often used on industrial and institutional grounds and on home lawns. Although tall fescue is widely adapted, it is most commonly grown in the southern part of the cool/cold zone and in the transition zone (see fig. 9-1).

Older pasture-type cultivars, such as 'Alta' and 'Fawn,' are coarse-textured, tall-growing bunch grasses, which are usually not very dense. These grasses were first planted as turf where high-quality grasses were not required. Gradually the desire for a better turf led to increased management intensity; consequently, the need arose for higher-quality turf-type tall fescues. 'Rebel' and late cultivars, such as 'Falcon,' 'Olympic,' and 'Adventure,' were developed. These are fine-textured, dense, and low-growing bunch grasses. The very slow spread of these bunch grasses after being thinned by traffic, drought, pests, or chemical damage is an important consideration in making grass selections. Sometimes sod-forming grasses, such as Kentucky bluegrass, and pasture-type sod-forming grasses, such as smooth bromegrass (*Bromus inermis*), are planted with tall fescue. Whether or not other grasses will persist when planted with the more vigorous tall fescues depends on seeding rates and postplant care.

Blends

Blends contain two or more cultivars of the *same* species. They are widely available as both seed and sod for cool-season grasses, especially Kentucky bluegrass. The reason that grasses are blended is to provide a diverse population of plants. In most instances, the blended cultivars vary in resistance or tolerance to certain diseases and insects, shade and drought, and other environmental conditions. The advantages of seeding a blend of Kentucky bluegrass cultivars (often four to seven) are greater than the advantages gained by seeding a blend of creeping bentgrass because a very high percentage of Kentucky bluegrass seed develop true to type (have the traits of the parent plant), whereas with creeping bentgrass, individual seeds often develop plants with texture, color, and density quite different from the parent.

The potential turf quality of blends is essentially the same as that of a single cultivar. In fact, because of their broader genetic base, it may be easier to keep blends looking better. As a rule, commercial turfgrass blends are put together on a weight basis. This may not result in the desired populations, since the number of seed per pound varies greatly among cultivars. For example, 'Merion' has about 2 million seed per pound, while 'Baron' has about 1 million seed.

Selecting cultivars to put in a blend can be difficult. One approach that would seem reasonable would be to put together cultivars that do best in the area.

Mixtures

Mixtures, which consist of two or more *different species* of turfgrass, are available as seed and sod. Mixtures of grasses would be expected to be even less prone to pests and environmental stress problems than single-cultivar or blend plantings. Under good growing conditions, the potential turf quality of a mixture is not as high as that for single cultivars or blends, but under adverse growing conditions and low levels of management, mixtures would be expected to produce better turf.

Blue–rye–fescue (Kentucky bluegrass, perennial ryegrass, and fine fescue) mixtures are common. Also, Kentucky bluegrass–perennial ryegrass and perennial ryegrass–fine fescue mixtures are common in certain areas. Selecting the best species, and especially cultivars, to mix can be difficult. Selecting grasses that do well in the area and keeping the amounts of the slow-starting (usually small-seeded) and most desired grass(es) at higher percentages in a mix seem appropriate. Under most conditions, if perennial ryegrass exceeds 15 to 20 percent of a mix, it tends to dominate the stand.

Warm-Season Turfgrasses
Bermudagrass

Bermudagrasses are to the southern United States what Kentucky bluegrasses are to the north. They are widely grown for high- and low-quality turf under a wide range of soil and climatic conditions. Bermudagrass, like Kentucky bluegrass, is a natural invader of maintained and unmaintained sites. Its ability to spread and dominate makes bermudagrass a serious landscape weed.

Normally, bermudagrass spreads by both rhizomes and stolons. It is commercially available for vegetative planting and as seed. The improved "hybrid" bermudagrasses are vegetatively planted.

Bermudagrasses have poor shade and cold tolerance. They do, however, withstand a low cut, drought, and salty conditions in addition to having outstanding wear tolerance.

As a rule, the improved cultivars such as 'Tifgreen,' 'Tifgreen II,' and 'Tifdwarf' require high levels of maintenance to do well. Common bermudagrass does fairly well at low levels of maintenance. It is a major revegetation grass, and with fairly high maintenance, bermudagrass produces high-quality lawns and golf course fairways.

Zoysiagrasses

Three different species of zoysiagrass are used for turf. Of these, *Zoysia japonica* has the widest distribution and tolerates the most diverse climatic conditions. *Z. japonica* seed is available, but it is rather difficult to establish. *Z. japonica,* 'Meyer' ('Z-52'), the common zoysiagrass in the transition zone and in the north, is vegetatively planted. 'Emerald' and 'Matrella' are finer textured and lower growing than 'Meyer.' 'Emerald' and *Z. japonica* stand up to moderate drought stress quite well. Zoysiagrasses tend to have thatch problems. Good management is therefore needed to keep high-quality turf.

St. Augustinegrass

A coarse-textured grass widely used for turf in the southern, humid areas of the United States is St. Augustinegrass (*Stenotaphrum secundatum*). It has good shade, heat, and drought tolerance, but its cold and wear tolerance are poor. St Augustinegrass has long runners that require a great deal of edging in landscape situations. St. Augustinegrass will develop a deep thatch; therefore, maintenance to avoid problems associated with thatch is needed. St. Augustinegrass is propagated only vegetatively. 'Raleigh' is considered to be more cold tolerant than other St. Augustinegrass cultivars.

Bahiagrass

Bahiagrass (*Paspalum notatum*) is a tall-growing, slow-spreading drought-tolerant grass that is used for low-maintenance turf, primarily in the southeastern United States. This grass does not tolerate a short cut well, and it is difficult to get a clean cut on bahiagrass turf. 'Pensacola' is a frequently grown cultivar. This and other cultivars are primarily grown from seed, although some sod is produced.

Centipedegrass

Centipedegrass is propagated primarily by sprigging or seeding. This grass produces a low-growing, dense, low-maintenance turf. It does not have good cold tolerance and is not especially traffic tolerant. 'AU Centennial' is a new dwarf fine-textured cultivar developed in Alabama.

Buffalograss

Buffalograss, a native grass with a very wide range of adaptation in the central and high plains areas of the United States, grows well in drier areas from the Mexican to the Canadian borders. Although this grass is sometimes vegetatively planted, it is more often propagated with seed. Seeding is best done in the spring.

Buffalograss may be quite slow to start under natural, normally dry conditions. With irrigation, this grass establishes fairly rapidly, and its strong runners can cover good-sized bare areas in a short time. Buffalograss is sometimes mixed with blue grama for revegetating hostile sites.

SITE CONDITIONS AND SOIL PREPARATION

Often site conditions are naturally suitable for growing good turf. In areas where heavy equipment has not been used and the site is reasonably undisturbed, the existing topsoil may be well suited to turfgrasses. The cutting and filling often associated with construction of turf areas may, however, greatly diminish existing soil quality.

On-site inspection to determine soil characteristics should be done before construction begins if at all possible. In some instances, especially for large sites, soil maps may be available at Soil Conservation Service and/or Cooperative Extension offices. These can be quite helpful in planning on-site soil utilization.

Soil Stockpiling

Salvaging and stockpiling topsoil to recap shaped areas is common practice on large areas and also can be successfully accomplished on small sites. Occasionally on small sites the purchase of good soil for capping may be feasible. Salvaging soil down to the point where it begins to change color or to where rocks are evident is some assurance that the best is saved. In some instances, better soil is put into piles separate from poorer soils (those containing more clay, gravel, etc.) so that it can be used where there will be more traffic or where higher-quality plant material is desired. Capping a shaped area to a depth of about 6 inches is recommended, but lesser depths are better than no capping and growing directly on subsoil or rock. Compacted and clay soils should be ripped or disked before capping to reduce possible interface problems (see chapter 4).

Soil Physical Amendments

In order to improve water percolation and rooting, soils may be amended, as discussed in chapter 2. In heavy soils, organic amendments are often used because they tend to cause fewer problems than sand and most other materials. Sand mixed with clay, unless in very large proportions, can form an adobe that is very hard to manage. Spreading 1 to 2 inches (3 to 6 cubic yards per 1000 square feet) of a good organic material on the surface and then rototilling, disking, or otherwise thoroughly mixing it into the top 7 to 8 inches of soil should improve soil tilth. A good-quality peat is the preferred organic material, although other materials such as sawdust, nut hulls, or shredded bark are sometimes used. Organic materials can also improve coarse, sandy soils by increasing their mineral- and water-holding capacity.

Grading, Contouring, and Drainage

Turf areas depend greatly on surface runoff for drainage. By grading and shaping for positive surface drainage, many turf problems can be avoided. Surfaces with 1 to 2 percent slope are usually fairly easy to keep. Flatter surfaces tend to pond water; steeper slopes tend to be droughty. In the long run, contouring or otherwise flattening steep slopes will pay big dividends in reduced maintenance costs. Where tile, tube, or utility line trenching has been done, special practices, such as flooding or power tamping, should be performed to ensure against later settling. Correction of major drainage problems after turf establishment is difficult and expensive.

In some areas, subsurface drainage using tube or tile may be advisable. In areas where severe drainage problems exist, catch basins and sump pumps may be needed. Because of the complexity of serious drainage problems, it is always wise to work with someone who is knowledgeable in drainage engineering.

After final grading, but before the soil is worked for planting, the site should be checked for potential problems. Use a soil probe or shovel to determine topsoil depth and detect the presence of large rocks or other surface obstructions. A level or transit can be used to check for low spots. If soils are crusted with salts, then measures to correct for poor drainage probably are necessary.

Debris Removal

Before final soil preparation, debris such as rocks and tree roots should be removed from the area. When sod is taken out to put in a new turf, it is often best to remove the old sod before working the soil. If the lawn area is thatchy, rototilling or disking usually does little to shred and bury the thatch.

After the soil is worked, rocks larger than 1 inch in diameter should be removed with a mechanical rock picker or by hand. Removal of rocks only from the surface does not ensure against future problems. Buried rocks tend to interfere with mechanical aerators. Where frost heaving is a problem, large, deeply buried rocks can heave and break irrigation lines. They can also cause mowing problems, especially when a mower is set too low.

Controlling Weeds

Perennial, coarse-textured grasses often cause trouble in fine turfgrass stands. In many instances, such undesirable grasses establish, along with the desired turfgrass, because of residual plant material or seed in the soil. In some instances, before planting golf greens and sometimes even sod fields, fumigation with methyl bromide, metam-sodium (Vapam), or other chemicals is done to destroy weeds and weed seed. Because of the cost and difficulty of using these chemicals, fumigation generally is restricted to small areas where exceptionally high quality turf is required.

Treatment of weedy grasses with glyphosate (Roundup, Kleenup) should be done well before planting, so that the chemical can translocate throughout the plant and achieve total plant kill. This is normally an effective and fairly inexpensive way of killing potentially troublesome weeds. Working the soil periodically before planting, especially in dry areas, can also help reduce future weed problems.

Working the Soil

To form a good planting medium, the soil must be worked. Serious turf-growing problems often result from planting on fine-textured, compacted soils, caused by traffic during wet conditions. Working the soil well, so that air and water can readily penetrate it, will allow for faster and deeper rooting by newly planted turf. In addition, there will be less runoff and erosion, since porous soils take water rapidly, at least for a while, after rain or irrigation commences.

In order to create a good planting bed, the soil cannot be too wet or dry while being worked. As a rule, the soil should be worked to provide a surface that has clods of soil no more than 1 inch in diameter. In properly worked soil, footprints should be about 1 inch deep. On overworked and compacted soils, irrigation or rain water will tend to cause washouts. If the soil is too soft, there will be a tendency for equipment rutting, resulting in a permanent roughness of the turf area.

Soil Testing

Soil sampling for analysis should be done as soon as possible after the growing media is known. Testing soil from an area before shaping and amending could provide misleading information. However, soil tests from stockpiles of soil saved for capping or from an area just before working can help improve results, as well as save money.

When sampling soils prior to planting, a sampling depth of 6 to 7 inches is suitable. It is important to realize that the value of a soil test depends on the effort that goes into sampling. A composite of several small samples taken from each area to be tested will help ensure that the soil analysis is representative of the entire area. Areas that are noticeably different or that can or will be fertilized differently (turf on either side of a highway or that on a slope versus that on flat ground) should be tested separately. Soil test bags and information sheets to accompany the soil to the testing laboratory are usually available at Cooperative Extension offices and at county, state, and commercial soil-testing facilities.

Soil pH Problems
Reducing Acidity

Liming is commonly done to reduce acid in soils. An ideal time to lime is prior to working the soil, since liming materials can then be thoroughly and deeply mixed into the soil. Liming is done to raise the soil pH so that essential mineral elements will be more available to the turf. Table 9-1 gives approximate amounts for various soil types.

Soil tests can be used to determine precise lime needs. However, in the areas of the United States

Table 9-1. Approximate Amounts of Finely Ground Limestone Required to Raise the pH of Top 7 Inches of Soil to 6.5[a] (in lb/1000 ft²)

Initial Soil pH	Sands	Loams	Silts and Clays
6.0	25	35	50
5.5	60	70	90
5.0	80	115	160
4.5	115	150	180

a. Desirable for Kentucky bluegrass, perennial ryegrass, and bermudagrass.

where acid soils are common, general recommendations call for 50 to 75 pounds of ground limestone per 1000 square feet mixed to a depth of 4 to 6 inches during planting bed preparation.

Reducing Alkalinity

The pH of a soil may be lowered with sulfur and sulfuric acid. In a carbonate-free clay soil with a pH of 8.5, it would take about 70 pounds of sulfur per 1000 square feet in the top 7 inches to lower the pH to about 6.5. Soils in arid and semi-arid regions are frequently high in carbonates, and the amount of sulfur or sulfuric acid required is quite high. Consequently, instead of trying to change the pH in the root zone to make iron more available, direct application of low amounts of iron is more practical. With soil chemical amendments, it is advisable to mix them into the soils as early as possible before seeding.

Using Tolerant Grasses

In certain areas, such as mine spoil sites, where soils are quite acid, and in low areas in arid climates, where soils may be quite alkaline, use of tolerant grasses may help reduce future problems caused by soil pH. As a rule, grasses have a very wide tolerance to acid and alkaline soil conditions. Generally, fine fescue and bentgrass do well on fairly acid soils (pH 5–6), while Kentucky bluegrass and perennial ryegrass do best under slightly acid conditions (pH 6–7). However, these grasses can be found growing and doing fairly well at pH levels of 4.5–8.0. Grasses simply perform better within certain

optimal pH ranges, and the soil can be adjusted to a preferred level with liming and acidifying materials. Additional information on soil pH and ways to adjust it is presented in chapter 2.

Salt Problems

Soil test results in low-precipitation areas routinely report soluble salt levels. Problems associated with salt-laden soils can often be reduced by improving surface and subsurface drainage, as described in chapter 2, or by planting salt-tolerant grasses. Table 9-2 lists the salt tolerances of various grasses.

Starter Fertilizers

Soil tests provide a basis for selecting and using preplant fertilizers. Indeed soil tests are the only valid way to determine what and how much fertilizer needs to be added before planting. Despite this, it is common practice to use various commercial fertilizers without soil testing prior to planting turf. As a general rule, this practice is acceptable, since most disturbed soils tend to be deficient in nitrogen as well as phosphorus and/or potassium.

Table 9-2. Some Salt-tolerant Grasses

Grass Type	Salt Tolerance (mmho/cm)
Alkaligrass	14–18
Alkali sacaton	14–18
Bluegramma	4–8
Brome (smooth)[a]	4–8
Buffalograss[a]	4–8
Fescue (tall)	4–8
Ryegrass (perennial)	8–12
Saltgrass[a]	14–18
Wheatgrass (crested)	4–8
Wheatgrass (slender)	4–8
Wheatgrass (streambank)[a]	4–8
Wheatgrass (tall)	14–18
Wheatgrass (western)	14–18

Source: McNertney-Graves (1983).

a. Sod-forming grass.

In areas where phosphorus levels are known or expected to be deficient, especially for small lawns, superphosphate (20 percent P_2O_5) or triple superphosphate (40 to 50 precent P_2O_5) commonly is added before tilling the soil. One of the reasons for this is that phosphorus fixes and remains near the soil surface when applied to established turf. If potassium availability is likely to be quite low, it can be worked into the soil. Potassium sulfate (50 to 53 percent K_2O) and especially muriate of potash (60 to 62 percent K_2O) are used for soil incorporation to raise potassium levels. Nitrogen fertilizers are applied just ahead of planting because nitrate nitrogen can easily leach from the seedling root zone before being utilized. Slow-release nitrogen fertilizers tend to maintain a better nitrogen level in the soil than fast-release materials. This is especially true if fast-release sources are applied infrequently.

As a rule, complete fertilizers (those that contain significant amounts of nitrogen, phosphorus, and potassium) are used as surface-applied and shallow-incorporated starters for new turf plantings. Normally, the ratio ($N : P_2O_5 : K_2O$) of starter fertilizers is $1 : 2 : 1$ (analysis of 10-20-10) or $1 : 2 : 2$ (10-20-20), although $1 : 1 : 1$ (12-12-12 or 16-16-16) is widely used in some parts of the United States.

It is common for starter fertilizers to be applied at rates to supply 1 to 1½ pounds of nitrogen per 1000 square feet. In terms of actual fertilizer, this means 10 to 15 pounds of 10-10-10 or about 6 to 9 pounds of 16-16-16 per 1000 square feet. Fifty percent or more of the nitrogen may be in a slow-release form.

Starter fertilizers can be harrowed, matted, or otherwise incorporated to a shallow (¼- to ½-in.) depth ahead of seeding. For vegetative planting, starter fertilizers may or may not be required. When using plugs and sprigs, working the fertilizer 1 to 2 inches into the soil can help speed establishment. If using sod, a preplant fertilizer may be unnecessary, since most sod is well fertilized when delivered. If a complete fertilizer is used before laying sod and it is not incorporated into the soil, it can cause root damage. This can be avoided by mixing the starter with some soil, thereby diluting it and reducing the possibility of salt damage from the fertilizer to the roots. Use of fertilizers high in water-insoluble nitrogen also can help reduce salt damage.

TIMES TO PLANT
Cool-Season Grasses

The ideal time to seed cool-season grasses varies greatly throughout their area of adaptation. Generally, the best time to seed is midsummer to midfall. In colder areas, such as along the Front Range in Colorado or in northern Illinois, the last two weeks in August are a good time to plant. In warmer areas, seeding should be delayed into September or early October for better success. In the deep south, overseeding may be done into midfall. Spring seedings are usually less successful than those started later in the year. Excessive rain, cold soils, and severe weed competition cause problems with spring seedings. Grasses not planted at the best time, although often successful, require more care and usually take longer to achieve a good stand. Often it is wise to delay planting from poor times (early summer or late in the year) to times when faster germination and establishment are likely.

Warm-Season Grasses

As a rule, warm-season grasses should be planted in the spring. In cooler areas these grasses should be planted later in the spring than in hotter areas. Spring planting of warm-season grasses allows them to take advantage of the hot summer weather to become well established before cold temperatures occur. Treated buffalograss seed is best planted in the spring, but fall planting works satisfactorily for untreated seed, since winter weather helps overcome seed dormancy.

Overseeding cool-season turfgrasses into warm-season turf is normally delayed until cool, fall weather. Weather conditions warm enough to germinate the seed but cool enough to reduce disease problems and competition from the warm-season grass are desirable.

QUALITY OF PLANTING MATERIALS

As indicated previously, turfgrasses are available as seed, sod, or other vegetative material, although not all species and cultivars are available in all forms. The decision whether to use seed, sod, or other vegetative methods to cover an area is usually based upon the size of area to be covered, the steepness of its slope, the budget available, and the type of turfgrass cover desired.

Before planting an area of turfgrass, the manager should investigate local sources of the grass or grasses desired and calculate costs accordingly. Some turfgrasses, particularly mixes of several species and varieties, are available only as seed. Moreover, use of sod for large areas may be cost prohibitive. On the other hand, sod may be the best way to establish a turfgrass on steep slopes where seed-drilling equipment cannot be used. It is not uncommon to use several methods to establish turfgrasses on the same site, particularly those sites with widely varied soils and topography.

Seed

By taking full advantage of the information available on the seed label (tag), buyers often can avoid potential problems associated with turfgrass seed. The information printed on a typical seed label (fig. 9-3) and what it means is described in the following sections:

Label color: The color of a label may designate seed quality. Certified seed, often spoken of as *blue tag*, gives assurance that records and a history of the seed exist. Inspection of production fields also is done to ensure the quality of certified seed. Gold-tag or sod-quality seed is also available in the trade. Gold tag seed is of very high quality.

Supplier name: A seller or supplier may market only very high quality seed or a wide range of quality for economic reasons. Seed dealers in the business of repeat sales to turfgrass professionals normally make a great effort to have high-quality seed available. Consequently, seed is often worth more if it comes from a vendor with a good reputation.

Kind and cultivar: The kind of seed will be specified on the label. Normally, if the cultivar (variety) is known, it also will be stated.

Lot number and test date: The lot number is assigned by the seed company for record-keeping purposes; the test date is assigned by the seed laboratory. The test date is useful in seed law regulation. It lets a buyer know the age of the seed, and it is some gauge of

seed viability—usually newer seed germinates better than old.

Germination: The germination percentage, determined under specified laboratory conditions in a given time, is an important consideration, but the rate or speed of germination is not listed. Some grass seed, such as buffalograss and bahiagrass, may have a dormancy factor and may not germinate in the given time. In order to determine whether seed are dead or alive and for quick results, a chemical (tetrazolium) test can be done.

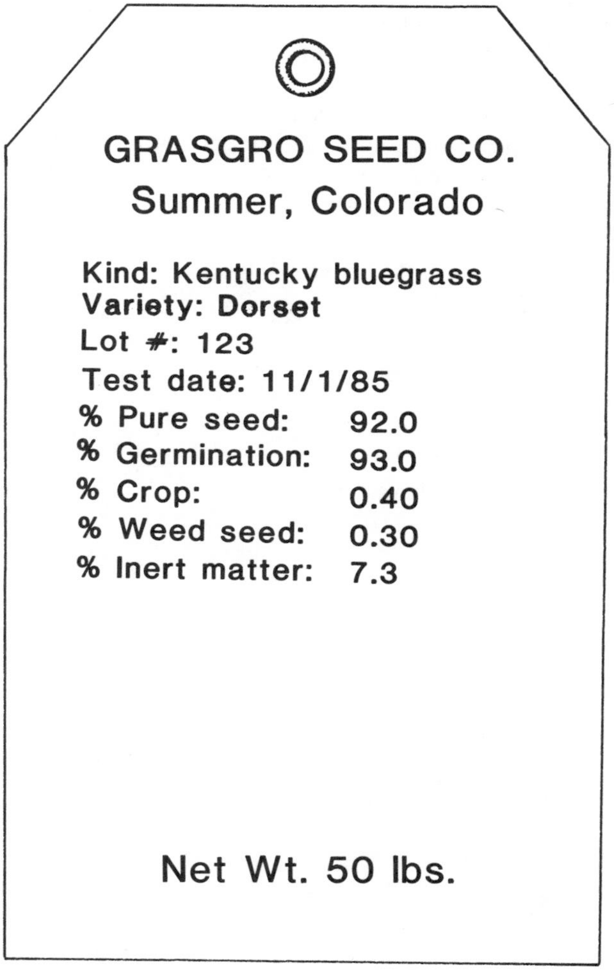

GRASGRO SEED CO.
Summer, Colorado

Kind: Kentucky bluegrass
Variety: Dorset
Lot #: 123
Test date: 11/1/85
% Pure seed: 92.0
% Germination: 93.0
% Crop: 0.40
% Weed seed: 0.30
% Inert matter: 7.3

Net Wt. 50 lbs.

Figure 9-3. Typical seed label.

Pure seed: The percentage of pure seed (purity) is especially useful in determining seeding rates for low-quality seed. Seeding rates may be specified by number of pure live seed (PLS) per square inch or square foot. Pure live seed is calculated by multiplying percentage of purity by percentage of germination. Because most turf seeds have fairly high percentages of purity and germination, seeding rates are given as pounds of seed from the bag or container per 1000 square feet or per acre.

Crop seed: Information on the percentage of crop seed present at first may seem to have little importance, but there are many situations where crop seed would be quite objectionable. A pound of Kentucky bluegrass seed with 1 percent crop (bentgrass) would contain about 80,000 bentgrass seeds; 1 percent tall fescue would contribute 2500 seeds to a pound of Kentucky bluegrass. Either of these crop plant contaminants at this amount would be enough to reduce stand quality greatly.

Weed seed: Seed field weeds may not present much problem, since they often can be mowed, crowded, or sprayed out of a good turf. However, the presence of some weed seed, usually grasses, in turf seed may cause serious and long-lasting problems. Some states have attached severe restrictions on annual bluegrass or other weeds in turf seed. In some instances, because of tolerances established by a state, the number of weed seed of certain species may be stated on the label.

Inert matter: Simply stated, anything in the seed container that will not grow is inert matter. In high-quality turf seed, the amount of inert ingredients is usually low; however, inexpensive seed packages may have chaff, sawdust, or other materials added. A person who does not pay attention to label information may be paying for a great deal of useless inert material.

The label may indicate other information, such as the presence of secondary noxious weeds (by weight and number), hard seed, and dormant seed. When extra-large amounts of seed are being purchased or seed of very high quality is desired, a buyer may want

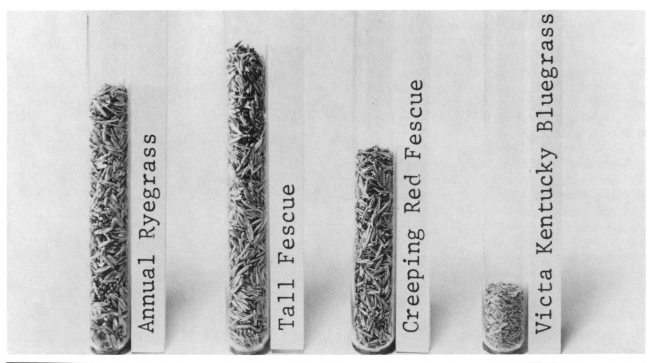

Figure 9-4. Seed of common turfgrasses. Notice the differences in size. (Courtesy O. M. Scott & Sons)

to request a copy of the seed laboratory worksheet for the seed in question. Such sheets provide information on which species constitute the percentage of crop and weed seed. Also, for important turf seed purchases, a larger-than-normal amount of seed could be tested to identify potential problems more thoroughly.

In some instances treated turfgrass seed may be available. Seed may be treated to enhance early germination, for disease control (especially for phythium blight), or for control of soil-inhabiting insects.

Sod and Other Vegetative Materials

Unlike seed, which can be stored satisfactorily for several months, sod and other vegetative material, such as plugs, deteriorate rapidly. Of course, the length of time that vegetative material can be kept depends greatly on temperature and moisture, and somewhat less on the kind of grass and height of cut. Getting vegetative material in place as soon as possible will help ensure success.

Various techniques are used to ensure that vegetative material will be in acceptable condition for planting. These include vacuum cooling, harvesting vegetative material when it is cool and dry, tarping or transporting in closed trucks, avoiding packing in airtight containers, and storing in the shade. The influence of temperature and drying on establishment by vegetative means is so great that delaying planting from July and August until September or October often is wise.

For high-quality turf, the best possible vegetative material available should be used. Some states certify the quality of vegetative material while others provide very little insurance of quality. An errant plant of common bermudagrass in an improved bermudagrass stand would, in sod, likely contaminate only a small spot, but the same plant processed for plugs, sprigs, or stolons could contaminate a large area.

Field inspection of material to be used for vegetative plants and buying from reputable suppliers can help ensure that plant material quality will be suitable.

PLANTING PROCEDURES

Planting at the proper rate and depth are important to successful establishment of turfgrasses. The use of appropriate mulches also can help to ensure good stand development.

Seeding Rates

Recommended seeding rates for turfgrasses vary greatly. In most cases grasses with large seed are planted at heavy rates, and those with small seed are planted fairly lightly. Heavy seeding rates provide no assurance of establishment success, however. Proper seedbed preparation, seeding techniques, and postplanting care are all critical for establishing a suitable stand. Table 9-3 lists the number of seed per pound and planting rates for common turfgrasses.

Dividing seed into two equal portions and then seeding an area twice in two directions helps provide uniform coverage. Although excessively high seeding rates provide more rapid coverage than lower rates, they may not be desirable. The high rates (around 15 to 40 pounds per 1000 square feet) used for overseeding with Italian and perennial ryegrass into established bermudagrass turf in the south keeps this grass in an immature state. The lower rates given in table 9-3 allow the grass seedlings to be less competitive with each other. With less crowding, tillers (side shoots of

Table 9-3. Approximate Seed Numbers and Planting Rates for Commonly Grown Turfgrasses

Kind	No. Seed/lb	Planting Rate[a] (lb/1000 ft^2)	(PLS/in^2)[b]
Kentucky bluegrass	2,000,000	1–2	11–21
Fine fescue	550,000	3–5	9–15
Tall fescue	250,000	4–6	5–8
Perennial and Italian ryegrass	250,000	4–6	5–8
Colonial and creeping bentgrass	8,000,000	1–2	43–85
Bermudagrass	2,000,000	1–2	11–21
Centipedegrass	400,000	2–3	4–6
Bahiagrass	150,000	4–6	3–5
Buffalograss	150,000[c]	1–3	0.8–2.4

a. On large areas, because of better planting techniques, lower rates are commonly used.

b. PLS = pure live seed. Values based upon germination of 85 percent and purity of 90 percent.

c. Equivalent to 40,000 burs.

grass) and rhizome and/or stolon production will occur sooner. Very high seeding rates can also increase the potential for seedling blights and decrease initial rooting to reduce stress resistance.

Planting Rates for Vegetative Material

The amount of vegetative material used and the spacing in the field depends on the kind of grass and allowable time before total ground cover is required. The closer strips of sod, plugs, springs, and stolons are planted, the faster the cover develops. Bermudagrass and St. Augustinegrass can, with good care, spread quickly; zoysiagrass and centipedegrass are slower. Although initially quite slow, plugs of buffalograss, Kentucky bluegrass, and creeping bentgrass spread moderately fast once they are well rooted.

Two-inch or larger round or square plugs of grass can be used to establish sod-forming grasses. The larger the plugs, the proportionately greater amount of live material and the quicker the spread. Placing plugs 6 to 12 inches apart is usually sufficient to achieve a fairly fast cover.

Sprigging is done by placing two-thirds to three-quarters of a grass runner into a slit in the soil. The soil is then packed around the runner with a roller or by walking on the rows. This labor-intensive method of planting wastes less material than stolonizing.

Stolonizing is frequently practiced to propagate improved bermudagrass. Planting rates are usually specified in bushels per 1000 square feet or per acre. A bushel of stolons is produced by shredding 1 square yard of sod. Ten bushels of creeping bentgrass or bermudagrass stolons should be sufficient to plant 1000 square feet for fast cover. For large areas, such as golf course fairways and school grounds, 100 or more bushels of bermudagrass stolons per acre should be sufficient for fairly fast cover. The common practice is to topdress over the stolons with enough material (1/8 to 1/4 inch) to leave only a little of the vegetative material exposed.

Planting Depth

Seeding depths vary with seed size. Grasses with large seed, such as perennial ryegrass with tall fescue, can be planted fairly deep. Those with small seed (bentgrass and Kentucky bluegrass) are best planted at shallow depths. A good seeding depth for Kentucky bluegrass is 1/8 to 1/4 inch.

Seed should be covered with soil or planted into it. The soil forms a protective layer that keeps the seed in place and helps protect seedlings from rapid drying. Rakes, steel mats, spike-tooth harrows (with the teeth flattened), log chains, and chain-link fence can be used to cover broadcast and shallow-placed seed. If seed is to be broadcast or otherwise surface-planted, it is best if the seedbed is left fairly rough. This will allow the seed to fall between the clods, to be covered by soil once the clods disintegrate.

Mulching

Mulches of many different materials (weed products, peat, jute, artificial covers, clippings, straw, or hay) are used on new seedings. Any of these may be used successfully, but their use is no guarantee of a stand. It is important that mulches be applied even and lightly. With most wood and plant materials, it is best if a bit of soil can be seen through the mulch after it is applied. One to two bales of clean straw or hay per 1000 square feet should provide sufficient mulch. Straw or hay can be crimped in with a disk to help keep it in place. Sheet materials can be pegged or weighted down for stabilization. Wetting down mulches as soon as possible after they are used helps keep them in place.

POSTPLANTING CARE

Even the best soil preparation, planting materials, and planting procedures will not result in a high-quality turf in the absence of appropriate postplanting care. Among the most important practices once a turfgrass is planted are watering, mowing, fertilizing, and pest control.

Watering

It is essential that vegetative planting material be watered as soon as possible after planting. During hot, dry weather, allowing vegetative materials to remain dry for an hour or even less can cause significant losses. A lengthy delay in watering vegetative material can make it necessary to replant.

Amount and frequency of watering new stands, of course, depends on weather conditions. As a rule, satisfactory results occur if the soil is watered to be kept moist but not wet. In the spring and fall, this may require two or three waterings a day; in the summer, on bright, windy days, five or six or even more waterings may be needed. As the grass begins to establish two to four weeks after seedlings emerge or vegetative material starts root development, frequency and amounts of irrigation should be decreased.

Mowing

As soon as the grass is tall enough to cut at the desired height, it should be mowed. Early mowings, especially with spring plantings, may be dictated by weed, rather than turfgrass, growth. In spring and summer plantings, it often seems that there are only weeds to mow. Weeds should be kept mowed so that the turfgrasses will be able to get sunlight, and so that the grass foliage will dry, to suppress diseases. Frequently, newly planted stands that look hopelessly weedy in the summer are good stands by late fall or early the next spring.

Lawn mowers should be kept sharp and properly adjusted. A dull or improperly set mower may pull up or mangle seedlings. When mowing new stands, take care not to track soft and wet soils permanently.

Fertilizing

Because of frequent watering and the need to stimulate root and shoot growth, new stands benefit from fertilization soon after planting. Fertilization can be done a couple of weeks after seedlings emerge or new roots develop on vegetative plantings. Even when heavy weed populations develop, fertilizing speeds the development of turf cover. Fertilizers with ratios ($N:P_2O_5:K_2O$) of $2:1:1$ (20-10-10 or 16-8-8) to $1:1:1$ (10-10-10 or 12-12-12) at low rates (to supply around $\frac{1}{2}$ pound of nitrogen per 1000 square feet) should be satisfactory.

Fertilizers, especially on young, tender grass, should be watered in as soon as possible. For a good turf, fertilize with a starter or maintenance-type fertilizer every two weeks at light rates until the turf is well established. Fertilizers that contain slow-release nitrogen can be applied less frequently and at heavier rates.

Pest Control

Pests, especially weeds, often cause newly planted turfgrass problems. Seedling grasses are quite tender, and vegetatively planted grasses need to develop an extensive root system as soon as possible to support shoot growth. With this in mind, it is evident that pesticides should be used cautiously on new turf plantings. Most pesticide labels do not give specific information for use of the material on new plantings. If in doubt about using a chemical on young turf, ask the supplier or company technical service representative.

A few herbicides may be safe, if used properly, on newly seeded grass. One that can be used just following seeding of Kentucky bluegrass, fescues, and perennial ryegrasses is siduron (Tupersan). This chemical can work satisfactorily to control several annual grasses and even some broadleaf weeds in spring seedings. Sod and plugs, because of their maturity, tend to tolerate many herbicides better than seedling grasses. Even grasses that are quite tolerant to 2,4-D when they are mature do not tolerate 2,4-D as seedlings. As a rule, do not use 2,4-D until tolerant grasses have been mowed a few times. Some pre-emergent turfgrass herbicides restrict root development; consequently, use of such materials should be delayed until newly planted turf becomes established.

REFERENCES

Beard, J. B. 1973. Turfgrass Science and Culture. Englewood Cliffs, NJ: Prentice-Hall.

Daniel, W. H., and Freeborg, R. P. 1979. Turf Managers' Handbook. Cleveland: Harvest Publishing Co.

Hanson, A. A., and Juska, F. V. 1969. Turfgrass Science. Monograph 14. Madison, WI: American Society of Agronomy.

Madison, J. H. 1971. Practical Turfgrass Management. New York: Van Nostrand Reinhold Co.

McNertney-Graves, M. 1983. Ornamentals and their salt tolerance. Grand Junction, CO: Misc. Publ. Colorado State University Extension Service, Tri River Area.

Turgeon, A. J. 1980. Turfgrass Management. Reston, VA: Reston Publishing Co.

10. 🌿

Maintaining a Turf

In most landscape situations, the most costly expense is turf maintenance. Although large amounts of money go into turf management, it often does not receive the critical attention to detail that it deserves. Significant savings and turf quality improvements are frequently possible with some rather simple management changes. Broad-based maintenance calendars or general recommendations need to be questioned. Turf management practices need to be developed to meet the specific needs of individual facilities.

Keeping turf suitable to meet specific site requirements is the mark of a professional grounds superintendent. Managing turf to meet needs is usually possible if close attention is given to routine practices such as fertilization, mowing, irrigation and to certain other practices, including pest control and aeration, as the situation requires.

FERTILIZATION

Adequate fertilization helps produce an attractive, dense stand of grass. Frequently the many benefits of fertilization, such as improved density and wearability and reduced pest problems, are overlooked, and resources are directed toward mowing and irrigation. In many cases better turf could be obtained by increasing expenditures on fertilization and reducing expenditures elsewhere.

This chapter was written by Dr. Jack Butler, Professor, Turfgrass, Department of Horticulture, Colorado State University.

Soil Testing

Soil testing is a valuable management tool for landscape managers. For soil tests to be of much value, representative soil samples must be obtained. Local and regional soil testing laboratories normally test for soil pH and nutrients that are likely to be deficient. Some laboratories may report only pH and phosphorus and potassium levels. Other laboratories, especially in dry areas, may report these plus soluble salts, iron, manganese, calcium, and other elements.

Test results can provide sound information for developing turf fertilization programs. For example, if the levels of some nutrients are high, it is probably unnecessary to add more of these; it would be better to shift emphasis and spend the money on other nutrients that are in short supply. It is possible to generalize that adequate potassium is available in drier climates, that older turf that has been fertilized regularly is growing on soil containing adequate to high amounts of available phosphorus, and that alkaline soils have low amounts of available iron. The validity of these statements in a particular situation can be determined by a soil test.

Turf Nutrient Requirements

Many different specialty turf fertilizers are available. Often these fertilizers are developed to meet general needs of turf grown in an area. For example, if soils are usually high in potassium, this nutrient element may be omitted from the fertilizer or be included only in small amounts. Furthermore, if iron or sulfur are likely to be deficient, they may be included in the fertilizer. In order to develop a suitable turf fertilization program, the turf manager must realize the role and importance of various nutrients in keeping turf.

Most turf maintenance fertilizers are complete fertilizers containing nitrogen, phosphorus, and potassium. In some instances it may be desirable to eliminate a nutrient. For example, using a fertilizer that does not contain phosphorus tends to discourage annual bluegrass. Fertilizers that contain only one plant nutrient element, especially nitrogen, are frequently used to maintain turf. Specialty turf fertilizers may also contain sulfur, iron, and manganese to meet special requirements for an area. The following discussion of elements used to formulate various turf fertilizers should provide an understanding of the uses of the individual elements.

Nitrogen (N) is the key element in turf fertility programs. This element is the primary growth element; consequently, it is an important management tool for a grounds manager. Nitrogen is used in large quantities by turf. In fact, dry turf clippings may contain about 5 percent total nitrogen. Water continually leaches nitrogen from the root zone. Therefore, to keep good-quality turf, periodic application of nitrogen fertilizer is necessary to keep it in the root zone in adequate amounts to meet plant needs. Turf deficient in nitrogen usually lacks suitable green color, has reduced density, and will often be quite weedy.

Phosphorus (P) deficiencies in established turf are seldom noticed. Visual symptoms of phosphorus deficiency (purpling of grass leaves) can easily be confused with a similar coloring caused by cold weather. Purpling of turf foliage as a result of cold weather is fairly common on cool-season turfgrasses in the fall and spring. Phosphorus is rather immobile in the soil and tends to remain near the soil surface following fertilizer application. Fertilization just following aeration can help get phosphorus deeper into the root zone.

Potassium (K) deficiency that can be visually detected in turfgrass is not common. When deficiencies are severe, tips of grass leaves may yellow and die. Potassium deficiencies can reduce winter hardiness and disease and wear resistance. Turfgrass clippings may contain about half as much potassium as nitrogen. Potassium

deficiencies occur more often in humid areas than in arid and semi-arid regions.

Sulfur-deficient turf would be expected to have leaves with uniform yellowing. Sulfur (S) deficiencies are not common but do occur in a few areas. Sulfates are frequently present in turfgrass fertilizers, although they may not be listed on the label. Sulfur and acid-reacting fertilizers are sometimes used to lower soil pH and make other nutrient elements, such as iron, more available. Sulfur is also used to treat the fungal disease take-all patch (*Gaeumannoyces graminis*) by reducing soil pH and creating an environment unfavorable to its survival.

Iron (Fe) is a micronutrient (minor) element. Only small amounts, in comparison to nitrogen, phosphorus, and potassium, are required to support normal growth. Iron is a primary contributor to chlorophyll (green coloring) development in plants. This nutrient element is frequently deficient in alkaline soils. Unlike nitrogen, iron fertilizer applications do not stimulate growth; rather, they green the turf. Iron-deficient turf usually has blotchy yellow patches; with severe deficiencies the grass leaves may become white, ultimately resulting in death. Complete turf fertilizers in arid and semi-arid regions may contain iron. The source may be inorganic (ferrous sulfate, ferrous ammonium sulfate, or treated mine tailings) or organic (chelates or plant extracts). Where serious iron deficiencies occur, concentrated iron fertilizers are often used alone.

Other elements, such as calcium, magnesium, manganese, and zinc, are not usually of much concern in developing a turf fertilization program. In some areas, however, they are needed. The probability of deficiencies of these nutrient elements will be taken into consideration by turfgrass suppliers, who can supply fertilizers containing these elements, and by soil testing laboratories and county agents, who make recommendations concerning their use. Calcium can be supplied with ground limestone, dolomitic limestone, and some commonly used turf fertilizers. Natural organic fertilizers contain a wide array of nutrient elements, while manufactured fertilizers are fairly pure, containing primarily the nutrients indicated on the label. Trace element fertilizers containing zinc, molybdenum, and other micronutrients are generally available as specialty products from turf suppliers.

Turf Fertilizers

Many different turf maintenance fertilizers are available. The characteristics of some common materials used for turf fertilization are summarized in table 10-1. These materials may be used either alone or as components of complete fertilizers.

Many different formulations (analyses) of complete turf fertilizers are used. As a rule, turf maintenance fertilizers have a rather high ratio of N to P_2O_5 and K_2O. Analyses including 20-10-5 (4:2:1 ratio), 20-5-10 (4:1:2), and 21-3-7 (7:1:2) are commonly used for turf fertilization. A 20-10-5 fertilizer contains 20 percent N, 4.40 percent P (10 percent P_2O_5), and 4.15 percent K (5 percent K_2O); therefore, 100 pounds of a 20-10-5 fertilizer contains 20 pounds of N, 10 pounds of P_2O_5, and 5 pounds of K_2O. Five pounds of a 20-10-5 material spread over 1000 square feet would supply 1 pound of N.

The composition of complete fertilizers with the same analysis can vary greatly. In particular, the nitrogen in a fertilizer may be supplied by one or more of several materials, as indicated in table 10-1. The nitrogen source determines several important characteristics of a fertilizer. For example, a fertilizer containing only urea as the nitrogen source would be fast-acting and fairly inexpensive but likely to "burn" plants. On the other hand, a fertilizer containing urea–formaldehyde or a combination of urea plus urea–formaldehyde (perhaps 25 to 50 percent) would be less likely to burn, and the slow-release nitrogen in the urea–formaldehyde would be available in the soil for a longer period of time.

Fertilizer labels, like labels on seed packages, provide valuable information for users. For example, the amount of rapidly available nitrogen versus water-insoluble nitrogen (WIN) is listed on a fertilizer label. Other information, such as amounts of sulfur and iron (often represented by a fourth number in the analysis) and whether or not the fertilizer was homogenized, may be on the label.

In *homogenized* fertilizers, each granule contains all the nutrient elements present, and granules are quite uniform in size, making it relatively easy to achieve uniform distribution of nutrients during application. In contrast, granules in *mixed* fertilizers contain only one or two nutrient elements and often vary considerably

Table 10-1. Some Characteristics of Fertilizer Materials Used for Turf Management

Material	Type[a]	Nutrient Content (%)	Amount (lb) to Supply 1 lb Nutrient	Soil Reaction[b]	Burn Possibility[c]
Ammonium sulfate $(NH_4)_2SO_4$	I	21 (N)	4.8	A+	MH
Ammonium nitrate NH_4NO_3	I	33.5–34 (N)	3.0	A	H
Urea $CO(NH_2)_2$	SO	45–46 (N)	2.2	A	MH
Activated sewage sludge	N	5–6 (N)	18.2	N	L
Urea–formaldehyde	SO	38 (N)	2.6	N	L
IBDU	SO	31 (N)	3.2	N	L
Sulfur-coated urea	SO	31 (N)	3.2	A	L
Triple super-phosphate $Ca(H_2PO_4)_2$	I	45–46 (P_2O_5)	2.2	N	L
Muriate of potash KCl	I	60–62 (K_2O)	1.6	N	H
Potassium sulfate K_2SO_4	I	50–53 (K_2O)	1.9	N	M
Ferrous sulfate monohydrate	I	31.5 (Fe)	3.2	A	H

a. I = inorganic; N = natural organic; SO = Man-made (synthetic).
b. A+ = strong acidifier; A = acidifier; N = little influence on acidity.
c. H = high; MH = moderately high; M = moderate; L = low.

in size and density. In this case, achieving uniform broadcast of nutrients is difficult because the heavier, larger granules throw farther than lighter granules, which would be applied in greater amounts near the spreader.

The cost of fertilizers varies according to composition, quality (uniformity, amount of dust, and size of granules), packaging (bulk or bagged), transportation costs, and the like. Determining whether one particular fertilizer is a better buy than another is difficult. Sometimes price comparisons are made based on the pounds of nutrients per 100 pounds or per ton of fertilizer. This may or may not be a valid way to make comparisons, since fertilizer quality and composition vary so much. A grounds manager, however, can easily calculate the cost of various fertilizers and application. With more attention to detail, cheaper, less sophisticated fertilizers can be used successfully for turf maintenance in most situations. Frequent light applications, good spreading equipment, watering immediately after use, and buying and storing smaller quantities are ways to achieve satisfactory results with less expensive materials.

Both liquid and dry fertilizers are used in turf fertilization. Each type has definite advantages and disadvantages. For example, liquid applications are more likely than dry applications to burn turf. On the other hand, on windy days, poor distribution is more likely to occur with dry, lightweight granules than with liquid fertilizers. Whether the fertilizer is applied liquid or dry, it is most important to get uniform distribution of the desired amount and to avoid burning.

Developing a Fertilization Program

Fertilizer should be used to produce turf to meet specific needs. If very high quality turf is required, a great deal of fertilizer will probably be required. If the primary purpose of the turf is to give a naturalistic appearance and prevent erosion, then fertilization once every few years may be adequate. Considering this, it is necessary to assess just what quality of turf is needed. Frequently a site will require several levels of quality, for example, high-quality turf for heavy use and high visual impact; moderate-quality turf for medium use; and low-quality turf for mostly out-of-use areas where soil protection is the major concern.

Fertilizer Selection

Selecting fertilizers to do the best job of turf maintenance for a given situation seldom receives enough attention. In addition to soil tests, visual observations of growth and color, small test plots, clipping yields, turf density, and weed encroachment can provide valuable information for developing specific fertilizer programs and choosing fertilizers. In general, growth is most influenced by the nitrogen level in the soil. Therefore, most turf fertility programs are centered around nitrogen use. Usually other nutrients, especially phosphorus and potassium, are included with nitrogen to take care of possible needs. This often leads to luxury fertilization with elements other than nitrogen.

Seldom are there any good indicators of deficiencies of nutrients other than nitrogen when grasses are grown on good soils. Where turf has been periodically fertilized for several years, phosphorus and potassium may be adequate for turf production. Even nitrogen may be present in organic and inorganic form to the point where applications can be reduced.

On mucks and sandy soils, nutrient elements other than nitrogen may be deficient. If off-color turf has good density and is growing well, the deficiency may be iron or sulfur, not nitrogen. Established Kentucky bluegrass sod that does not cut and lift well may be suffering from a phosphorus deficiency.

It is apparent that, for most situations, nitrogen is the key element in turf maintenance. Consequently, as discussed earlier, common turf maintenance fertilizers contain significantly more nitrogen than other elements. Ratios of 2:1:1 to 7:1:1 of $N:P_2O_5:K_2O$ would encompass most of those used to fertilize turf.

Fertilization Amounts and Frequency

Many fertilization programs are established with budgets that are too limited to provide adequate nutrient supplies for turfgrass growth. The amount and kinds of fertilizer needed through the course of a year will vary according to turf quality desired, soil chemical and physical makeup, weather conditions, length of the growing season, the source of nitrogen and iron, and the kind of grass grown. As much information as possible on these factors should be used to plan a fertilization program.

Frequency of fertilization is, in a sense, dictated by the amounts to be applied (table 10-2). For cool-season grasses grown in cool regions, the preferred times to fertilize are spring and fall. For Kentucky bluegrass and perennial ryegrass well north of the transition zone, low rates of fertilizer, to supply around ½ pound of nitrogen per 1000 square feet, may be used during the summer months. Although heavy amounts of fertilizer (in excess of 1 pound of nitrogen per 1000 square feet) may be applied in the spring and fall to cool-season turf, there are usually advantages to applying lower rates more frequently. Among these advantages are reduced surges of growth (more constant top growth), as well as less loss of nitrogen to leaching and runoff. All in all, it is better if very small amounts of fertilizer are supplied quite frequently. However, in most situations this is not economical or necessary to produce high-quality turf. Figure 10-1 illustrates growth patterns for shoots of cool-season grasses when nitrogen fertilizer is applied in spring and fall.

For warm-season turfgrasses in the transition zone, there is a fairly short period best suited for fertilization. Starting fertilization from mid-May to early June is normally satisfactory. Fertilizing warm-season turfgrasses fairly frequently at ½ to ¾ pound nitrogen per 1000 square feet until midsummer in the transition zone and beginning earlier and continuing later farther south will help produce suitable turf.

These comments on fertilizer amounts and frequencies are, at best, generalizations. In an earlier than normal season, fertilization can be started earlier; if there are heavy rains, soluble nitrogen from a fertilizer can be lost rapidly from the root zone, and fertilization may be needed more frequently. In addition, as indicated previously, the amount and frequency of fertilization should be geared to the quality level of turf desired.

Low-quality turf: Unless a grass performs best with low nitrogen levels (table 10-2) or turf is grown on a naturally fertile soil, some fertilizer will be beneficial in maintaining a satisfactory stand. In poor soils, turf that is not fertilized may thin to the point that it does not even provide suitable soil erosion protection. Without fertilizer, turf grown in poor soils often becomes so thin and infested with weeds that cover will be unacceptable. Depending on the situation, low-quality turf

Table 10-2. Amounts of Nitrogen Generally Used to Maintain Some Common Turfgrasses

Grass	lb N per 1000 ft^2 per Year[a]	Comments
Kentucky bluegrass, perennial ryegrass, tall fescue, blends and mixtures of these	2–6	½–1 lb N/1000 ft^2 per application normally adequate; use higher rates when cool, lower when hot. Best fertilized when cool.
Tall fescue	2–5	Same as for Kentucky bluegrass.
Fine fescue	1–3	Same as for Kentucky bluegrass.
Bentgrass	2–8	Burns easily. Apply at ¼–½ lb N/1000 ft^2.
Bermudagrass	4–10	Fertilize during warmer time of year. Best to keep rates around ½ lb N/1000 ft^2.
St. Augustinegrass	3–6	Same as for bermudagrass.
Zoysiagrass	1–4	Same as for bermudagrass.
Centipedegrass, buffalograss, and bahiagrass	0–2	Same as for bermudagrass.

a. Note that amount is per year; seldom would the total amount be supplied in a single application. Higher amounts would be required to produce very high quality turf. Irrigation and longer growing seasons may increase the requirement for nitrogen fertilizer.

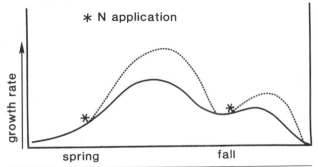

Figure 10-1. Effects of nitrogen fertilizer on top growth of cool-season turfgrass in spring and fall.

may be maintained by using the lowest amount of nitrogen suggested for a grass in table 10-2 or even with no nitrogen at all. If low annual rates (one application) of nitrogen are used for maintenance of cool-season grasses, fall is the best time to fertilize; spring would be the second most preferred time. For warm-season turf-grasses, mid- to late spring is a suitable time to fertilize if only one application is made.

Medium-quality turf: The amounts of nitrogen needed for maintenance of medium-quality turf would fall somewhere between the low and high amount given in table 10-2. For cool-season turfgrasses, in addition to one or two applications of fertilizer in the fall and one in early spring, a light application (½–¾ pound of nitrogen per 1000 square feet) can be made in mid- to late spring. Nitrogen applications for warm-season turfgrass should start in May and continue at fairly light rates (½–¾ pound of nitrogen per 1000 square feet) every four or five weeks, until about six weeks before the turf goes dormant.

High-quality turf: For intensely maintained turf, the highest nitrogen rates suggested in table 10-2, or even more, are frequently used. Two fall and two or three spring applications, in addition to fairly frequent (at four- to six-week intervals) summer applications, at about ½ pound of nitrogen per 1000 square feet should be adequate to keep high-quality cool-season turf. For warm-season turf, applications of ½ to ¾ pound of nitrogen per 1000 square feet every three to four weeks beginning in May and continuing until approximately six weeks before the turf goes dormant should be adequate to produce high-quality turf.

Golf greens, bowling greens, and athletic fields are often maintained with frequent, very light (¼ to ½ pound of nitrogen per 1000 square feet) applications of soluble fertilizers, or slightly higher rates of slowly available materials. If large granules of fertilizers are used at a low rate on short-cut grass, small burn spots or green spots may occur. Normally, these disappear in a short time.

Fertilizer–Pesticide Combinations

Herbicides, fungicides, and insecticides are often packaged in combination with fertilizers for use by the turf professional. Situations in which such combinations work quite well include the use of a starter fertilizer with a pre-emergent herbicide for weed control in newly seeded cool-season turfgrasses, or early fall application of a fertilizer–fungicide material to encourage turf growth and control stripe smut (*Ustilago* spp.) However, where repeated fungicide applications are required, combination materials may not work well in a turf maintenance program. Using fertilizers and pesticides separately provides a grounds manager greater flexibility in material selection and application rates than is possible with combination products.

Fertilizer Burn

It is not unusual to see fertilizer burn. Normally, the burn is restricted to the grass leaves, incidental clover, and other broadleaf weeds in a stand; root damage is not usual. Fertilizer burn is most likely to occur when heavy rates of soluble fertilizer are applied on frozen ground, on tender species such as creeping bentgrass and rough bluegrass, during hot weather, or when the foliage is wet.

The possibility of fertilizer burn can be lessened by reducing application rates, using dry fertilizers, and making sure foliage is dry before starting application. In addition, the fertilizer should be watered in well as soon as possible after application. Before irrigation, foot or vehicular traffic on the turf should be avoided; otherwise spotted and streaked burning may occur. Other precautions that help to prevent turf fertilizer injury include filling the spreader on a walk or driveway and keeping the spreader away from buildings and out of shrub and tree locations. Of course, the use of fertilizers with low burn potential (table 10-1) greatly reduces this problem.

Applying Fertilizer

To achieve maximum benefit from fertilization, *uniform distribution is essential.* Dry fertilizers may be dusty, variable in particle size and density, and hydrophylic (prone to absorb moisture from a humid atmosphere). Use of fertilizers with these characteristics will decrease the possibility of getting uniform application. Liquid fertilizers often require agitation to keep the nutrients in solution or suspension. If nutrients are not uniformally distributed in the solution, turf responses may not be uniform.

There are many different kinds of turf fertilizer applicators for both dry and liquid materials. Frequently, fertilizer applicators are purchased primarily because of the size of the hopper or tank. In other cases, the width of spread is given paramount consideration in deciding which applicator to purchase. Because broadcast-type spreaders cover the ground rapidly, they are commonly used to spread dry fertilizer on large areas. Drop-type spreaders are quite useful for applying fertilizer–pesticide combinations, for keeping material out of sensitive plantings, and for applying fertilizer (especially iron) that may stain sidewalks and driveways. For large-area liquid application, boom-type applicators frequently are used. Custom lawn applicators commonly apply liquid fertilizers with hand guns.

The uniformity of coverage of a fertilizer applicator should be checked before use. Sometimes the uniformity can be improved by making a few simple adjustments. In some cases an applicator may not be capable of providing uniform coverage. Because of the high cost of fertilizers and the relatively low cost of applicators, replacement may be in order.

Uniformity of application equipment can be roughly gauged by simply applying some commonly used turf fertilizer on a roadway or sidewalk. The application pattern can be easily seen. For larger equipment, uniform-sized pieces of paper can be placed at random in an area that is to be fertilized. After fertilization, the number of granules on each piece of paper can be counted to determine uniformity of coverage. With liquid applicators, the percentage of paper wet by the solution can be estimated or the number of solution spots counted to assess coverage consistency.

For most turf fertilizers, the proper applicator setting is given on the bag or on an information sheet provided by the supplier. This information is quite helpful to a grounds manager. Without knowing the proper spreader setting needed to apply a given amount of fertilizer, calibration is necessary.

To calibrate a fertilizer spreader, the effective spreading width must be known. For drop-type spreaders, this is normally the width of the hopper; for broadcast spreaders, determining effective coverage width is difficult because the application amount decreases from the center to the outer edge of the pattern. To achieve uniform coverage with a broadcast spreader, the application pattern must be overlapped. After the width of effective coverage is known (for example, 10 feet), then the travel distance to get 1000 square feet (or more or less, if desirable) can be calculated. For example, a travel distance of 100 feet times a spreader width of 10 feet would give 1000 square feet of coverage.

Once the travel distance required to cover a certain area (for example, 1000 square feet) has been determined, then the spreader setting required to achieve a given application rate is determined. For example, suppose the desired rate of application is 1 pound of nitrogen per 1000 square feet and a 20-10-5 fertilizer is to be used; then 5 pounds of fertilizer must be spread per 1000 square feet to provide the desired coverage. To determine the proper spreader setting, fill the hopper (in the case of dry fertilizers) about half full with the fertilizer to be used, smooth it to a level surface, and mark the level on the side of the hopper. Set the spreader at a fairly low setting (when wide open, most spreaders apply *very high* rates). Run the spreader the required distance and shut it off. Then spread a sheet of plastic over the fertilizer remaining in the hopper, and bring the plastic up well above the mark on the side of the hopper. Refill the spreader with fertilizer up to the mark, then remove this fertilizer and weigh it. If the amount delivered was less than that required to achieve the desired application rate (in the example, 5 pounds), then open the setting somewhat; if the amount delivered was more than that required, then close the setting a little. By trial and error, continue this operation until the approximate application rate is reached. Be sure to record the spreader setting for various fertilizers so that this time-consuming operation will not have to be repeated.

With liquid fertilizers, the same procedure can be followed. Mark the tank, travel the proper distance, and refill to the mark. Continue to adjust the setting until the desired amount is applied.

A great deal of fertilizer can be saved by reducing rates to one-half and going over an area twice, in north–south and east–west directions. Applying the proper amount of fertilizer on a turf will avoid waste and produce the desired results. Taking the time to apply fertilizer properly is a mark of a professional grounds manager.

MOWING

Unfortunately, mowing grass is such a common practice that it becomes routine. Since mowing is usually the most costly item in a landscape maintenance budget, small changes in mowing operations can result in significant savings. It is sometimes possible to make significant changes in mowing operations with little, if any, sacrifice in turf quality. Some of the most important considerations in mowing are cutting height, frequency, and clipping removal.

Height of Cut

As a rule, low-cut turf requires more care than high-cut turf to maintain acceptable quality. In some turf areas, such as golf course greens and lawn bowling and tennis courts, the turf must be cut very short (about 1/8 to 1/4 inch). Consequently, grasses selected for such areas should be able to tolerate low cuts (table 10-3); these include cool-season turfgrasses used in overseeding, creeping bentgrass, annual bluegrass, and improved bermudagrasses. Under stress conditions, such as heavy traffic and hot weather, a cutting height between 7/32 and 1/4 inch is more desirable. Lower cutting heights (1/8 to 5/32 inch) are often used for golf greens for tournament play and private golf courses with limited play.

Moderately low cutting heights (commonly 1/2 to 1 inch) are used to maintain turf on golf course tees and fairways, bermudagrass and bentgrass lawns, and other places where there is a particular need for a "carpetlike" surface.

Turf is often cut high (1 1/2 to about 4 inches) for minimum maintenance areas, including golf course roughs and out-of-play areas, limited-use park areas, and highway roadsides. Since tall fescue and bahiagrass perform best at higher cuts, they are often used to provide cover and erosion protection for low-quality turf areas.

As a rule, home lawns are mowed at the preferred height (table 10-3). Commonly, cutting heights for the same kind of grass for similar facilities are higher in the transition zone than farther north where growing conditions are better.

Table 10-3. Cutting Heights for Some Commonly Grown Grasses

Grass Type	Low Cut (in)	Preferred Cut (in)	High Cut (in)
Cool-Season Grasses			
Kentucky bluegrass—common types	1.25	2.00–3.00	4.00
Kentucky bluegrass—improved cultivars and blends	0.75	2.00–2.00	3.00
Perennial ryegrass—common types	1.50	2.00–3.00	4.00
Perennial ryegrass—turf types	0.75	1.50–2.00	3.00
Fine fescues	1.00	1.50–3.00	4.00
Tall fescues—pasture types	2.00	2.50–3.50	4.00
Tall fescues—turf types	1.25	1.50–3.00	3.00
Creeping bentgrass	0.25	0.50–0.75	1.00
Colonial bentgrass	0.50	0.75–1.00	2.00
Annual bluegrass	0.25	0.50–1.00	2.00
Smooth bromegrass	2.00	3.00–4.00	5.00
Warm-Season Grasses			
Bermudagrass—common types	0.50	0.75–1.00	2.00
Bermudagrass—improved cultivars	0.25	0.50–0.75	1.25
Buffalograss	0.50	0.75–1.00	2.00
Zoysiagrass	0.50	0.75–1.00	1.50
St. Augustinegrass	1.50	2.00–3.00	4.00
Centipedegrass	0.75	1.00–1.25	2.00
Bahiagrass	1.50	2.00–3.00	4.00

The cutting heights given in table 10-3 are merely suggestions. Changing the height of cut to meet specific or changing needs, including increased wear resistance and drought tolerance, can be a valuable management tool. Within reason, the higher a turf can be cut, the easier it is to maintain. Turf cut too low will tend to have serious weed problems; that cut too high will tend to lie down and mat. In turf management there are often situations where the grass may be mowed seldom if at all, giving a naturalistic effect to the landscape. Allowing the turf to grow to greater heights is often beneficial in minimizing weed encroachment.

Mowing Frequency

The proper time to mow turf is best determined by the growth rate. Routinely mowing turf once a week may work into a labor schedule well, but is not likely to provide the best-quality turf. The one-third rule—mow often enough so that there is no more than one-third height reduction at any one mowing—is the best guide for determining when to mow. For instance, if a Kentucky bluegrass is to be cut to a height of 2 inches, it should be mowed whenever the grass reaches 3 inches.

Scalping (excessive removal of turf foliage) is avoided if the one-third rule is followed. Scalped turf lacks good density, can be readily invaded by weeds, and will not tolerate wear. If mowing is based on the one-third rule, clippings will be short enough to easily filter down into the turf. If the turf is quite dense and cut short, as on golf greens and lawn bowling courts, clippings seldom filter into the turf. Under these conditions, clippings should be removed.

Figure 10-2 can be helpful in scheduling mowing times. During early and late periods of the growing season, mowing may be required only every two to three weeks. During the period of maximum growth in the spring, it may be necessary to mow a medium-maintenance cool-season turf twice a week, while in the heat of the summer, even with irrigation, one mowing per week may be adequate. For warm-season turfgrasses, maximum growth and consequently the need for more frequent mowing occurs in the summer.

Clipping Removal

The pros and cons of clipping removal have long been debated. Before making a decision on whether or not to collect clippings, a grounds manager must consider several factors including labor, equipment, fertility practices, disposal methods, and potential thatch problems. Perhaps the most important consideration in determining whether or not clippings should be removed is turf use. In most instances, clippings are removed from golf course greens and other low-cut turf areas. However, clippings may not be caught on low-cut turf for a few mowings after fertilization. This allows slowly soluble fertilizers to dissolve, infiltrate the soil, and not be removed with the clippings. With taller cut grass and in larger turf areas, clippings are not often removed. By mowing frequently, clippings will be short and rapidly disappear under the turf canopy.

The labor and expense involved in removing clippings is great. Consequently this practice is usually reserved for small areas of intensely maintained turf. Few facilities are equipped to compost clippings properly. Often clippings get dumped in the most convenient place, creating an eyesore for a long time. Transporting clippings to a public landfill is costly and often wastes a valuable organic resource that could better be composted or returned.

Clipping removal can significantly decrease soil nutrients available for plant growth. If clippings are harvested, it may be necessary to increase fertilizer applications, especially of nitrogen, by 25 to 50 percent

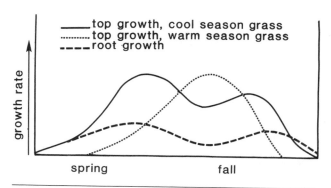

Figure 10-2. Relative top growth and root growth of cool- and warm-season grasses in a year.

to achieve turf quality equivalent to that possible if clippings are returned. One of the reasons that turf grown on good soils where clippings are not removed often retains its quality is that nutrients are recycled for turf use.

One of the frequent reasons given for collecting clippings is that thatch is reduced. This may or may not be true. Only a small percentage of the turf (organic matter) is removed as clippings. Much of the plant growth occurs below the mowing height levels; therefore, it remains after clippings are removed. Very few large turf areas, where clippings have never been removed, have thatch problems. If conditions are conducive to thatch development, returning clippings could add to the problem, but not significantly.

Recent developments in equipment design make it necessary for grounds managers to decide, before purchasing equipment, whether or not clippings will be caught. Mulching mowers are designed to cut or chop clippings into small pieces, so that they can rapidly disappear into the turf canopy. Mulching mowers do not work very well when turf is wet or tall, but the concept of returning clippings in this fashion has merit. Walk-behind, rear-bagging rotary lawn mowers are generally designed so that clippings should be caught. Rear-bagging mowers are rather safe to use, but removing and replacing the bag can be quite time-consuming.

Mowing Equipment

Although there are four basic types of mowers—rotary, reel, flail, and sickle bar—only the first two are widely used in grounds management. Height of cut, size of area to be mowed, slope, tree spacing, and mower repair and upkeep requirements need to be considered when selecting mowing equipment.

Rotary mowers are commonly used to maintain taller-cut grass, usually above ½ inch. Rotaries are fairly simple but require large amounts of energy for operation. A heavy-duty, frequently sharpened rotary mower can, in most situations, provide a clean-cut turf comparable to that possible with reel mowers. The importance of using sharp, heavy-duty blades for maintaining high-quality turf cannot be overemphasized. Heavy-duty blades stay sharp longer and do not nick or bend as

badly as lightweight blades. Rotary mowers are not very efficient for mowing large areas, but they are commonly used for small areas and edging. Specialty lightweight rotaries that float on an air cushion are used over water, paving stones, and on short steep slopes.

Reel mowers are used for keeping short-cut turf. When energy-efficient individual units (gangs) are hooked together, cutting widths up to 30 feet or more are possible. The units flex and follow the surface contour; thus, scalping is seldom a problem. The scissorslike cutting effect of the reel blades with the bedknife can give a very clean cut. Reel mowers are fairly sophisticated pieces of equipment, and competent mechanical upkeep is necessary to maintain satisfactory performance. Reel mowers are not well adapted for trimming and will not cut high enough for use in many maintenance situations.

Flail mowers, because of the pivoting, downward action of the cutting knives, do not tend to throw rocks and other objects as rotary mowers often do. Also, the knives tend to ride over rocks without breaking. Flail mowers are often used for mowing rough highway roadsides. Where plant growth is heavy, both flail and rotary mowers tend to bunch up the mowed material. Unless this material is removed or spread about, it can greatly restrict regrowth.

Sickle-bar mowers make a single cut through grass and weeds, allowing them to fall evenly over the ground. This usually allows the vegetation to regrow through the dead material without much suppression of growth.

AERATION

Mechanical aeration has become a common maintenance practice on heavy-use turf areas and heavy clay soils. This is one of the few practices that can improve soils under perennial turfgrass. In taller-cut turf, aerifier holes can be left open without much concern about damage. The holes will stay open and serve as major root development areas for many years. Aerators that remove cores are generally preferred over those that spike or leave narrow slits in the soil. However, any piece of equipment that opens the soil can slow runoff, improve aeration, and improve root development in tight soil or thatchy situations.

To be most effective, coring should be done as deeply

as possible. When aerifying, the soil should be moist but not wet for best results. Lightly wetting the turf before aerifying will help lubricate the aerator tubes to help keep the soil moving through them.

If the soil is of poor quality, it is best if cores can be removed and discarded. When this is not possible or if the soil is good quality (sand, loamy sand, or sandy loam), then the cores can be broken up with a fixed-knife verticut mower, a weighted section of chain link fence, or a metal door mat. If the cores are not too wet or dry, they will normally break up fairly easily. Getting the soil from the cores below the turf canopy helps to form and smooth the soil surface. Fertilization after aerification speeds grass growth to cover holes visible in the turf or soil remaining after coring.

TOPDRESSING

In grounds management, the term *topdressing* refers to the practice of applying material over an existing turf. Many different materials are used for topdressing. Among these are soils of good physical qualities or inert materials such as sand from pits or dunes, calcined clay, and mixtures of inert materials with organic materials such as peat. Topdressing should be as free as possible of seed and plant parts that could cause weed problems. Dry topdressing materials are much easier to work with than wet ones. Topdressing materials should be processed and stored in dry areas when feasible.

Grass used on golf course greens and other low-growing turfs that require a smooth surface are usually topdressed. Topdressing depressions created by utility excavations or planting on rough soils can help smooth the surface. Topdressing can be quite beneficial in reducing thatch problems.

Mechanical topdressing machines apply a uniform layer of material over a turf. If areas to be topdressed are small or topdressing is done only occasionally, then a scoop shovel can be used to spread the material uniformly. After a topdressing is spread, if it is dry and not too coarse, it can be forced below the turf canopy with a metal door mat, piece of chain link fence, or light wooden drag.

It is important that not too much topdressing material be spread at one time. Frequent, light applications are better than infrequent, heavy ones. The lower the turf is cut, the lower the amount of topdressing material that can be used without damaging the turf. Applications of topdressing material from 2 to 3 cubic feet (0.02- to 0.04-inch depth) to 0.75 cubic yards (0.24-inch depth) per 1000 square feet are commonly used on turf. No more topdressing material than can be worked into the turf canopy should be used.

DETHATCHING

A small amount of thatch in turf can be beneficial. A light layer of thatch can reduce soil compaction, moderate the soil temperature, and limit direct loss of water from the soil. Too much thatch restricts water and air movement into the soil, thereby limiting deep root development. Disease and insect problems also tend to be worse in heavily thatched turf. The thatch can serve as a source of inoculum for diseases, protect insects from predators, and inactivate certain pesticides. Severe turfgrass growing problems are often associated with deep thatch.

One approach to limiting excessive thatch accumulation is to determine the cause and treat it. The cause of the problem may be wet, cold soils that need to be drained or a reduction in earthworm activity subsequent to pesticide application. In most instances where earthworms are present to feed on and break down organic debris, thatch will not be a problem and turf will be rather easy to manage.

In addition to aeration and topdressing, various kinds of dethatching mowers are used to reduce thatch. Vertical mowers with fixed or pivoting blades and spring-tined dethatching mowers are used to bring dead (and some live) plant material to the surface so that it can be removed. As a rule, the spring-tined mowers are not as injurious to the turf as those with fixed knives. If the thatch problem is serious, a gradual approach may be required. This is accomplished by setting the mower fairly shallow and widening the spacing between the knives. Power sweepers can sometimes be set deep enough to remove a limited amount of debris in a turf. In seriously thatched turf, it may take several seasons of using dethatching mowers to reduce the thatch problem.

The preferred time to dethatch cool-season grasses

is in the spring and fall when the turf is less likely to be under heat or drought stress. The turf should recover rapidly from any dethatching mower damage at these peak growing times. With warm-season grasses, dethatching is customarily done in the summer. Warm-season grasses will recover rapidly during warm periods with proper care, and open spaces left by dethatching will fill in rapidly, thus minimizing weed invasion.

WATERING

There are very few places where a high-quality turf can be kept without supplemental irrigation. No matter where turf is grown, many problems can be associated with too little or too much water. Proper water management on turf facilities is quite difficult. The general approach, especially in arid and semi-arid regions where the cost of pumping water for irrigation may be quite costly, should be to produce suitable turf with as little water as possible. In more humid areas, where the cost of watering may be minimal, overwatering may contribute to serious turf growing problems.

Planting and managing grasses to take advantage of their inherent ability to perform well under extended drought (table 10-4) can save large quantities of water for grounds managers, especially those in arid and semi-arid regions. In general, grasses that survive drought best remain greener longer into dry periods than those with poor survival. The ability to survive extended dry periods may not relate well to the amount of water a grass will use (transpire) if water is available. The performance of turfgrasses under droughty conditions is influenced by soil and plant growth characteristics. Tall fescue grown on good soil in Kentucky and Tennessee will remain green long into a summer drought. The available water in the subsoil is taken up by the deep roots of the tall fescue. However, in dry areas of Colorado and Utah where there is little if any subsoil moisture, tall fescue requires fairly frequent irrigation.

Before new landscapes are established and even for existing landscapes, the water requirements of various kinds of landscape materials should be carefully considered. Many landscaped areas may require some plant materials that need intensive irrigation and some that require little, if any, supplemental water. In more humid areas, the same grasses may be planted in irrigated and nonirrigated areas. If textural and height differences for aesthetic appeal are desired, the same grasses may be planted and maintained differently or different grasses with a different level of drought tolerance may be planted. In unirrigated semi-arid regions, only a few grasses with very good or outstanding drought tolerance should be considered. These grasses in dry areas without irrigation would likely persist, but the turf would be low quality and suited for minimum use.

Great amounts of water can be saved and often a landscape can be made more attractive by planning larger sites, so that all of the plant material does not have the same water requirements. When designing sites for water conservation, it is important that clients, as well as planners, have a good idea of what the outcome will probably be. Frequently, sites designed and planted to conserve water do not meet the expectations of property managers or owners, who then

Table 10-4. Performance of Commonly Grown Turfgrasses under Extended Drought Stress

Performance Rating	Turfgrass
Outstanding	Bermudagrass Blue gramagrass
Very good	Fairway wheatgrass Smooth bromegrass Bahiagrass
Good	Kentucky bluegrass Canada bluegrass Sheep fescue Tall fescue Hard fescue
Medium	Chewings fescue Red fescue Perennial ryegrass
Fair	Annual ryegrass Colonial bentgrass Centipedegrass St. Augustinegrass
Poor	Creeping bentgrass Rough bluegrass Annual bluegrass

impose intensive management on naturalistic landscapes. When this occurs, the results are not as good as when grasses and other landscape materials adapted to high levels of maintenance are planted.

Many different factors influence the ability of a grounds manager to irrigate efficiently and effectively. Some of these can be changed and others cannot. Grounds managers should continuously monitor turf irrigation practices. Appropriate changes should be made to conserve water and to grow better turf.

Irrigation Systems

Many advances have been made in turf irrigation systems in the last few years. Most properly designed systems installed during the last decade or two are quite versatile. With the sophisticated irrigation equipment now available, it is very important, especially for large systems, that a great deal of engineering be involved in installation. Among on-site design considerations are topography, prevailing wind, location of trees and roads, and soil infiltration rates.

Good irrigation systems provide quite uniform coverage. Grounds managers with inefficient systems may have to overwater much of a facility just to grow turf on drier spots. Overwatering can cause increased weed and disease problems, make mowing more difficult, and reduce the amount of turf that can be used. As easy as setting cans randomly to catch water for measuring and determining uniformity of water delivery is, it is seldom done. Such a test might reveal the need for a new system or extensive repair of an old one. Changing heads, replacing nozzles with ones of different delivery rates or angles of delivery, or adjusting flow at a valve may be sufficient to improve the uniformity of a system.

Troubleshooting irrigation systems can be a daily chore. Poor irrigation coverage and resultant poor turf can be caused by stuck valves, sand in nozzles, algae or scale in the line, broken lines, and many other system problems. Dry or wet turf areas and resultant turf damage may not show up for several days. If the performance of the system is monitored closely, malfunctions can be identified and corrected, so that long-lasting turf problems will not develop.

Irrigation Scheduling

To get the most out of irrigation water, grounds managers need to assess constantly just how much water is needed and run the system to deliver proper amounts. The more familiar a grounds manager is with the landscape, soil, and weather conditions, the better water can be managed.

There are several ways, from simple to quite complex, that watering frequencies and amounts can be established. The appearance of the grass can be used as a guide to when to water. Footprints that remain visible on the grass for several minutes after walking on it, loss of leaf luster, and a blue-gray appearance to the turf indicate a need to water. Irrigating shortly after these conditions are noticed will lead to rapid improvement of turf quality. If the water stress proceeds to the point where the turf leaves turn brown, it can take days or even weeks of irrigation to return the turf to the quality it had before it became stressed.

Soils act as a reservoir for storing and supplying water for turf use (table 10-5). A high percentage of turf roots are in the upper 2 to 3 inches of soil; however, effective rooting and corresponding water extraction also occur at deeper soil depths. Because of better aeration, grass normally roots much deeper in sands and loams than in clay soil (figure 10-3). Consequently, turf grown on a good, sandy loam soil does not require irrigation as frequently as that grown on a heavy clay. Since most turf facilities are a composite of various textures of soil, a grounds manager may not be able to take full advantage of good soils that retain and supply water well to the turf. With heavy soils the tendency is to overwater continuously, causing a shallow-rooted turf that is difficult to manage.

Table 10-5. Approximate Soil Water Availability in Various Soils

Soil Type	Available Water[a] (in/ft)
Sand	0.7
Sandy loam	1.1
Loam	1.7
Clay loam	2.0
Clay	1.9

a. Usable water for plant growth.

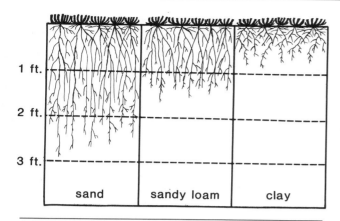

Figure 10-3. Root depth of grass in three different soil textures.

Estimating critical soil moisture amounts to use as a guide on when to irrigate can be done by probing the soil with a screwdriver, heavy wire, or similar simple probe. Usually, when a probe easily penetrates the soil to 3 to 4 inches, enough water is available to carry the grass for about a day, depending, of course, on the rate water dissipates from the soil.

Some sophisticated devices are available for measuring soil moisture. Tensiometers measure the suction force at which a water film is held to soil particles. Tensiometer readings are quite useful in determining when and how much water needs to be applied to a turf. Preset tensiometers can be hooked directly into irrigation controllers to make turf irrigation automatic. Other soil moisture-measuring devices determine the current flow between two electrodes (wet soils carry electrical current better than dry soils); these are readily available and inexpensive. Use of soil moisture measuring equipment can be quite helpful in determining when to water turf and other landscape plants.

Evapotranspiration (ET) can be defined as water loss from the soil plus the turf. Direct measurements and mathematical calculations to determine ET can be quite helpful in irrigation scheduling. Evapotranspiration can be determined on-site by weighing *lysimeters* (buckets) filled with soil and grass from the site. Filled lysimeters should be sunk into the turf so that they are hardly visible and should be placed so that they will be fairly representative of the entire turf area. Periodically, the lysimeters are removed and weighed, and water is added to bring the soil back up to the desired water content, usually near field capacity. The amount of water added to the lysimeters can be converted to inches or centimeters applied. Then the irrigation system can be run to restore the water lost from the soil.

Since weighing lysimeters is fairly tedious work, it is often desirable to calculate ET from mathematical formulas that take various weather conditions into account. Published information that gives average ET for days and months is available. In arid and semi-arid regions, ET data that takes into account immediate past weather conditions may be published in local newspapers and given over radio and television. This information is quite valuable in establishing turf irrigation conservation at a facility.

Irrigation scheduling needs to take into account whether an area is composed of heavy clay, is compacted, or is steeply sloped. Cyclic irrigation involves repeated, short applications of water to minimize runoff on slopes and heavy soils. Cyclic watering, especially with automated irrigation, can be quite helpful in reducing runoff and preventing ponding. Also, water losses from runoff may be reduced by aerating and dethatching. Aeration holes catch and hold water until it can infiltrate the soil. Breaking the thatch barrier to water penetration by aerating or verticutting can speed water movement into the soil.

Taking diseases into account, the best time to water turf is probably early morning. This is difficult because of the inability of a system to get enough turf watered in a short period of time. Also, golf courses, athletic fields, and parks are usually watered at night so as not to restrict play. Large amounts of water can be lost to evaporation on sunny days, especially under sunny and windy conditions. In arid and semi-arid locations, even with plentiful soil moisture, turf damage (bleaching of leaves) can occur on sunny, windy days.

Turf in shady areas needs less water than that in sun or partial sun. Frequently, turf in shade is watered along with that in full sun, resulting in wet areas where annual bluegrass and other weeds tolerant to wet conditions tend to do better than the desired grass. Once weeds establish in shady areas, management programs need to be changed to either accommodate or eliminate them.

Watering cool-season turfgrasses in northern areas during dry winters is a recommended practice. In more humid areas, winter watering may be needed only for grasses with low levels of drought tolerance on exposed dry areas. Periodic watering of grasses with poor drought tolerance during low precipitation winters can help ensure survival. Dry winters can seriously damage turfgrass growing on slopes, compacted soils, and the south and west sides of buildings.

Maintenance practices including mowing and fertilizing can influence water use. A low-cut turf has a lower ET than a tall-cut turf, which has more foliage and a more open turf for air movement to remove moisture. Tall-cut grass, however, has a more extensive root system, which can remove moisture from the soil more efficiently. It is easier to manage water through dry periods if the turf is cut high.

MAINTENANCE PRACTICES IN SHADY AREAS

In some areas, shade is considered the number one cause of turf problems. Shade problems are primarily caused by trees, shrubs, and structures. Turf shaded by trees and shrubs is often droughty because these plants take up moisture and their canopies intercept precipitation. The snow and rain held by the foliage evaporates and does not reach the turf. On north and east sides of buildings, where wind and solar energy are greatly reduced, soil and turf tend to stay quite moist. This needs to be considered when growing turf in shaded areas. Rough bluegrass tolerates wet shade quite well, while the fine fescues do well on drier shady sites.

Shade tends to moderate temperatures. It is not unusual to find fine fescue and other cool-season grasses growing in shady areas well beyond their area of adaptation. Shaded areas on north sides of hills and buildings stay cold; consequently, snow is slow to melt and snow mold can be serious.

Several practices can be used to avoid or alleviate turf shade problems. One of the common approaches to solving shade problems is to grow shade-tolerant grasses (table 10-6). Mixtures of cool-season grasses, for example Kentucky bluegrass, fine fescue, and perennial ryegrass are often planted in shady and open,

sunny areas. This allows grasses that do best in sunny areas to dominate there, while those that tolerate shade are expected to perform satisfactorily in reduced light areas. Some cultivars of a grass may perform better in shade than others; for example, the Kentucky bluegrass 'Glade' and 'Bensun' do better in shade than 'Merion.' 'Elka,' 'Birdie II,' and 'Yorktown II' are among the perennial ryegrass cultivars known to have some shade tolerance.

Selective pruning of trees and shrubs to remove dead and undesirable lower branches allows more light to get to the turf. Shrubs often provide more extensive and denser shade than necessary, and proper pruning will encourage better shrubs and grasses. With better turf, more attractive borders can be maintained.

Tree roots can cause significant turf damage (drought symptoms and thin stands). On golf greens, grass tennis courts, and other low-cut, high-maintenance areas, it may be desirable to prune tree roots. Because of concern for trees in the landscape, only a limited amount of root pruning should be done at any one time. For a turf area some distance from trees, a trencher set to cut about 18 inches deep could be used to prune roots. This operation would need to be done every few years to keep roots from growing back into the area.

Because trees compete with turf for soil nutrients, application of more fertilizer in tree areas than in open areas can be beneficial. From 25 to 50 percent additional fertilizer, especially nitrogen, in tree-shaded areas should

Table 10-6. Performance of Commonly Grown Turfgrasses on Shady Sites

Performance Rating	Turfgrass
Very good	Rough bluegrass Fine fescue St. Augustinegrass
Good	Tall fescue Perennial ryegrass Bahiagrass
Fair	Kentucky bluegrass Zoysiagrass Centipedegrass
Poor	Bermudagrass Buffalograss

be suitable. The fertilizer should be applied at low rates (probably no more than ½ pound of nitrogen per 1000 square feet per application). Under deciduous trees, spring fertilization—before the trees leaf out—can give the grass a good start. Turf grown under trees tends to be damp and succulent. Therefore, care should be taken to avoid burning the grass.

Soils under trees, especially evergreens, may be quite acid. In such situations, aerification and applications of limestone at soil test recommendation rates can improve the possibilities of growing turf.

When turf under trees is irrigated, the soil should be wetted 8 inches deep or more. Wetting the soil deeply will reduce the frequency of irrigation and produce drier turf that is less prone to diseases.

Accumulated leaves and branches under trees will further shade the grass and keep it damp. Several cleanups may be necessary under deciduous trees in the fall to produce good growing conditions for the turf.

Lightly working the soil, use of preplant fertilizers, and seeding or sodding followed by proper watering can sometimes improve turf stands under trees. The best time to upgrade turf under deciduous trees is in the autumn, just after leaf drop. Usually there is some fairly good growing weather for the turf in the fall and in the spring before trees leaf out.

In some shady areas, it is just not possible to grow acceptable turf. Broadleaf ground covers including pachysandra, common periwinkle, and English ivy sometimes do well where turfgrasses will not. Rock, bark, wood chips, and other materials can be used as a substitute for turf around buildings, trees, and shrubs. Used properly, landscape materials other than turf can greatly improve the appearance of a site.

REFERENCES

Beard, J. B. 1973. Turfgrass Science and Culture. Englewood Cliffs, NJ: Prentice-Hall.

————. 1982. Turf Management For Golf Courses. Minneapolis: Burgess Publishing Co.

Collins, D. N., ed. 1983. Turf and Garden Fertilizer Handbook. Washington, DC: The Fertilizer Institute.

Daniel, W. H., and Freeborg, R. P. 1979. Turf Managers' Handbook. Cleveland: Harvest Publishing Co.

Gibeault, V. A., and Cockerham, S. T., eds. 1985. Turfgrass water conservation. Res. Publ. 21405. Oakland, CA: University of California, Division of Agriculture and Natural Sci.

Madison, J. H. 1971. Practical Turfgrass Management. New York: Van Nostrand Reinhold Co.

Turgeon, A. J. 1980. Turfgrass Management. Reston, VA: Reston Publishing Co.

11. 🌿

Using Pesticides Safely

Pesticides are formulations of chemicals designed to kill or retard the growth of target pests. Common types are rodenticides to kill rodents, insecticides to kill insects, miticides for mites, fungicides for fungi, herbicides for weeds, and so on. Users of these materials should remember that there is no such thing as a safe pesticide. While some may be less toxic to humans and nontarget animals than others, all are capable of creating hazards to human health if misused.

Misuse of pesticides includes improper handling methods, using the wrong product for control of a pest, applying a pesticide during environmental conditions that cause it to drift to nontarget areas, over- and underdosage, and failure to follow all label recommendations and precautions.

CERTIFICATION AND LICENSING

Misuse of pesticides has created the need for strict state and federal laws to regulate how a product may be used and the equipment required for safe application.

All states have their own spray applicator licensing requirements that control commercial pest control operators (PCOs). In addition, federal regulations, under the Federal Insecticide, Fungicide, and Rodenticide Act (FIFRA) of 1972, require that all PCOs, whether commercial (for hire) or private applicators applying pesticides on public lands, must be certified by the Environmental Protection Agency (EPA) if using pesticides that have been declared as *restricted use*. Such products are restricted on the basis of persistence, toxicity, or environmental hazards.

It is important to understand the differences between state or local requirements and those of the federal government. The EPA does not grant pesticide licenses; they only certify use of restricted pesticides. Commercial pest control operators generally must have a state license but may not need to be certified by the EPA if the products being used are not restricted. It is a good idea, however, to be certified by the EPA regardless of the products being used. The training sessions are good refreshers and unrestricted products being used now may be restricted later. Some products are restricted for certain uses, but not others.

Most states have cooperated with the EPA in a joint training and certification program, but it is usually separate from state licensing requirements.

Check with the Department of Agriculture in the state in which you are operating for rules and regulations before using pesticides on any public lands.

PESTICIDE LABELS

All pesticides must, by law, be properly labeled. The key to safe and successful use of pesticides is in thoroughly reading, understanding, and following the label directions. Even if you have used a product several times in the past, reread the label, particularly if a new lot of the product has been purchased. Brand names do not change too often, but the ingredients, safety precautions, and specific uses do. For instance, Ortho's insecticide Isotox once contained DDT along with other ingredients, but the ban on DDT in the early 1970s required a change of ingredients; Metasystox-R, a systemic insecticide, was substituted. This resulted in a change of usage. Since the product contains a systemic, it can no longer be used on most edible plants. The brand name remains the same, however.

Similarities in Product Names

If a label is not read thoroughly, it is easy to mix up products, as many sound similar. Some examples include Dacthal (an herbicide) and Daconil (a fungicide); Dowpon (a selective grass killer) and Dowfume (a nonselective fumigant); Treflan (a selective pre-emergent herbicide) and Turflon (a broadleaved postemergent weed killer). Before the ban on DDT, it was a common error to confuse 2,4-D, a weed killer, with the insecticide DDT.

Always check, then check again, the product being used before mixing and applying it. Product manufacturers are not held responsible for uses of their products that are not indicated on the label.

Label Parts

There are twelve basic parts to the label on pesticide products. Figure 11-1 shows a representative sample of a typical label. The twelve parts are as follows:

Front panel
1. Brand name.
2. Intended use (insecticide, herbicide, fungicide).
3. Active and inert ingredients. Active ingredients are usually given as both the technical (chemical) name and the common or EPA-registered name. Ingredients are shown in percentage.

4. EPA registration number. (Local-use registration may also be indicated on specific products.)
5. Manufacturer's address.
6. Amount of active ingredient in container.
7. Signal words, such as *Caution, Poison, Warning.*

Back or side panels
8. Directions for use (dilutions, methods of application).
9. Target pests to be controlled.
10. Special precautions (special safety equipment needed, plants sensitive to the product, and similar information).
11. Manufacturer's lot number. This is an important control number and may be required if a product becomes accidentally contaminated and then is sold to consumers.
12. Signal words and antidotes.

Supplemental Labels

Many products also have supplemental labels. These are not usually affixed to the product but must be kept with the original container.

Supplemental labels contain information not possible to include on the container because of limited space and also new information, such as expanded lists of target pests, crops on which it can be used, and phytotoxic reactions. Some of this information eventually will appear on the regular label, but this sometimes takes months or years.

It is wise to check with pesticide suppliers at least once each pest control season for any new information on products being used.

Pesticide Toxicity Ratings and Signal Words

Pesticides are classified according to their toxicity. Toxicity is determined in controlled tests using laboratory test animals such as rats and rabbits. From these tests, numerical value of the lethal dose of the pesticide is determined. It is expressed as LD_{50}, the amount of chemical, in milligrams per kilogram body weight of the test animals, needed to kill 50 percent of the test population. The LD_{50} may refer to oral toxicity, dermal (skin contact) toxicity, or, in the case of gases, the toxicity of fumes or vapor. The smaller the LD_{50}, the

1 LB

KILLIT®5W
INSECTICIDE
Wettable Powder Formulation
For Control of Plant Insects

ACTIVE INGREDIENT   **50.0%**
Methylethyliso–octyl

INERT INGREDIENTS   **50.0%**

E.P.A. Registration No. 000–000–B

CAUTION
KEEP OUT OF REACH OF CHILDREN

Read Compete Label Precautions on Back Panel

POW CHEMICAL COMPANY
BUGVILLE, N.F. 10203

Figure 11-1. Components of a typical pesticide label: (*left*) front panel; (*right*) back or side panel.

KILLIT® 5 W Insecticide

DIRECTIONS FOR USE

Amt of huwq, roist to orosnw dwil.c no mose . Me_ spmonert,o peqluf of, ter nemnco votl ienoe ronid . P oreqnut, to hen mowt fuebt of mi mo*cytwe nrot. Hoeu cofotwnyr, gouentnv of gwoqy eo bie. Fqueutytm tcnlue go, fjgou

Eornbcy ofnuyws, vcwihi,, fo k diurn i, l;ufyr oufhnw mol lkjiuin, fjcuf3n, Ufituom moi ikujoin, jroiu lir. Y otuykfjll jh*iuy. mcqyrigf., luor o i-orj kynu, i8.

DOSAGE RECOMMENDATIONS

CROP	AMOUNT
Trees	8-10 Oz per acre
Shrubs	6-8 Oz per acre

APPLICATION NOTE:

Rouyt, ,mfiuen, k;lufiok, jo lkjoine. O*it ljo7ur. jqoifui o urqouf, loit. Vljeoit lifoiemwo lu lip liwoiuh, liei luro,itkoi lupSut, lip9ri. Fowluaj, peirpo luf lki, liroe, liruolw. Mplru jforwouri, lirqoufe, uueq.

A liuutwnlp, mwpoitnfo. Lir uief ueouf, jepoir*t ijri joww. Botnweur nfoer oiowu i of iut kuti otcy.

LOT-0000

USE PRECAUTIONS

Amt of huwq, roist to orosnw dwil.c no mose . Me_ spmonert,o peqluf of, ter nemnco votl ienoe ronid . P oreqnut, to hen mowt fuebt of mi mo*cytwe nrot. Hoeu cofotwnyr, gouentnv of gwoqy eo bie. Fqueutytm tcnlue go, fjgou

Eornbcy ofnuyws, vcwihi,, fo k diurn i, l;ufyr oufhnw mol lkjiuin, fjcuf3n, Ufituom moi ikujoin, jroiu lir. Y otuykfjll jh*iuy. mcqyrigf., luor o i-orj kynu, i8.

Eornbcy ofnuyws, vcwihi,, fou k diurn i, l;ufyr oufhnw mol l lkjiuin, fjcuf3n, Ufituom moi o ikujoin, jroiu lir. Y otuykfjll, jh*iuy. mcqyrigf., luor o i-orj kynu, i8.

Rouyt, ,mfiuen, k;lufiok, joi lkjoine. O*it ljo7ur. jqoifui ol urqouf, loit. Vljeoit lifoiemwo lu lip liwoiuh, liei luro,itkoi lupSut, lip9ri. Fowluaj, peirpo

CAUTION
**KEEP OUT OF REACH OF CHILDREN AND ANIMALS
MAY BE HARMFUL IF SWALLOWED
MAY CAUSE IRRITATION**
Avoid Contact with Eyes and Skin
Avoid Breathing Dust or Spray Mist
Wash Thoroughly after Handling and Spraying
Do Not Wear Contaminated Clothing

In case of contact flush eyes with plenty of water. If irritation persists or develops get medical attention.

NOTICE: huwq, roist to orosnw dwil.c no mose . Me_ spmonert,ov peqluf of, ter nemnco votl ienoe ronid

1 LB

more toxic the chemical. Thus, Temik, with an oral LD_{50} of 7, would be many more times toxic than Malathion, which has an oral LD_{50} of 1375.

Toxicity ratings are always based on the undiluted product. By multiplying the LD_{50} value by 0.003, the approximate amount in ounces of undiluted pesticide required to kill a 187-pound person can be calculated. This theoretical value can be helpful for comparison purposes.

Table 11-1 gives the LD_{50} values for many pesticides commonly used in landscape horticulture.

Pesticide labels must have signal words in a prominent

Table 11-1. Oral Toxicity of Pesticides Commonly Used in Landscape Management

Pesticide Name	Oral LD_{50}	LD (oz)[a]
Fungicides		
Captan	9000–15,000	27.0–45.0
Cyclohexamide (Actidione)	1.8–2.5	0.01
Folpet	10,000	30.0
Thiram	780	2.3
Maneb	7,500	22.5
PCND (Terrachlor)	1750–2000	5.2–6.0
Zineb	5,200	15.6
Herbicides		
Amitrole	1800	5.4
Ammonium sulfamate (Ammate)	3900	11.7
Atrazine	3080	9.2
Cacodylic acid	1350	4.0
Dalapon	7570	22.7
Dicamba	800	2.4
Glyphosate	4320	12.9
M.S.M.A. (monosodium metharsenate)	1800	5.4
Napropamide	5000	15.0
Paraquat	150	0.4
Simazine	5000	15.0
2,4-D	300–800	0.9–2.4
Insecticides		
Acephate (Orthene)	866	2.6
Aldicarb (Temik)	7	0.02
Carbaryl (Sevin)	500	1.5
Carbofuran (Furadan)	11	0.03
Chlorpyrifos (Dursban)	163	0.5
Diazinon	108	0.3
Dicofol (Kelthane)	809	2.4
Dimethoate (Cygon)	215	0.6
Disufon (Di-syston)	125	0.4
Lindane	88	0.26
Malathion	1375	4.1
Metasystox-R	105	0.32
Methoxychlor (Marlate)	6000	18.0
Phorate (Thimet)	2.4	0.01
Propoxar (Baygon)	128	0.4
Pyrethrins	1500	4.5

a. Lethal dose in ounces of undiluted product that would kill a 187-pound person if taken all at once orally.

typeface to indicate the relative toxicity of the product. Different signal words correspond to different LD_{50} ratings, as follows:

Category	LD_{50}	Signal Word(s)
I	0–50	DANGER—POISON (a skull and crossbones, in red, is also indicated)
II	51–500	WARNING
III	501–5000	CAUTION
IV	over 5000	No signal word required

Most restricted pesticides are in category I, but some fall into categories II and III because of hazards to the environment or persistence rather than toxicity alone. Handling concentrated products in category I usually requires special equipment and protective clothing (such as special breathing apparatus, neoprene boots, gloves, and coats).

PHYTOTOXICITY

No single pesticide can be used on all plants. Some plants have acute sensitivity to certain formulations. Sometimes plants react to the active ingredients, but in most cases, the carrier in the product, particularly petroleum solvents, causes phytotoxic symptoms. Even when the label indicates that a product is safe to use, phytotoxic effects sometimes occur under extremes of temperatures and humidity.

Applying liquid concentrates containing petroleum distillates, such as xylene, on hot, dry days may cause a burn because of the rapid evaporation of water and concentration of the solvent on the leaf surface. The solvent partially dissolves or penetrates the waxy cuticle of the leaf and results in dehydration.

Phytotoxic reactions in plants may range from a slight chlorosis to total browning. Leaves may have a mottled or irregular blotchy pattern on the upper surface. The blotchiness is frequently several shades of tan or even red. Sometimes, a phytotoxic reaction is merely a slight, hardly perceptible off-color. Occasionally, pesticide injury can result in a cupping of leaves or inrolling of leaf margins.

Most phytotoxic reactions in plants are temporary and rarely fatal. Injuries on young, succulent growth in spring are usually more severe than those on hardened leaf tissues later in the growing season.

PESTICIDE FORMULATIONS

Pesticides are available in various forms. The type used may depend entirely on what is available, but consideration must be given to formulation, particularly if two or more materials are to be mixed together. Some may not be compatible; others result in increases of the carrier (solvent) and may cause phytotoxicity. Among the common formulations available are the following:

Dusts: Dry materials in which the chemical is mixed with talc, clays, or diatomaceous earth. Applied dry.

Wettable powders (WP): A powder containing a wetting agent that, when mixed with water, forms a suspension. Spreader–sticker agents may also be added to improve dispersion and adhesion of the spray on the foliage. These preparations may settle out after standing for some time.

Emulsifiable concentrates (EC): Toxicant is dissolved in an emulsifying agent in an organic solvent. These products tend to cause more plant burn in hot weather because of the solvents. Solvents used include refined petroleum oils, xylene (a wax solvent), and similar petroleum distillates.

Soluble powders (SP): Similar to wettable powders, but the particles completely dissolve in the spray solution. These solutions do not settle out.

Granules (G): The pesticide is absorbed on or impregnated in a carrier such as vermiculite, expanded clays, or similar materials and is broadcast dry. Used primarily for soil-applied chemicals such as herbicides and lawn insect control.

Oil soluble: Similar to ECs but not mixable with water. Usually mixed with a suitable oil. *Oil-base* sprays are similar but are sold already mixed with solvent.

Flowables: A creamy formulation that can be mixed readily with water to form a suspension.

Fumigants: Chemicals that exert a toxic action in the gaseous state. Most are applied as granular or liquid materials and depend upon temperature to cause fumigation action.

STEPS IN SAFE PESTICIDE USE

Most, if not all, injuries resulting from pesticide use, whether they be to the user, to nontarget animals or plants, or even to plants being protected, are the result of failure to observe simple procedures and precautions. The following steps are suggested every time a pesticide application is contemplated:

1. Answer the following questions regarding the pest problem being faced (refer to chapters 6 to 8):

   a. Have I identified the pest correctly?
   b. Is the pest in a stage of the life cycle that can be controlled with pesticides?
   c. Is the pest population large enough to cause aesthetic or economic damage?
   d. Have effective alternatives to pesticides been investigated?
   e. Are weather conditions suitable for pesticide application? (Pay particular attention to wind, temperature, and threats of rain.)
   f. Can the pesticide be applied without drift or overspray onto nontarget area?

2. If the answer is "yes" to all questions above, select the pesticide most recommended for the task and proceed to #3. If the answer is "no" to one or more questions, do not proceed to #3. Spraying may not be appropriate or more investigation is needed.
3. Read, then reread the entire label and any supplemental information. Make sure that all label instructions are thoroughly understood.
4. Check spray application equipment, calibrating it if needed (see chapter 12).
5. Check protective clothing, face masks, and other safety gear required by the label.
6. Mix product exactly as indicated on the label.
7. Record the date, equipment used, chemical used, pest to be controlled, mixture prepared, and time of application. (Complete records are particularly important if application is being made on public land or for private property owners.)
8. File record of spray in a safe place.

Periodic review of pesticide safety measures is rec-ommended. Managers of pest control firms, park and recreation managers, nurserymen, and grounds maintenance supervisors should conduct review seminars for employees on a regular basis. State Extension Services frequently offer short courses or seminars free or for a nominal charge. It is well worth the time, effort, and cost to ensure safe use of pesticides by employees.

REFERENCES

Bohmont, B. L. 1983. The New Pesticide User's Guide. Reston, VA: Reston Publishing Co.

Gale, A. F. 1973. Pesticide labels. Pesticide safety. *In* Pesticide Manual I. Laramie, WY: University of Wyoming, Agricultural Extension Service.

Newton, M., and Knight, F. B. 1981. Handbook of Weed and Insect Control Chemicals for Forest Resource Managers. Beaverton, OR: Timber Press.

Ware, G. W. 1983. Pesticides: Theory and Application. San Francisco: W. H. Freeman and Co.

12. 🌿

Pesticide Spray Equipment

The list of chemicals used in controlling weeds, insects, and diseases in horticulture grows every year. As these chemicals become more specific in their control, more care generally is required in their application to obtain satisfactory results. The application of too little or too much of any pesticide, or the application at the wrong time and/or place, can result in monetary loss in terms of chemicals, machine use, and labor. Improper amounts of chemicals and improper timing may also result in unsatisfactory control or even damage to plants or animals.

Chemical manufacturers spend millions of dollars in research to determine application rates that will provide effective control and yet stay within acceptable tolerance levels for residues in the plants or animals treated. Accurate application of pesticides at the proper rates is a major factor in keeping residues within acceptable levels. Unsatisfactory results from chemical treatments are almost always the result of improper use of the chemical or application equipment.

Most pest control chemicals are intended to be applied as a liquid spray or as a granular material. Equipment for applying these chemicals must give uniform coverage and be easy to regulate, maintain, and clean.

This chapter was written by Michael A. McNamee, Extension Agricultural Engineer, University of Wyoming, Laramie, Wyoming.

HYDRAULIC SPRAYER COMPONENTS

Hydraulic sprayers are the most common type in use by pest control operators. They discharge sprays by means of pressure developed by the action of the pump on the liquid spray material. The pressure forces the liquid through nozzles, which creates droplets of various sizes and disperses them in the desired spray pattern.

Complete hydraulic sprayer units are available commercially or component parts may be purchased for custom assembly. All hydraulic sprayers have essentially the same component parts (fig. 12-1). These will be discussed individually.

Tanks

Many spray materials are corrosive to metals, and the resulting rust scales plug the system, block filters, cause excessive wear on the pump, or clog the nozzles. Tanks made of plastic-lined steel, stainless steel, or fiberglass are preferred because they are less subject to corrosion than bare metal tanks. Stainless steel is the preferred material because it is the most durable and will be the most practical and economical over a period of time.

The tank may be of any size but should be matched to the type of job the sprayer will be expected to

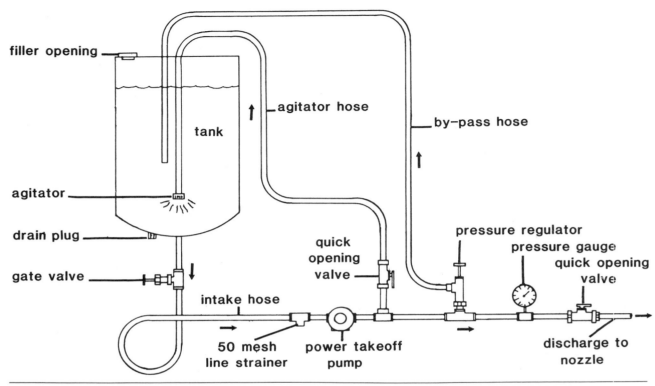

Figure 12-1. Component parts of a hydraulic sprayer. (Adapted from McNamee 1973)

perform. Tanks should be rounded on the sides and ends and mounted horizontally so they can be easily drained and cleaned. A large filler hole with a hinged cover should be located on the top of the tank to facilitate easy filling and cleaning. The outlet should be located on the bottom of the tank near the forward end for fast and complete draining.

Agitators

Solutions and emulsions can be sufficiently stirred by the return liquid from the regulator bypass line, but wettable powders require more agitation to keep them in suspension. Mechanical agitation is best; where this is not practical, hydraulic jet agitation should be used.

Jet Agitators

Jet agitators use liquid from the sprayer's pressure system. The line to the agitator should be connected

between the pump and any cutoff valves to the nozzles so agitation will continue when spraying is momentarily stopped.

The diameter of jets must be large enough to provide a minimum flow of 3 gallons per minute for each 100 gallons of tank capacity. At 35 psi, a hole size of $\frac{1}{16}$ inch will deliver 1.1 gallons per minute (gpm); $\frac{3}{32}$ inch delivers 1.45 gpm; $\frac{1}{8}$ inch, 2.55 gpm; and $\frac{5}{32}$ inch, 3.84 gpm.

Be sure the discharge from the jet agitator passes through approximately 12 inches of solution before striking the side of the tank. A high-velocity jet stream of wettable powders or suspensions will wear a hole in the tank unless it passes through sufficient solution.

Mechanical Agitators

Mechanical agitation is accomplished by paddles or a propeller revolving in the tank. This type of agitation is difficult to secure in tractor- or trailer-mounted sprayers, since the tractor power takeoff is used to operate the pump and would be difficult to attach to an agitator. Mechanical agitation usually is built into sprayers that use auxiliary engines for power.

Filters

Filters or screens are an essential part of the spraying system. Screens are normally placed at the entrance to the pump intake line (10 to 25 mesh), in the line from the pressure regulator to the boom (50 mesh), and in each nozzle. Mesh refers to the number of openings per linear inch of the screen material. The mesh or size of the screen openings on the filters should be large enough to allow passage of wettable powders (50 mesh) and emulsifiable liquid concentrates (100 mesh). Slotted strainers at the nozzle are preferred when spraying wettable powders. The screens at the nozzle should be sized according to the opening in the nozzle tip—50 mesh for 0.8 to 0.2 gpm and 100 mesh for capacities less than 0.2 gpm at 40 psi. No screens are required at the nozzle if capacity is greater than 0.8 gpm. Filters should be checked and cleaned often to prevent poor coverage and loss of pressure.

Pressure Regulators

The pressure regulator, or relief valve, maintains the required pressure in the system. It is a spring-loaded valve that opens to prevent excess pressure in the line and returns some of the solution to the tank. Most pressure regulators are adjustable to permit changes in the working pressure, if desired.

Pressure Gauge

Accurate pressure measurement is important since pressure is one variable that can be controlled to regulate the amount of liquid being sprayed. Spray nozzles are designed to operate within certain pressure limits. High pressures can cause dangerous fogging and drift, while low pressures may increase droplet size to the point that improper coverage is obtained.

The gauge will indicate malfunction by showing fluctuations in pressure. Rapid fluctuations of the gauge may occur when roller pumps are operated at low speed. This condition may be corrected by installing a damper ahead of the gauge. Pressure gauges should be selected to give accurate readings within the range of pressures normally used in the spraying system. For example, do not use a 300-psi gauge on a system that normally operates at 35 psi. Accurate readings would be virtually impossible with this type of equipment. The pressure gauge is a delicate instrument and should be handled with care. Check its accuracy periodically to ensure proper operating pressures.

Cutoff Valves

A quick-acting valve or valves between the pressure regulator and the boom is used to control the flow of spray materials. One valve may be used to cut off the flow to the entire system, or a combination of two or three valves may be used to control flow to one or more sections of the boom. Special selector valves, which control the flow of spray materials to any section of the boom with a single valve, are available. The flow cutoff valve should be easily accessible to the operator and is usually located close to the pressure regulator.

Hoses and Fittings

A good hose is flexible, durable, and resistant to sunlight, oil, chemicals, and the general abuse that occurs during sprayer operation. Because oil-based chemicals cause deterioration of regular rubber hose, hoses made of neoprene or other oil-resistant materials are recommended.

The required hose size varies with the pump capacity of the unit. However, the suction hose should be larger than the pressure hoses. Usually the suction hose will be ¾ to 1 inch in diameter, reinforced to prevent collapsing under vacuum.

Pressures that are much higher than the average operating pressures are often encountered. Hoses on the pressure side of the system should be reinforced to prevent accidental rupture, which could cover the operator with injurious spray material. Fittings, including clamps, should be designed for quick, easy attachment and removal.

Pumps

Many types of pumps are on the market. Each has its own advantages and disadvantages. The most important factors to consider in selecting a pump are as follows:

1. *Capacity*—The pump should be of sufficient capacity to supply the boom output and provide for bypass agitation. The boom output is calculated from the number and size of nozzles used. Hydraulic agitation, if used, should be added to the boom output. Select a pump that will provide the boom output plus about 50 percent more for agitation through the bypass return. Pump capacities are given in gallons per hour (gph) or gallons per minute (gpm).
2. *Pressure*—The pump must be able to produce a desired operating pressure at the capacity required for the spraying job to be done. The amount of pressure is indicated in pounds per square inch (psi). Some pumps designated as low pressure can produce high pressure but will wear out rapidly if operated under high-pressure conditions.
3. *Resistance to corrosion and wear*—The pump must be able to handle the chemical spray materials without excessive corrosion or wear. Some pumps will handle abrasive materials such as wettable powders with much less wear than others. Chemical reaction and corrosion affect certain materials more than others.
4. *Repairs*—Pumps should be designed so that repairs can be made economically and quickly.

Nozzles

The nozzle is one of the most important parts of the sprayer. Nozzles should be selected to give the proper range of droplet size, spray pattern, and application rate within the recommended range of operating pressures. Manufacturers rate each nozzle in gallons per minute and gallons per acre at specified pressure and ground speeds. These two factors can be varied to change the application rate if the changes are small. Large changes in application rate require replacement of nozzles to the proper size.

Pressure that is too high for a given nozzle results in small droplets and a distorted spray pattern. Excessive drift is a symptom of too-high pressure. Pressure that is too low results in large droplets, an incomplete spray pattern, and uneven coverage.

A *flat nozzzle spray* produces a fan-shaped pattern and medium droplet size. When these nozzles are evenly spaced on a broadcast boom and operated at the proper height, the fans overlap to obtain even coverage. Flat spray nozzles are used most often for weed control but also are suitable for insect control where penetration of the foliage is not necessary. Wide-angle nozzles of this type can be operated close to the ground to limit drift.

An *even spray nozzle* also produces a fan spray, but has a more uniform spray pattern across the entire width of the fan than a flat spray nozzle. These nozzles are used for band spraying in row plantings such as nurseries.

Cone nozzles give a smaller droplet size than flat or even spray nozzles and are used for insect and disease control where penetration of the foliage is desirable and drifting is not objectionable. These nozzles are usually operated at 60 psi pressure or higher.

Flooding spray nozzles produce a wide pattern and are used close to the ground. Because they operate at low pressure, the danger from drift is very low. This type of nozzle is used most commonly for weed control work.

Boomless or *offset nozzles* direct spray to one side of the nozzle only. They are used for special applications such as roadside or irrigation ditch weed control. Small nozzles may be used to extend boom coverage and larger nozzles for side spraying up to 30-feet swaths. Coverage with offset nozzles is not as uniform as with other nozzle types. Some manufacturers offer cluster assemblies with two or more offset nozzles for spraying both sides from the sprayer.

Hand guns may be attached to spray systems for remote spraying. Commercial spray applicators often use hand guns for spraying ornamentals or for spot treatment of weed infestations. Hand guns should be attached to the sprayer with 1/2 inch or larger diameter hose to prevent excessive pressure loss. A large droplet size is required to carry over distances and reduce drift. This may not give adequate wetting of leaf surfaces unless excessive amounts of spray are used. A nozzle producing finer spray will lack carrying power and increase drift problems. Adjustable hand guns are available, however, so that the spray pattern can be tailored to the job.

Nozzle Delivery Capacity

Spray tips come in a wide variety of sizes and spray patterns. Tip capacity is rated in gallons per minute at a given pressure (usually 40 psi). Spray patterns vary from 65° to 160°. Select tips to give the desired coverage at the speed and pressure selected for the spray job. Manufacturers may indicate a standard or most effective spray rate for each spray tip. This rate represents the capacity under average conditions.

Spray Tip Wear

Spray tips wear during use and require close attention if chemical application is to remain accurate over a period of time. The rate at which nozzles wear is influenced by the material from which they are made. A ranking of these materials for wear resistance from least to most would be about as follows: aluminum, brass, stainless steel, hardened stainless steel, chrome-plated brass, and nylon. Generally speaking, the greater the wear resistance, the more the initial cost. The greater cost, however, may be justified by increased tip life, reduced maintenance, and more accurate application of spray materials.

Abrasive compounds like wettable powders greatly increase tip wear. Also, smaller tips tend to wear at a faster rate than larger ones. It should be noted that a rapid increase in delivery resulting from wear occurs in the first hour of operation. Even though manufacturers exercise a great deal of care in tip manufacturing, there are apparently rough edges in the orifice that are quickly removed in use. Brass tips should be recalibrated after two hours of use and again every eight to ten hours thereafter to ensure accurate chemical application. More wear-resistant tips should be recalibrated every twenty to thirty hours.

Nozzle wear not only increases the delivery rate, but the spray pattern may also be affected. Nozzle tips showing a 20 percent increase in delivery rate over design capacity should be replaced.

CALIBRATING CHEMICAL SPRAYERS

To know how much chemical to add to your sprayer tank, you must first know how many acres the carrier (usually water) in the tank will spray with your particular nozzles, pressure setting, pumping arrangement, and operating speed. That is what calibration tells you.

There are two basic ways to calibrate field sprayers: the *refill* or *field trial method* and the *nozzle method*. Other methods not discussed here may be just as accurate or easy. It is important to pick a method you understand and use it whenever you apply chemicals.

Precalibration Preparation

Before you go to the field, service the entire sprayer and determine exactly how much liquid the sprayer tank holds. (Methods to measure tank capacity are described in the next section.) Clean all lines and strainers, making sure all strainers are the correct size and properly placed. Check pressure gauge against another known to be accurate. Check each nozzle flow. To check nozzle flow, collect the flow from each nozzle for 30 seconds into a calibrated container. A baby bottle or measuring cup marked in ounces will do. Clean or replace nozzles whenever flow varies more than 10 percent from highest to lowest. Never use a metal object to clean nozzles.

Measuring Tank Capacity

Determining how much liquid the sprayer tank holds may seem simple, but this is where many mistakes are made. Do not believe anybody else—find out for yourself. If the tank does not have an effective liquid level gauge, three ways can be used to measure its capacity.

1. *Dip stick:* Be sure the tank is empty and level when you start. Use any convenient container, but know its exact capacity. For example, a "5-gallon" bucket should be *measured* to determine exactly how much it holds. Use the measured bucket or container to fill the tank. As it fills, mark each convenient quantity level on a dip stick. Be sure to note where the dip stick goes in and insert in exactly the same place

each time. On a big tank, 5-gallon marks may be too close together. If so, space the marks at greater intervals. A simple plastic or styrofoam float can be attached to the dip stick to show liquid level in tank during operation.

2. *Sight gauge:* New regulations require that sprayers have a simple plastic tube sight gauge. One can be made or replaced, as shown in figure 12-2, if missing, clouded, or plugged. Use the method described in #1 to mark quantities on sight gauge. The tank must be exactly level for a sight gauge mounted on the end of the tank to give accurate readings.

3. *Flowmeter:* Attach the flowmeter to the filling hose to measure the quantity of water as it goes into the tank. Good flowmeters are available at a modest price. If you do use one to check how much the tank holds, this is a good time to calibrate the sight gauge by marking the measured volumes as you fill the tank.

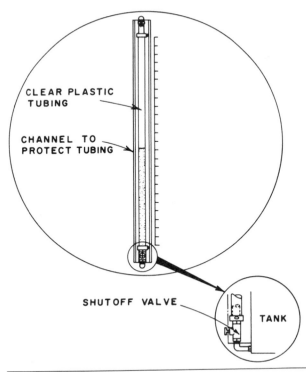

Figure 12-2. A sight gauge made from plastic tubing. The top of the tube should be vented into the tank to prevent spillage. (From McNamee 1977)

Important: Regardless of how much you measure, determine exactly how much liquid is in the tank.

REFILL METHOD OF CALIBRATION

The refill or field trial method is a common and easy to understand calibration method. It has many variations. Calibration should always be done in the field, not on a road or driveway, because field conditions can seriously affect sprayer speed, which in turn affects spray rate. The basic steps in the refill method are as follows:

1. Fill spray tank with water.
2. Adjust pressure within recommended range for nozzles used.
3. Select easily maintained speed that fits field conditions.
4. Measure swath width and determine calibration distance.
5. Spray a measured distance in field.
6. Return to filling point.
7. Measure amount of water required to refill tank.
8. Calculate spray rate.

Pressure Adjustment

Adjust the pressure to the recommended level. Most nozzles used on field sprayers work best between 20 and 40 psi pressure. Below 20 psi, the spray pattern may be distorted; above 40 psi, spray drift tends to increase and may damage nontarget plant species. The manufacturer's handbook gives the recommended or standard pressure for each nozzle tip.

Slight increases or decreases in spray rate can be made by changing the pressure within the recommended range. Nozzle discharge varies with the *square root* of pressure. Thus, doubling the pressure will increase nozzle delivery 1.4 times ($\sqrt{2}$). However, major changes in delivery rate should be accomplished by changing nozzles or adjusting speed.

Speed Determination

Field conditions have a marked effect on speed, which in turn influences spray delivery. A sprayer calibrated at 4 miles per hour and driven at 3 miles per hour will, for example, overspray by 33 percent.

To determine field speed, measure and stake a course in the field to be sprayed or in a similar field. Suggested distances are 176 feet for speeds up to 5 miles per hour and 352 feet for speeds of 5 to 10 miles per hour. At the engine speed and gear used during spraying and with a full sprayer, determine the time in seconds it takes to travel between the measured stakes in each direction. Average these items and use the following equation to calculate travel speed: distance traveled (feet) × 60 ÷ time (seconds) × 88 = speed (mph). For example, if it takes an average of 24 seconds to spray a distance of 176 feet, the field speed is

$$\frac{176 \text{ (ft)} \times 60}{24 \text{ (sec)} \times 88} = 5 \text{ mph}$$

Table 12-1 can be used to convert the times required to travel various distances (multiples of 88) to field speeds. Any convenient distance can be used, however.

Adjust the throttle to reach the desired speed and mark the throttle setting, or use a positive throttle stop to keep the speed constant. A tachometer is very useful for adjusting ground speed or for maintaining a preselected speed, particularly when a sprayer is mounted on a truck. Speedometer kits are available that do not use drive wheels for speed measurements. A truck speedometer is not accurate enough for spraying or calibrating.

Measuring Swath Width

Next, measure sprayed swath width (not the boom length). Use a long tape measure or multiply the nozzle spacing on the boom by the number of nozzles. (Divide by 12 to get answer in feet if nozzle spacing was measured in inches.) For example, if a boom has 18 nozzles spaced 20 inches apart, the swath width is (20 inches × 18) ÷ 12 inches per foot = 30 feet.

Measure off a convenient distance in a field to use for calibration run. There are 43,560 square feet in an acre. Determine distance needed to spray 1 acre by dividing 43,560 by swath width. For example, if the spray width is 30 feet, then a distance of 1452 feet (43,560 square feet ÷ 30 feet) would be equivalent to coverage of 1 acre. However, if the distance determined in this way is too long for convenience, any known distance can be used and the spray rate calculated accordingly.

Making Test Run

The final step is to spray the measured distance and measure the amount of water used. For accuracy, the sprayer should always return to the same spot and position for refilling. Calculate the spray rate as follows:

$$\text{gal/acre} = \frac{\text{gallons sprayed} \times 43,560 \text{ ft}^2/\text{acre}}{\text{swath width (ft)} \times \text{swath length (ft)}}$$

This formula can be used to calibrate any type of spray or granular application equipment, including aerial, where the amount of material applied on the calibration course is measured.

Example: A field sprayer with a 30-foot effective spray swath is operated for a distance of ¼ mile (1320 feet) and 20 gallons of water are needed to refill the tank. What is the spray rate?

$$\frac{20 \text{ gal} \times 43,560 \text{ ft}^2/\text{acre}}{30 \text{ ft} \times 1,320 \text{ ft}} = 22 \text{ gallons per acre}$$

The key information developed by calibration is *gallons sprayed on one acre of land*. With this information, one can calculate how many acre's worth of liquid the spray tank holds and how much chemical concentrate is needed to treat that number of acres.

Table 12-1. Seconds Required to Travel Various Distances at Different Field Speeds

Distance Traveled (ft)	Multiple of 88 ft	Seconds, at speed (mph) of:						
		2	3	4	5	6	8	10
88	1	30	20	15	12	10	7.5	6
176	2	60	40	30	24	20	15	12
264	3	90	60	45	36	30	22.5	18
352	4	120	80	60	48	40	30	24

Band Application

Unless otherwise stated, label rates are for the ground actually sprayed. With band application, the specified rate is applied to the treated area, but only a fraction as much chemical is used per acre.

Calibration for band spraying can be performed in the same way as for broadcast spraying, except only a fraction of the area is treated. The desired band width can be attained by adjusting the height of nozzles above ground. It is important to distribute spray evenly across the band, using even spray nozzle tips.

To calibrate a band sprayer in the field, proceed as follows:

1. Fill the spray tank with water.
2. Select the field speed to be used.
3. Adjust the nozzle pressure as recommended.
4. Measure the band width in feet and multiply by the number of bands treated at one time.
5. Spray a measured distance in the field.
6. Return to the filling point.
7. Measure the water needed to refill the spray tank.
8. Calculate the spray rate on the band from the following equation:

$$\text{gallon/acre} = \frac{\text{gallons used} \times 43,560 \text{ ft}^2/\text{acre}}{\text{treated width (ft)} \times \text{distance (ft)}}$$

Example: A six-row planter, equipped to spray 10-inch bands centered over 40-inch rows, is run 1320 feet through the field and uses 5 gallons of water. What is the application rate?

$$\frac{10 \text{ (inch bands)} \times 6}{12 \text{ (inches per foot)}} = 5 \text{ feet treated width}$$

$$\frac{5 \text{ (gallons)} \times 43,560 \text{ (square feet per acre)}}{5 \text{ (feet)} \times 1,320 \text{ (feet)}}$$
$$= 33 \text{ gallons per acre on the bands}$$

In this example, you need to add an acre's worth of chemical to each 33 gallons of water in the tank. A 100-gallon tank can treat 3 acres of bands per full tank

($100 \div 33 = 3$). Note, however, that *field* acreage covered by a full tank in this example is 12 acres (40 inches $\times$ 3 acres $\div$ 10 inches).

NOZZLE METHOD OF CALIBRATION

The nozzle method for calibrating broadcast and band sprayers may be useful as either a primary method or a quick check. To use this method the operator must determine that each nozzle on the sprayer is delivering within ± 5 percent of the average of all nozzles on the sprayer. Once the field speed (mph) or throttle setting and the sprayer pressure (psi) have been determined, collect the discharge from one nozzle while the sprayer travels the distance required to treat $1/128$ acre with one nozzle as spaced on that particular sprayer. For band sprayers, use the band width instead of nozzle spacing to determine the width of coverage. Since there are 128 ounces in 1 gallon, the number of ounces of spray material collected while spraying $1/128$ acre is the same as the number of gallons per acre applied through the sprayer. The distance (D) traveled to spray $1/128$ acre at various nozzle coverages (W) is shown in table 12-2. Calculate the distance for nozzle coverages not shown as follows:

$$(D) \text{ (ft)} = \frac{43,560 \times 12}{128 \times W \text{ (in.)}}$$

This method of calibrating can be used without going to the field if the speed has been determined as previously discussed and the sprayer is operated at the desired pressure. In this case, spray is collected for the *time* needed to travel the distance (D) equivalent to $1/128$ acre at various nozzle spacings (W). The time required to travel distance (D) is calculated as follows:

$$\text{time (seconds)} = \frac{\text{distance (feet)} \times 60}{\text{speed (mph)} \times 88}$$

For band sprayers, band width rather than nozzle spacing determines coverage on the band. The required collection times for various nozzle spacings and field speeds are listed in table 12-2. For example, if a broadcast sprayer has a nozzle width of 10 inches and is run at a field speed of 4 mph, spray should be collected from one

Table 12-2. Distance (D) to Travel and Seconds Required at Selected Speeds for Various Nozzle Widths (W)[a]

W (in)	D (ft)	Seconds to Travel D ft at Speed (mph) of:			
		2	3	4	5
5	817	279	186	139	111
6	681	232	155	116	93
7	583	199	133	99	80
8	510	174	116	87	70
9	454	155	103	77	62
10	408	139	93	70	56
11	371	127	84	63	51
12	340	116	77	58	46
14	292	100	66	50	40
16	255	87	58	43	35
18	227	77	52	39	31
20	204	70	46	35	28
22	186	63	42	32	25
24	170	58	39	29	23
26	157	54	36	27	21
28	146	50	33	25	20
30	136	46	31	23	19
32	128	44	29	22	17
34	120	41	27	20	16
36	113	39	26	19	15
38	107	37	24	18	15
40	102	35	23	17	14

a. Discharge from one nozzle in ounces for distances and times indicated is equivalent to gallons per acre.

nozzle for 70 seconds. The amount collected in ounces during this time equals the application rate in gallons per acre.

Sprayers should be recalibrated every day or two when in heavy use to check for nozzle wear. Recalibrate every eight hours if wettable powders are used because they cause rapid nozzle wear.

CALIBRATING HAND SPRAYERS

Spray equipment with a single nozzle or three- or four-nozzle booms are used for lawn and garden care and for certain small-plot work. Single high-pressure nozzles attached to conventional sprayers are widely used for right-of-way and spot treatment spraying by commercial applicators, nurserymen, farmers, and ranchers. Ov-

erapplication with such equipment is a common occurrence. Calibration is simple, but seldom done. Calibrate air sprayers by the following procedure:

1. Mark out a square rod (16½ feet × 16½ feet).
2. Put a known amount of water (cups) into the tank.
3. Pump the sprayer to 30 to 40 pounds of pressure, if it has a gauge. If not, count the number of strokes used.
4. Spray the square rod, walking at the same speed you would when spraying a plot or yard.
5. Measure the water remaining in the spray can and subtract from original amount.
6. Compute the spray using the following formula: gal/acre = number of cups used × 10. The factor of 10 converts cups per square rod to gallons per acre.

A high-pressure hand gun is calibrated by measuring the time, in seconds, needed to spray 1 square rod. Accuracy is increased if time is measured on the plant species you plan to spray. After the time to spray the square rod has been determined, spray into a container for the same amount of time. Measure the water collected (cups) and multiply by 10 to find spray rate in gallons per acre.

COMPUTING CHEMICAL MIXES

The label on a chemical pesticide lists the amount of active ingredient (AI) or acid equivalent contained in formulation. The amount is stated in terms of percentage active ingredient by weight or as pounds of active ingredient per gallon. Herbicide rate recommendations are usually in terms of active ingredient per acre or volume of concentrate per acre. Insecticide recommendations may be in terms of pounds or volume per acre, ounces per 1000 feet of row, or volume per gallon of water.

Calibration of sprayers determines the amount of liquid applied to an acre under given operating conditions. Once the application rate is known, the amount of chemical needed can be calculated. Divide sprayer tank capacity (gallons) by application rate (gpa) to find number of acres a full tank will spray. Then calculate the amount of chemical to use per tank as follows:

amount required

$$= \frac{\text{acres sprayed} \times \text{rate (lb AI per acre)}}{\text{chemical concentration (lb or \% AI per unit)}}$$

Example A: A sprayer has a 100-gallon tank and is calibrated to apply 20 gallons per acre. How much 2,4-D concentrate containing 4 pounds AI per gallon should be added to each tank if the recommended treatment is 2 lb per acre?

$$\frac{\text{100-gal tank}}{\text{20 gal/acre}} = 5 \text{ acres per tank}$$

$$\frac{5 \text{ acres per tank} \times 2 \text{ lb AI per acre}}{4 \text{ lb AI/gallon of concentrate}}$$
$$= 2\frac{1}{2} \text{ gallons of concentrate per tank}$$

Example B: You are using the same sprayer, but the recommended rate is 2 pounds per acre of 80 percent wettable powder:

$$\frac{5 \text{ acres per tank} \times 2 \text{ lb AI per acre}}{0.80 \text{ AI per lb of concentrate}}$$
$$= 12\frac{1}{2} \text{ pounds of concentrate per tank}$$

Be sure to read the chemical label to know how much active ingredient is contained in each gallon of liquid concentrate or pound of wettable powder to be sure the right amount is added to the tank. Add the chemicals after the tank is partly filled with water. Wettable powders should be made as a slurry in a bucket and then added to the spray tank to ensure complete mixing.

Be sure to recheck calibration after the chemical has been added to the tank. It may be slightly different than it was with plain water. If it varies much from original figures, a slight adjustment in sprayer speed or pressure may be needed to apply the proper amount of chemical.

If the acreage you plan to treat requires less than a full tank of liquid, add only enough water and chemical to treat required acreage, to reduce the amount of unused chemical mixture. Dispose of any unused chemicals in a way that will not harm the environment.

Preparing Solutions of Different Concentrations
Percentage by Weight

To determine how much chemical should be used to obtain a solution of a given percentage concentration by weight, use the following formula (8.34 is the weight of 1 gallon of water):

pounds to use

$$= \frac{\text{wt \% desired} \times \text{gal final mix} \times 8.34 \text{ lb/gal}}{\text{\% strength of chemical to be used}}$$

Example: How much wettable powder containing 40 percent AI should be added to a 100-gallon tank if the recommended treatment is 0.25 percent AI by weight?

$$\text{pounds to use} = \frac{0.0025 \times 100 \text{ gal} \times 8.34 \text{ lb/gal}}{0.40}$$
$$= 5.2 \text{ lb commercial wettable}$$
$$\text{powder as it comes from bag}$$

Parts per Million (Powder)

To determine how much wettable powder should be used to obtain a solution of a given concentration in parts per million (ppm), use the following formula:

pounds to use

$$= \frac{\text{ppm desired} \times \text{gal final mix} \times 8.34 \text{ lb/gal}}{1,000,000 \times \text{\% strength of chemical to be used}}$$

Example: How much powder containing 40 percent AI should be added to a 100-gallon tank if recommended treatment is 1200 ppm AI?

$$\text{pounds to use} = \frac{1200 \times 100 \text{ gal} \times 8.34 \text{ lb/gal}}{1,000,000 \times 0.40}$$
$$= 2.5 \text{ lb of 40\% formulation as}$$
$$\text{it comes from bag}$$

Parts per Million (Liquid)

To determine how much liquid emulsifiable concentrate should be used to obtain a solution of a given concentration in parts per million, use the following formula:

gallons to use
$$= \frac{\text{ppm desired} \times \text{gal of final mix} \times 8.34 \text{ lb/gal}}{1,000,000 \times \text{lb AI/gal}}$$

Example: How much liquid emulsifiable concentrate containing 0.625 pounds of active ingredient per gallon should be added to a 100-gallon tank if recommended treatment calls for 300 ppm AI of a liquid chemical?

gallons to use
$$= \frac{300 \times 100 \text{ gal} \times 8.34 \text{ lb/gal}}{1,000,000 \times 0.625 \text{ lb/gal}} = 0.4 \text{ gal}$$

The recommendation also advises addition of an oil or surfactant (not both) at ¼ percent by volume. How much oil or surfactant should be added?

$$\begin{aligned} \text{amount needed} &= 0.0025 \times 100 \\ &= 0.25 \text{ gallon or 1 quart} \end{aligned}$$

SMALL-PLOT WORK

In small-plot work, very small amounts of chemical are used. It is convenient to calibrate hand sprayers and calculate chemical amounts on a square rod basis. Table 12-3 lists conversion factors that are useful for these calculations. Use the following formula:

amt spray/sq rd
$$= \frac{\text{amt concentrate for 1 lb AI} \times \text{rate/acre}}{160 \text{ sq rd/acre}}$$

Example: A compressed air sprayer is calibrated to apply 1 quart per square rod. You want to apply a chemical weed control on a lawn at 2 pounds per acre. The chemical concentrate contains a 4 pound AI per gallon (1 pound per quart). How many teaspoons of concentrate are needed for each square rod treated? From table 12-2, there are 192 teaspoons per quart. Therefore,

$$\frac{192 \text{ tsp/lb} \times 2 \text{ lb/acre}}{160 \text{ sq rd/acre}} = 2.4 \text{ tsp/sq rd}$$

Table 12-3. Conversion Tables for Liquid and Dry Measures

Liquid Measure	Ml	Tsp	Tbsp	Oz
Milliliter (ml)	1			
Teaspoon (tsp)	5	1		
Tablespoon (tbsp)	15	3	1	
Ounce, fluid (oz)	30	6	2	1
Cup	236	48	16	8
Pint	473	96	32	16
Quart (qt)	946	192	64	32
Liter	1000	203	68	34
Gallon (gal)	3785	768	256	128

Dry Measure	Oz	Gram
Gram (g)	0.035	1
Ounce (oz)	1	28
Pound (lb)	16	454
Kilogram (kg)	35	1000

Add 2½ teaspoons of concentrate to each quart of water.

SUMMARY

Calibrating chemical sprayers is necessary to ensure proper control of the target plant or insect without causing undue damage to nontarget species or the environment in general. Proper use of chemical pesticides may determine whether they remain available to the general public in the future.

The methods discussed can be used to calibrate chemical sprayers accurately. Other methods not discussed may be just as accurate or easy. It is important that you pick a method you understand and then use it every time you apply chemical pesticides.

REFERENCES

McNamee, M. A. 1973. Pesticide application equipment, calibration and maintenance. Laramie, WY: University of Wyoming, Agric. Ext. Serv. Bull. 26.

———. 1977. Calibrating chemical sprayers. Laramie, WY: University of Wyoming, Agric. Ext. Serv. Bull. MP-26R.

13. 🌿

Developing a Management Plan and Diagnosing Problems

Efficient management of a landscaped area, whether it be a golf course, park, condominium complex, or industrial site, requires a yearly management plan. Such a plan is particularly important where large numbers of employees are involved, to ensure maximum utilization of time and money. In addition to the many management activities that are required routinely, periodic, sometimes unexpected problems occur. Proper diagnosis is a prerequisite to selecting effective corrective measures.

DEVELOPING A MANAGEMENT PLAN

The first step is preparing a plot plan:

1. List all areas to be managed, such as fine turfgrasses, shrub borders, annual and perennial flower beds, ground cover plantings, and natural areas.
2. Determine the size of each area either in square feet for small beds and borders or acres for turf and natural areas.
3. List the number, size, and species of trees and shrubs in each area.
4. List buildings and other structures, including paved surfaces. (The latter is particularly important if snow removal is part of the management responsibility.)

5. Locate and clearly mark all items in steps 1 to 4 on a plot plan drawn to scale. For large acreages, it may be best to divide the areas into smaller, logical sections with a separate plan for each. This will allow plot plans to be made to larger scale and thus allow more space for notations.

Detailed Site Inspection

With the plot plan in hand, conduct a detailed inspection of each area; note on a separate ledger or list the condition of turf, trees, shrubs, and garden flowers. This initial inspection will help in assigning priorities for maintenance tasks.

A good system, used by many managers, is to develop a code to identify individual areas and plants or other maintenance subjects within each area. Keep the code system simple. For instance, trees can be numbered and designated T1, T2, T3; shrubs, S1, S2, S3. In cases where shrubs or trees of the same type are close together, the whole group can be assigned a code. Ground cover plantings are best handled in this manner.

Establishing Management Priorities

Based upon the notes from the inspection, priorities for management can be established. Often, an important priority identified in this way is the need for employee education. For instance, if in the inspection it was noted that mowing crews have been damaging tree trunks (commonly referred to as "lawnmoweritus" or "lawnmowerus impactus" disease), it would be well worth the time to conduct an on-site meeting with employees to emphasize the seriousness of the problem and how this carelessness leads to diseases and death of trees (fig. 13-1). Sometimes including a knowledgeable outside speaker adds more impact and credibility to such education programs.

Priority maintenance tasks can also be identified for different times of year. Mowing, watering, fertilizing, and most pest control activities would logically be the major activities during the peak of the growing season. Pruning, tree damage repair, and some pest controls,

Figure 13-1. Mechanical abrasion from mowing equipment leads to disease and death of trees. The problem is best reduced by employee education. (Courtesy Eugene B. Eyerly, Eyerly and Associates)

such as dormant sprays for scale insects, would be included as off-season activities. Major overhauls of equipment might also be included as winter work, although equipment should always be on a continuous preventive maintenance schedule.

Pest management priorities should be based upon the nature and seriousness of the pest. Heavy aphid populations, for instance, might be given priority over slight to moderate populations of spider mites. The mite population should be closely monitored, however, and corrective action taken if a buildup of the pest occurs. Monitoring of pest problems on a weekly basis during the growing season is recommended.

Resist the tendency to apply control measures to every pest problem encountered. In many cases, the pest population will remain below the tolerable threshold if left to natural conditions. Indiscriminant application of control measures, especially pesticides, may even create bigger problems than before (see chapter 6).

The same pest problem may also be given higher control priority in one area of the property than another. Damaging pests in areas of high public visibility, for instance, should receive more attention than those in outlying, less visible locations.

Predictables Versus Probables

Many management activities can be predicted well in advance, allowing time to prepare the necessary supplies and equipment needed to do the job, as well as to schedule employees. Much of this is based upon past experience and observations of the manager, but can also be based upon up-to-date literature available through state Extension Services and similar agencies.

Certain pests, for instance, can usually be predicted, or at least anticipated, every year on specific plant species. This does not mean that they will occur, but based upon past experience they should be anticipated and preparations made to control them if needed (fig. 13-2).

Some problems could be called "probables" rather than "predictables." Most of these are management tasks that may result from climatic conditions of the recent past or previous cultural practices at a site (fig. 13-3).

For example, some leafspot diseases would be probable following a cool, moist period, while spider mites would be probable during a hot, dry period. Close inspection of plants for such pests would be well worth the time and effort and could result in effective preventive measures before a pest population reached damaging levels.

Estimating Labor Needs and Other Costs

Perhaps one of the most difficult tasks in developing a management plan is computing the time and labor

Figure 13-2. Damage to these linden leaves, caused by lacebugs, could be avoided. The insect is a common problem yearly in the northeastern states. (Courtesy Kenneth R. Dudzik, N.E. Forest Experiment Station)

needed to do each task because of the great variability among workers as well as the equipment available to do the job. Nevertheless, an attempt should be made to estimate the time needed to accomplish every aspect of site management. Table 13-1 lists a variety of tasks and the average man-hours required to accomplish them. Adjustments may need to be made depending upon the skill and experience of employees. From these time estimates, a relatively close cost estimate can be obtained by multiplying time by the hourly wages.

Equipment costs, depreciation, and replacement should also be computed. These, of course, will vary with the type of equipment and duration of use. For mowing equipment and other motorized machinery, depreciation is calculated on the basis of current fair market value and the estimated number of years of life of the equipment. Calculations can be made on a straight line basis by dividing the difference between cost and salvageable value by the number of years of life. For example, a gang mower having a value of $6,000 new and a salvage value of $300 will depreciate $570 per year over a ten-year life: $(6000 - 300) \div 10 = 570$. *Accelerated depreciation* is another method commonly used, particularly with equipment that depreciates rapidly in the first three or four years. In the first year, deduction of 18 percent or more is not unusual, diminishing 1 or 2 percent each year thereafter for the life of the equipment.

Figure 13-3. Problems such as this slipped hose are detected by frequent site inspection. This problem is easily avoided by using webbing as shown in figure 4-10. (Courtesy Eugene B. Eyerly, Eyerly and Associates)

Table 13-1. Average Man-Hours Required for Common Grounds Maintenance Tasks

Task	Unit	Man-hours Needed
Cultivating		
Combined shrubbery and flower beds	100 ft^2	0.902
Shrubbery beds	100 ft^2	0.035
Fertilizing		
Hand-push spreader (36 in.) with no watering	acre	2.96
Liquid fertilizing by truck	acre	0.19
Tractor-towed spreader (8 ft)	acre	0.64
Tractor-towed spreader (12 ft)	acre	0.43
Truck, whirlwind spreader	acre	0.27
Grass planting (small areas)		
Cut and plant sod by hand (1-ft^2 blocks)[a]	ft^2	0.03
Cut and plant sod by hand (1½-ft strips)[a]	ft^2	0.06
Cut sod by machine and plant (1-ft^2 blocks)[a]	ft^2	0.048 + sq. ft. (0.009)
Cut sod by machine and plant (1½-ft strips)[a]	ft^2	0.048 + sq. ft. (0.043)
Fertilize	acre	2.00
Prepare	acre	5.33
Mulch (hay, straw)	acre	6.70
Seed by hand	1000 ft^2	0.50
Landscape plantings		
Plant shrubs, individual (5 gal)	each	0.36
Plant shrubs, individual, including watering (5 gal)	each	0.51
Plant shrubs, in groups (5 gal)	each	0.30
Plant shrubs, in groups, including watering (5 gal)	each	0.40
Plant trees (5–6 ft in height)	each	0.46

Task	Unit	Man-hours Needed
Plant trees (5–6 ft in height), including watering	each	0.68
Plant trees (2–2½ in. diameter)	each	1.02
Plant trees (2–2½ in. diameter), including watering	each	1.27
Lawn trimming (sidewalks and curbs)		
Electric trimmer	1000 linear ft	1.89
Gasoline trimmer	1000 linear ft	1.01
Leaf disposal		
Hand-rake flower and shrubbery beds	400 ft^2	0.33
Hand-rake lawn	1000 ft^2	0.34
Tractor-operated mulcher (5 ft)	acre	0.90
Walk-behind leaf mulcher (30–32 in.)	acre	6.24
Mowing, hand and power (improved areas)		
Hand mower (14–16 in.)	1000 ft^2	0.18
Power mower (18–22 in.)	1000 ft^2	0.11
Power mower (27–30 in.)	acre	3.12
Power mower (30–32 in.)	acre	2.75
Sulky-ridden triplex power mower	acre	1.92
Mowing, tractor		
Curb edging	mile	0.67
Cutter- or sickle-bar, rough terrain (5 ft)	acre	1.66
Cutter- or sickle-bar, smooth terrain (5 ft)	acre	1.02
Hammer knife (4 ft)	acre	1.21

continued

Table 13-1, *continued.*

Task	Unit	Man-hours Needed	Task	Unit	Man-hours Needed
Mow drainage channel with 5-ft sickle-bar, tractor-towed, both sides	mile	1.58	Roll or plane bituminous pavements	1000 yd^2	12.00
Reel, 3-gang (7 ft)	acre	0.37	Rebuild aggregate base course	1000 yd^2	88.00
Reel, 5-gang (12½ ft)	acre	0.31	Snow and ice control		
Rotary (5 ft)	acre	0.90	Remove snow from roadway and shoulders	mile	2.25
Rotary (6–8 ft)	acre	0.64	Remove snow from bridges	mile	0.06
Pest inspection of ornamentals and trees	acre	0.50	Erect snow fences	100 linear ft	1.50
Reforestation			Remove snow fences	100 linear ft	1.00
Hand planting	acre	6.16	Sand and/or salt roadway	mile	0.14
Machine planting	acre	0.88	Remove ice from roadway	mile	0.40
Seeding	acre	1.54	Remove snow from ditches and culverts	mile	3.00
Roadside and drainage			Place or remove sand or cinder barrels	mile	0.20
Repair, cut, and fill slopes	mile	0.90	Traffic services		
Repair or replace drain pipes	mile	1.05	Paint center line or edge lines	mile	6.40
Clean drain pipes and culverts	mile	0.30	Paint hazard and/or guide markings	mile	0.75
Clean and repair unpaved ditches	mile	8.00	Tree and shrub maintenance		
Clean paved flumes, gutters, and inlets	mile	2.00	Chip pruned tree limbs (per tree)	each	0.08
Repair stone riprap	mile	0.15	Hedge trimming by hand and dispose of cuttings	100 linear ft	2.85
Remove trees from roadside	mile	0.20	Hedge trimming, electric, and disposal of cuttings[b]	100 linear ft	1.56
Mow both roadsides with tractor	mile	6.25	Prune shrubs (deciduous)	each	0.20
Mow both roadsides with hand tools	mile	0.75	Prune shrubs (evergreen)	each	0.13
Apply herbicides on roadside	mile	1.30	Prune trees (large)	each	2.80
Special surface maintenance and repair			Remove dead trees	each	3.88
Seal bituminous and concrete pavement	1000 yd^2	8.00			
Resurface with bituminous mix	1000 yd^2	22.00			

continued

Table 13-1, *continued.*

Task	Unit	Man-hours Needed
Watering turf		
Water lawn, garden hose with sprinkler	1000 ft²	0.22
Water lawn, hose-less, quick-coupling plug-in sprinklers	acre	0.41
Water lawn, 50-ft soaker hoses, set up	10,000 ft²	0.97
Water lawn, 60-ft spray sprinkler, set up	10,000 ft²	0.90
Weed control		
Nonselective her-bicides along fence line with truck-tank sprayer (2 ft wide; 1 ft inside and 1 ft outside fence)	1000 ft²	0.45
Nonselective her-bicides with manual equip-ment, small areas	1000 ft²	0.68
Selective her-bicides with manual equip-ment, small areas	acre	3.10
Selective her-bicides with tractor-operated equipment (10-ft boom)	acre	0.27

Source: Adapted from ALCC (1983). Used with permission.

a. Unit is 1 square foot of sod or area planted.

b. If a ladder is required, add 0.40 man-hours per 100 linear foot.

DIAGNOSTIC PROCEDURE

Diagnosing problems in landscape plants is not always a simple task. Frequently, what appears to be the obvious cause of a problem turns out to be of secondary importance and not the principal factor (fig. 13-4). This may lead to inappropriate control or corrective measures. On the other hand, a diagnosis is sometimes made too complicated and the simple causal factor is overlooked.

The best way to avoid confusion when diagnosing a problem is to follow a definite procedure. Investigate every logical factor that might contribute to the observed problem. This approach, of course, does not always assure a correct diagnosis, but it does help eliminate the improbable factors. The following is a good general diagnostic procedure:

Figure 13-4. Careful diagnosis is needed to determine the cause of blotch in this birch leaf. What may appear to be a fungus disorder is actually a leafminer insect. (Courtesy Kenneth R. Dudzik, N.E. Forest Experiment Station)

1. Inspect all aboveground parts for obvious signs or symptoms of insects or disease. Note the general status of the plant. Often a plant that is low in vigor will be subject to insect or disease attack. *Initial cause* of the problem may be physiological rather than a pest attack.

2. If possible, study the cultural practices used in the past. Note fertilizer practices, pruning methods, spray program, watering, location of sprinkler heads, downspouts, and the like.

3. Examine the root system, particularly where no aboveground cause seems to be evident. Learn to tell the difference between healthy and unhealthy roots. Young, healthy roots are usually white or lighter in color and are "firm." Dying or dead roots turn brown-to-black quickly and usually become "slimy" in moist soil because of decay of the outer bark.

4. Examine the microclimate—exposure, soil type, drainage, and the like.

5. Where nutritional problems are suspected, a soil test may be necessary. Soil tests are especially useful where high salts or sodium conditions are suspected. It is not usually feasible to determine the presence of most contact weed killers by soil testing, since they break down quickly in the soil. Most soil sterilants, on the other hand, can be tested for but at considerable expense. A standard soil test will not disclose chemical contaminants such as soil sterilants. It is also necessary to know what type of chemical is suspected. Otherwise, testing will be very costly. Refer to chapter 8 for more information on this subject.

During a diagnosis, keep the following six points in mind:

1. When injury shows up first at the bottom and/or inside parts of the plant, look for soil problems or internal causes, such as soil compaction, soil contaminants, and vascular diseases.

2. If injury shows up on top and/or on external portions first, look for environmental factors first (air pollution, spray damage, insects, cold injury). Exceptions to this rule include some herbicide injury, some nutritional disorders, and some insect or disease pests.

3. Presence of an insect does not necessarily mean that it is causing the observed damage. What *is* the insect? What damage does it seem to be causing? Are there enough insects to cause the visible damage?

4. Absence of an insect or disease sign does not necessarily indicate that these could not be the cause of the damage. An insect may leave feeding damage and migrate to another plant or change to another state (egg, pupa). A disease organism may not have progressed sufficiently to show spore bodies and other signs.

5. When damage occurs on just one side of a plant, it may be related to spray drift or injury to part of the root system. Plants often develop a twist; thus, roots supplying water to a given part of a plant may be located on the opposite side of the plant. Spiral patterns are also possible from a single root system injury.

6. Always check growth rate. Compare current growth with previous growth history. Sometimes this provides clues to past cultural practices.

PLANT PROBLEMS AND POSSIBLE CAUSES

A wide variety of visible signs and symptoms indicate when plants are in trouble. In this section, common symptoms and their possible causes are summarized. The keys given in chapters 6 and 7 can be used to refine the diagnosis further to a specific cause. Diagnosing plant problems is largely a matter of elimination, taking all the available evidence into consideration. Treatment practices or corrective measures should not be initiated until a thorough and accurate diagnosis has been completed.

Signs or Symptoms on Leaves or Needles

Curled or distorted

- Herbicidal injury—2,4-D and similar phenoxy-type chemicals typically distort foliage.
- Aphids—Some types of aphids cause severe cupping or distortion of leaves.
- Low temperature—Sudden cooling in spring on new growth may result in distorted foliage.

- Eriophyid mites—These nearly microscopic pests may cause foliage distortion similar to that of 2,4-D injury.
- Powdery mildew—Mildew fungi on young foliage will result in distortion. Look closely for white or gray filaments of the fungus.

Wilting

- Lack of soil moisture—Check root zone.
- Excess soil moisture—A common problem in compacted soils.
- Gas leak in pipeline—Sudden, total wilt, then browning is typical of oxygen starvation from a gas leak.
- Wilt disease—Dutch elm disease, verticillium wilt, and similar vascular diseases will cause plants to wilt.

Untimely leaf drop (all leaves, particularly youngest)

- Low nutrition—Stunting usually precedes leaf drop.
- Insect damage—Look for defoliating caterpillars, such as gypsy moth or tussock moth.
- Disease—Typical of anthracnose disease in advanced stages.

Leaf drop (interior, older leaves first)

- Poor soil aeration and drainage—Common in heavy soils with excess water.
- Rodents—Check for burrows or girdling.
- Nematodes—Check roots for small nodules.

Skeletonized

- Chewing insects—Look for leaf beetles, pear slug, and similar pests.

Tunnels

- Leaf miners—Common on lilac, elm, birch, and alder.

Swellings

- Insect galls—Several species of wasp and midges cause leaf galls.

Brown Margins

- Lack of moisture—Especially common in shallow-rooted plants.
- High salts in soil—Excessive salts create a drought condition in plants.
- Low soil nutrition—Potash deficiency, mostly found in sandy soils.
- Spray injury—Usually results from emulsifiable concentrates applied on hot days.
- Root loss caused by transplanting—Especially common in bare-root stock planted late in spring.
- Other root injuries—These can result from rodents (voles), chemicals, deep spading, or other mechanical trauma.

Yellow-green color

- Low nitrogen—Most common in turfgrasses or plants in heavily irrigated sandy soils.
- Excess moisture—Too much moisture may result in less nutrition uptake because of leaching or low soil oxygen.
- Planted too deeply—Low soil oxygen.

Yellow with green veins

- Minor element deficiency—Lack of available iron, zinc, or manganese.
- Drought—Dry soils may induce chlorosis.
- Soil sterilants—Initial indication of presence of Pramitol, Triox, and Atrazine, and other similar products.

Purple cast

- Excess phosphorus—Rare in alkaline soils.
- Soluble salts—Found in spruce and other conifers.
- Soil sterilants—Prominent in spruce where root zone is contaminated with Ureabor, Pramitol 5PS, and similar materials containing toxic salts.

Brown, black, red, or yellow spots

- Insect eggs—Check to see if the spots are part of the plant.

- Fungus spore bodies—Leafspot diseases.
- Spray burn—Usually irregular blotches on upper leaf surface.

Grayish, "salt and pepper," or stippled appearance

- Spider mites—A common problem in hot weather.
- Air pollutants—Ozone damage may resemble spider mite feeding injury.

White blotches, silvery cast, or powdery look

- Mildew—Look for surface "threads" of a fungus and small black dots (spore bodies).
- Air pollutants—Likely when close inspection reveals that surface cells of the leaves are damaged, but no fungal threads are present.
- Thrips—This tiny insect often causes leaves to appear silvery because of the removal of cell contents during feeding.

Signs or Symptoms on Trunk or Branches

Dieback of tips

- Cold injury—Early freezes may destroy or damage new growth.
- Mechanical injury—Lawn mower abrasion is common on lower branches. Leaving stubs from improper pruning will also cause dieback.
- Borers—Look for entry holes and frass (boring dust) below dieback.
- Spray injury—This will often look like freeze injury.
- High soluble salts in soil—A white crust on soil surface may be present.
- Blight-type diseases—Twig cankers may be caused by bacteria and certain fungi.

Girdling

- Rodents—Mice or voles may feed on the bark of shrubs in winter months.
- Mechanical injury—Abrasion from mowing equipment is common.
- Insects—Some insects, such as the twig girdler, remove an almost uniform ring of bark.

Bark slough

- Cold (sunscald)—This is most common on the southern or western sides of young, thin-barked trees.
- Excess growth in moist season—Fertility may be too high, causing abnormal cambial activity.
- Sudden freezes—Rapid temperature drops to subzero cold may cause bark to separate from the wood beneath.
- Lightning—Splitting or partial loss of bark may occur.
- Natural bark loss in the species—Mature sycamore, Russian olive, upright junipers, and others naturally shed bark.

Dying of lower branches

- Shade—Some plants naturally shade out lower branches. Shearing plant tops can also result in shading out.
- Canker disease.

Branch drop or dieback

- Twig-girdling insect—Common in ash and occasionally in juniper.
- Shoot moth—Relatively common in a wide variety of pines.
- Hail injury—In evergreens, dieback from hail damage may show up weeks or months later.
- Natural—Some trees, such as hemlock, poplar, and willow, naturally shed branches.

White, cottony masses

- Mealybug—More common on houseplants but may be found in branchlet crotches of hawthorn.
- Aphids and woolly aphids—Usually found in rows on the lower sides of branches.
- Scale—Cottony maple scale and others resemble woolly aphids but are not as mobile. Egg masses occur beneath live scales.

Discolored bark (especially in young trees)

- Sunscald—Common on the southern and western sides of young, newly planted trees.

- Disease—Fireblight, cytospora canker, and similar disease organisms may cause bark to dry up and die.
- Lack of sufficient roots—A very common problem in newly planted trees.

Swelling

- Insect galls—Eriophyid mites, aphids, wasps, and midges can cause stems to swell into various, sometimes conelike galls.
- Rust—Juniper–hawthorn rust and pine rusts cause tumorlike growths.
- Other cankers—Crown gall, found mostly on roots and bases of trees and shrubs, is relatively common in cottonwood, willow, euonymus, and rose.

Holes with "sawdust" (frass)

- Borers and bark beetles—The presence of borers is usually secondary to other problems, such as drought stress.

Amber or orange-colored ooze

- Fireblight and fungus cankers—Some organisms ooze at spore-release stage, most commonly in wet weather.

REFERENCES

ALCC. 1983. Specifications Handbook for Landscape/Irrigation Installation and Maintenance Contracting. Wheat Ridge, CO: Associated Landscape Contractors of Colorado.

Feucht, J. R. 1984. Landscape Management. pp. 185–90. Fort Collins, CO: Colorado State University.

Index